The Voice of a Medieval Woman

St. Elizabeth of Hungary as a Franciscan Penitent

In The Early Sources for Her Life

by

Lori Pieper, SFO

Second Edition

New York

TAU CROSS BOOKS AND MEDIA

2016

ISBN

Paper: 978-0-9907756-4-5
EPUB: 978-0-9907756-3-8
Kindle: 978-0-9907756-5-2

Library of Congress Control Number: 2015910238

Cover Design: Lori Pieper

Cover Image: Detail of a crucifixion by Vincent de Groot, dated 1528, in the Sint-Elisabethkirche, Grave, the Netherlands. Used under the Creative Commons License.

The work shows St. Elizabeth in her Franciscan habit as the protector of a group of (Franciscan?) Beguines (See Chapter VII).

Acknowledgments

This work could not have been finished without the help of a great many people. I want to thank especially Sister Margaret Carney, OSF and Sister Ingrid Peterson, OSF for their encouragement and helpful comments as the project developed. Felicitas Schmieder, Barbara Haggh, and Anne Schuchman graciously volunteered their help in obtaining microfilms of manuscripts and rare printed works. Anne in particular offered many insights on medieval religious women from her work on Umiliana dei Cerchi.

Dr. Maryanne Kowaleski helped me greatly by opening vistas of research on women's history to me, and challenging me to explore different avenues of scholarship. Dr. Wayne Storey encouraged my interest in manuscript studies. Most of all, I could not have completed this work without my mentor, Dr. Richard Gyug, who was always patient and constantly available. His vast store of knowledge of hagiography, liturgy and medieval Latin were invaluable, and I cannot thank him enough for offering to photograph the Valenciennes manuscript for me on his own trip to France when other avenues were blocked.

Finally, I want to thank my parents, John and Betty Pieper, who taught me the value of hard work and perseverance and who never failed to believe in me. This work is dedicated to them.

Contents

Abbreviations. ix
Note from the Minister General .xi
Foreword to the First Edition xiii
Foreword to the Second Edition xv

Chapter

I. Introduction 1
II. Sources and Problems of Interpretation 26
III. The Franciscan Tradition on Elizabeth. 50
IV. The Anonymous Franciscan and His Sources 73
V. Elizabeth's Vocation: Choosing Poverty. 96
VI. Elizabeth's Vocation: Living the Franciscan
        Life 161
VII. Elizabeth's Influence on the Women's
        Franciscan Movement. 215
VIII. Conclusion. 243

Appendix: Table of the Anonymous Franciscan and
        His Sources 251
Bibliography. 273

Abbreviations

Publications

AASS	*Acta Sanctorum*
AB	*Analecta Bollandiana*
AF	*Analecta Franciscana*
AFH	*Archivum Franciscanum Historicum*
AF	*Bullarium Franciscanum*
BHL	*Bibliotheca Hagiographica Latina medii aevi*
CF	*Collectanea Franciscana*
EF	*Études Franciscaines*
FS	*Franziskanische Studien*
MF	*Miscellanea Franciscana*
MGH SS	*Monumenta Germanica Historiae. Scriptores*

Manuscripts

CA 34, 35, 91 = Cambrai, Mediathèque Municipale, MS. 34, 35 and 91.

D = Douai, Bibliothèque Municipale, Cod. 864.

K = Koblenz, Landeshauptarchiv, Abt. 701, No. 122.

H = Heidelberg, Universitätsbibliothek, Cod. Pal. Germ. 105.

T = Trier, Stadtbibliothek, Cod. 1173/475 8.

V = Valenciennes, Bibliothèque Municipale, MS. 508 (467 -- T. 4. 25.)

Quotations from the Vulgate in notes and commentary are from

Vulg. = Robertus Weber, OSB. *Biblia Sacra Iuxta Vulgatam Versionem.* Stuttgart: Württembürgische Bibelanstalt, 1969.

Tertius Ordo Regularis Sancti Francisci
Minister Generalis

To all Franciscan brothers and sisters of the Third Order Regular, to all Secular Franciscans, and to all Franciscans and those devoted to St. Elizabeth (of Hungary) and St. Francis, Peace and Good!

The year 2007 is a significant one for our Franciscan Order. We celebrate the 8th centennial of the birth of our patroness Elizabeth. This event encourages us to have an encounter with her person, her Franciscanism and her holiness. We have to recognize that the knowledge we have of her life is very limited.

We also know that the means required to overcome this limited knowledge are not at hand. With this motive, we want to put into your hands the present biography of the Saint. Lori Pieper's work is carefully written, and fulfills the demands for a critical history. It takes as its foundations the most genuine sources, which go beyond the legends. It presents the life of St. Elizabeth framed in the society of her time and in the Franciscan penitential movement.

Our desire is that this work will be an instrument that allows all of us to have an encounter with St. Elizabeth– with her person and remarkable holiness. May this knowledge of the Saint stimulate our sensibility, not only to fruitfully celebrate this centennial, but also to encourage and to strengthen our commitment to the world of the suffering and abandoned.

Our purpose is that our stirred-up charity will lead us to pour balm on the wounds of our society, to dry tears, and to pour out a bit of our hearts where mercy is lacking.

We beg God and St. Elizabeth that after having studied her life, every one of us will be able to repeat in our heart, "I believe in love."

Fr. Ilija Zivkovic
Minister General, T.O.R.
Rome, 2007

Foreword to the First Edition

Five years after I defended my dissertation on St. Elizabeth of Hungary, I am very happy to be able to offer it for publication. Thanks to the help of the Minister General of the TOR, Fr. Ilija Zivkovic, and the Vicar General, Fr. Michael J. Higgins, I am able to do so in time for the celebration of the eighth centenary of Elizabeth's birth in 2007.

In addition to abbreviating the text somewhat and making it more accessible to non-specialists, I have taken the opportunity to correct some errors in the text and translations from Latin and German and to update a few references.

I hope that my work will be a useful step in the journey, which will continue during the centenary year and beyond, toward a deeper knowledge of this valiant women and inspiring saint.

Lori Pieper, SFO
December 2006

Foreword to the Second Edition

I am happy to finally be able to present the second edition of this study based on my dissertation, which looked into the sources for the life of St. Elizabeth of Hungary and how their authors understood her relationship to the Franciscans and the Third Order. I have taken the opportunity to correct a few errors, but otherwise the text has not been altered from the 2007 edition.

Since that edition was published, I have gone on to research the lives of several saints for a series of posts for the Tau Cross Books and Media website, including St. Rose of Viterbo, Bl. Pietro Pettinaio, St. Amato Ronconi, Lady Jacoba dei Settesoli and others who were or who have been proposed as Third Order members. In time, I hope to publish some of them as full biographies. This research has confirmed my belief that more than legalities are needed in trying to understand the early history of the Third Order and its members.

Not long ago, I came across this passage from Fra Mariano of Florence, who might be considered the first true historian of the Franciscan Third Order. Writing his treatise on the subject in 1521, the 300th anniversary of the order's founding, he commented on the difficulties in determining whether or not someone was a tertiary:

> Some people have wanted to say that [St. Elizabeth] did not belong to the Third Order, because "in her legend we don't find it expressly stated; for this reason, we can only conclude that she didn't belong to the Third Order." And the same answer is given about St. Louis the king of France and St. Yves of Britany and St. Elzear. There are two reasons why it is not expressly stated in their

histories that they belonged to the Third Order. The first is because this Order, from its beginning up to the time of Pope Nicholas IV,[1] was not called an Order, but those who professed it were called brothers and sisters, and by some penitents . . . But then Nicholas IV in his bull that begins *Supra montem catholice fede* began to call it an Order, and it was entitled the Order of Penitents. The second reason is because the said saints in their legends are not called "of the Third Order" because the Order of Friars Minor did not intervene in their canonization, but they were canonized at the request of secular lords; and therefore since they weren't proposed by the Third Order of St. Francis, they were not registered in the bulls of canonization [as being] of this Order, but indeed [were such] by their penitence and humble and abject dress, as is manifested by St. Louis, of whom his legend says that he did not wear scarlet or green, but humble dress. . . And even though St. Elizabeth dressed in gray, rather in grey tending to back, nonetheless St. Bonaventure[2] says that she dressed in the habit and cord of the Minors, and did not otherwise name the Third Order.[3]

This passage reflects precisely what I discovered: that in the thirteenth century up until the promulgation of *Supra Montem* in 1289, there were a number of factors influencing whether someone was perceived as belonging to the Third Order. Among them is the use of a Franciscan-style cord and habit, as does the anonymous sermon Mariano attributes to St. Bonaventure.[4]

Another point Mariano mentions has also been confirmed by my own research: the recognition (or not) of a saint as a Third Order Franciscan often depended on the interest of the Franciscans in her cult or canonization process. The Franciscans did not have an influence on Elizabeth's cult or her canonization process, but in this case, instead of a secular lord, it was another group of religious, the Teutonic Order, that did. As a result, Elizabeth's true relationship with the Franciscans and the Third Order was obscured for a long time.

I hope that my work will encourage further research along these same lines for other early penitents, so that the history of the medieval Third Order will be clarified, and the light of its saints will shine ever more brightly on those who look to them for inspiration.

Lori Pieper, OFS
Pentecost Sunday, 2016

Notes

[1] Mariano wrote "Innocent" here, he but clearly meant "Nicholas," as his conclusion shows.

2 Mariano is referring the sermon long attributed to St. Bonaventure, but that should be attributed to another Franciscan writer, perhaps Conrad of Saxony or Servasanta da Faenza (See Chapter II).

3 Mariano da Firenze, Il trattato del Terz'Ordine o vero "Libro come Santo Francesco istituì et ordinò el Tertio Ordine de Frati et Sore di Pentientia et dell dignità et perfectione o vero Santità Sua." Ed. Massimo D. Pape (Roma: Ed. Analecta TOR, 1985), pp. 481-82.

4 The author writes: "A sign of her perfect humility was the cord and habit of the [Friars] Minor, which she adopted as best she could" (See Chapter VI)

Introduction

The Mystery of a Saint

For almost eight centuries, St. Elizabeth of Hungary (1207-1231) has been celebrated as a saint and as the patroness of the Franciscan Third Order Secular and Third Order Regular. She is loved for her dedication to the poor. Yet the details of her life are still too little known. Though there is an abundance of contemporary sources for her life, there is also an abundance of later legends. Only in the twentieth and twenty-first centuries has there been any sustained attempt to disentangle the facts from the legends.

When I began my studies on Elizabeth, I was surprised how much work was still to be done on the sources, and how many of them still remained unpublished. One of the results of my early research was the uncovering of the complete text of a source that up until then was known only in fragments: The Anonymous Franciscan. My interest in this new source, with its many unknown details about Elizabeth's life, led me to study all of the sources in light of the methodological questions that have recently been raised by historians. Many have questioned how the truth about saints can be distinguished from later legends and from societal constructions of sanctity, and how medieval women's authentic voices can be found in works written from the viewpoint of a male-dominated society. I wanted to discover a method for studying the sources for Elizabeth's life that would address these concerns.

I also became acquainted with another important and controversial question: in what way was Elizabeth a part of the Franciscan movement? Was she indeed, as many writers have stated, a member of the Third Order? What type of religious life did she lead after her husband's death?

The goal of this work is to illuminate Elizabeth's life by a new study of the sources, and to answer these questions, so that her life might be brought into the mainstream of historical study.

Elizabeth's Life

The bare outlines of Elizabeth's life have long been well-known. Born in 1207, the daughter of King Andrew II of Hungary and his German wife, Gertrude of Andechs-Meran, Elizabeth was betrothed at the age of four to Ludwig IV, the young son of Landgraf Hermann I of Thuringia and taken to Wartburg castle there, to be brought up there with her future husband. They married in 1221, when Elizabeth was fourteen and Ludwig twenty-one. It was a happy marriage, which produced three children, Hermann, Sophia and Gertrude. Elizabeth shunned the pomp and frivolity of court life, and dedicated herself to the relief of the poor in her husband's territories. She emptied the granaries to feed the poor during a famine in 1226, and built a hospital for the poor at the foot of Wartburg castle, where she nursed the sick herself.

Elizabeth aided the first group of Franciscans who came to Eisenach around 1225 by giving them a church. A Franciscan lay brother named Rodeger was her first spiritual advisor. She spun wool for the clothing of the poor and the habits of the Friars Minor. At times she would dress in rags in front of the women of her retinue, and speak of the day when she would go begging for the love of God. In accordance with the injunctions of her confessor, Conrad of Marburg, she refused any food that might have been unjustly exacted from the peasants by her husband's officials.

In 1227, Ludwig set out on crusade with Frederick II, but fell ill and died in Italy while waiting to embark for the Holy Land. Soon afterwards, persecution broke out against the young widow. Most historians in the past believed that Elizabeth was forcibly expelled from the Wartburg at her brother-in-law Heinrich's instigation. Others have thought that the expulsion took place elsewhere. Some modern historians, however, believe that Elizabeth voluntarily left the Wartburg rather than violate her conscience about eating food unjustly extorted from the poor. In either case, she is described as being reviled and persecuted by many of the powerful in the land and suffering from many hardships.

Desiring to consecrate herself to religious life, Elizabeth made her renunciation of the world in the Franciscan church in Eisenach on Good Friday, March 24, 1228. She moved to Marburg in Hesse, on the outskirts of her husband's territories. There she put on religious garb (the "gray habit"), along with several female companions, and built a hospital named for St. Francis, where she devoted herself to serving the sick and poor.

Elizabeth died on November 17, 1231, when she was only twenty-four. She was buried in her hospital chapel, amid universal mourning by the local people. Almost immediately she was the focus of tremendous popular devotion, and a number of spectacular miracles were reported at her tomb, which soon became a pilgrimage place drawing people from all over Europe. She was canonized by Pope Gregory IX in 1235. A magnificent Gothic church was built in Marburg to house her remains.

Elizabeth has remained a popular saint from the Middle Ages until now. There is a large amount of hagiographic writing, medieval and modern, about her, but much about her life and personality is still obscure. A critical approach is badly needed, and here is where the methodological issues mentioned above arise.

Critical Questions

Finding Women's Voices

The first important question raised by study of Elizabeth is one fundamental to women's history: how can historians find the authentic voices of medieval women, especially religious women, in a society where they were considered inferior, and where their individual spiritual experiences were often either ignored or forced into officially determined channels by the male hierarchy? Women's experiences were examined, evaluated and written down for posterity by men; as a result, the women's own views of their experiences were often lost.

Some feminist historians have attempted to answer these questions by new readings of traditional texts that attempt to find the hidden reality of women's history within the tradition as it was developed by men. As Rosemary Radford Ruether has said, those texts which are produced in a context of patriarchy also "contain resources for a critique of patriarchy." These resources include overlooked passages, interior contradictions and even silences in the texts.[1]

Many feminist historians are developing critical methods which can be used to examine texts by and about later medieval religious women, particularly those which purport to be their work, or a collaboration between them and male writers. These scholars study what these texts tell us about the relationship between the woman mystic and the male scribe in order to learn from them about gender dynamics in medieval society.[2] They use methods developed in recent years for separating the different perspectives in literary works.[3] (Some of these recent studies are discussed below in the section on medieval religious women). We can learn a great deal through these methods both about individual men and women and women as a group in society.

Hagiography

A second critical question of historical method is: how can we reconstruct both history and the relationship between the individual and society in the study of hagiography? In the 1970's and 80's, interest in demography, anthropology and sociology led to a number of attempts at quantitative studies of saints' lives, that is, attempts to gather statistics about a large number of saints, and to use the results as a source of information about medieval culture. One of the first to use this method, Pierre Delooz, argued that the "saint" (as opposed to the "person") was a construct of medieval society, and since it is the saint who appears in hagiography, it is the saint and medieval beliefs about saints, not details about individual holy people's lives, that we should seek in hagiography.[4] A number of such quantitative studies of the saints were written in the early 1980's, including those by Michael Goodich and Weinstein and Bell.[5]

With the rise of women's history, a number of studies were devoted to women saints and mystics, including the examination of texts attributed to them and medieval lives of them, in hopes of recovering something about women's experiences. Some of the common features noted in the lives of women saints include miracles and other supernatural occurrences, visions, fasting, and other severe ascetic practices, intense identification with the suffering Christ, and Eucharist-inspired visions. There are different interpretations of this pattern. Weinstein and Bell believed that this intense interior life and emphasis on bodily suffering could be attributed to the private rather than public nature of women's lives, and their internalization of the misogyny of their culture.[6] Bell discussed the psychological motives for the fasting of women saints, and found some similarities to the psychology of modern anorexics, though he admitted that "holy anorexia" had a predominantly spiritual goal.[7]

Other historians did not use statistics as such, but looked for broad characteristic patterns in saints' lives. Caroline Walker Bynum studied a number of medieval women who practiced extreme fasting and charitable distribution of food, often accompanied by flagellation, even self-mutilation, and intense Eucharistic devotion. Bynum attributes these practices to a complex web of associations between women and food in medieval culture. Women saw themselves as food for others, and identified with the flesh of the suffering Christ, which is offered as food to Christians in the Eucharist.[8]

Not everyone was satisfied with the quantitative or other mass approaches. Aviad Kleinberg questioned how representative quantitative studies of medieval sanctity really are. He pointed out that the results are affected by the small number of saints studied by historians, the problem of categorizing saints, the frequent bias in lists towards Italian saints and the papal politics involved in choosing saints to canonize.[9] Nor have the new studies of female saints mentioned above solved the various questions about religious women's lives. They do not tell us whether the described form of behavior is a common or an unusual response among women, or how to understand women whose lives, for one reason or another, do not correspond to the predominant pattern. Nor do they tell us whether the pattern itself fairly reflects medieval women's lives, or is itself a creation of a hagiography largely written by male clerics.

In fact, this view of women's spirituality as being determined by bodily experiences and visions is now being balanced by studies of medieval women's own words compared to those of their male biographers; in some cases, the women themselves often gave less importance to these experiences than the men did. Catherine of Siena's writings, for instance, show significantly less emphasis on mystical experiences involving the body than do the writings of her confessor, Raymond of Capua; her descriptions of her mystical experiences occur in the context of her apostolate and political involvement, while for Raymond they are a fascinating subject in themselves. This leads Karen Scott to wonder "whether the female mystics known to us only through hagiographic accounts would appear less otherworldly and conventionally holy if we had access to their writings as we do in Catherine's case."[10] Beatrice of Nazareth, a Belgian religious, also seems to have been interested in a mysticism that would free her from the use of bodily images, while her male biographer insisted on the importance and reality of these images.[11] Nor do studies using the mass approach place the saints or their cults in an individual context. For instance, Bynum has been criticized for fitting female saints into too rigid a pattern by not paying enough attention to the differences between women mystics and downplaying their erotic imagery.[12]

In the 1980's, the focus of scholars began to change as developments in literary and historical studies led them to undertake more in-depth examination of particular saints, their cults and their literary and cultural contexts through examination of individual texts.[13]

For instance, Aviad Kleinberg has studied the relationship of saints during their lifetime to their "public," that is, the local or religious communities which helped create the idea of them as saints. Their admirers and biographers tended to see them in a very personal and revealing way. Often the saint collaborated, consciously or unconsciously, in the formation of his or her own hagiographic portrait. Kleinberg found that all levels of hagiography are not the same; often the earliest accounts, such as those by eyewitnesses in canonization processes, provide the most "irrelevant" personal details, those which bring the human being into focus, while later accounts tend to focus on the core of sanctity, which, because it is based on a list of standardized virtues, becomes less personal and more conventional.[14]

Recent works on the literary collaboration between female mystics and their male scribes also see the recording of sainthood as the result of the personal relationship between a woman and an admirer or admirers who helped create the image of her sanctity.[15] A saint's community relationships could be very complex, as in the case of the Franciscan tertiary Umiliana dei Cerchi, who, though a virtual recluse in her family home, had a large audience, beginning with her own female servants, and including about thirty local female tertiaries and some local friars, among them her confessor, all of whom were interviewed by her biographer, Vito da Cortona. The resulting collective portrait, though controlled by Vito, gives us an idea of the workings of a whole religious circle in Florence, in which the women's testimony might well have affected the male biographer's view.[16]

A new type of source was added to hagiography in the thirteenth century, and was being solidified during Elizabeth's lifetime: the papal canonization process, which required the firsthand testimony of eyewitnesses to a saint's virtues and miracles. The testimonies about Elizabeth's life are one of the early examples of such a process. The study of canonization processes has proven to be a fruitful field for the investigation of medieval concepts of sanctity. The existing processes from the thirteenth century to the end of the Middle Ages have been the subject of statistical study in a monumental work by André Vauchez.[17] But even the statements by eyewitnesses, like most court testimony, are never wholly objective, and can show the effects of biases and political or ecclesiastical pressures. To many it seems that the canonization process, reflecting the already-existing view that a particular person is a saint, simply provides us with a saint's legend, as do other hagiographic texts, rather than personal details or accurate history. This suspicion is partly confirmed but also modified by the study made by Jacques Paul of the canonization process of St. Louis of Anjou, which began in 1308. Paul discovered that the local promoters of the cause relied on two Franciscan friars who had known the saint for drawing up the list of questions the interrogators would use. These friars framed the questions in such a way as to elicit replies conforming Louis' life to that of St. Francis and to the views of the Franciscan Spirituals. Many of those who knew the saint less well were strongly influenced by this questionnaire and gave stereotyped replies in conformity with it. But the plan did not entirely succeed. A number of those closest to Louis contradicted the biased questionnaire, and offered their own very detailed memories that did not conform to the pre-determined view. Paul concluded that the testimonies in the process, studied in context, could provide both genuine historical testimony about a saint and evidence of a legend in the making.[18]

Some feminist historians, on the other hand, are particularly suspicious of the evidence coming from such official processes. Catherine Mooney studied the various types of information available about St. Clare of Assisi: her own writings, the depositions of the nuns who knew her and testified at her process in 1253, and the biographies written by clerics. The testimonies of the nuns described Clare as being but little inferior in her holiness to the Blessed Virgin, an opinion apparently elicited from them by the male interrogators. Later biographers turned this into Clare's imitation of Mary, whereas Clare herself had written of her own following of Christ. Mooney decided that "the women's testimony, whatever it may have been when orally delivered, would then be recorded, abbreviated, or omitted entirely according to the judgment of the supervising males."[19] Similar concerns are raised by Dyan Elliot in her study of the way that Dorothy of Montau's confessor, John Marienwerder, worked to shape her cult and affect her canonization process. John wrote down Dorothy's revelations, spread propaganda for her sanctity after her death, and took a role in drawing up the questionnaire used at the process. The contribution of Dorothy's previous confessor was much less prominent; in the end, John's view of her holiness was the one remembered.[20]

Early processes like Elizabeth's, however, which took place while the method was still being developed, may not have been as formulaic. Vauchez found that none of the processes carried out before 1260, with the exception of the one for St. Dominic, used a questionnaire for the examination of the saint's virtues; in these cases, the answers of the witnesses were more spontaneous. Another benefit that Vauchez found in early canonization processes is that unlike other hagiographic texts they were not literary productions. While the questions were asked by the clerical elite, those who responded came from all classes of society, and offered a variety of viewpoints on what constitutes holiness.[21]

Though they are difficult to interpret, the unique features of these eyewitness testimonies require historians to develop a methodology for studying them that recognizes their nature as eyewitness reports and legal documents, as well as their role in the formation of hagiographic legends. This applies to Elizabeth's case as well, all the more since these questions have as yet scarcely been raised in regard to her process.

The Women's Religious Movement

Elizabeth was prominent in her time not only due to her position as a member of royalty, but also to the example of her life, both as a laywoman and a religious, which served as an inspiration to many other women. When her contemporary, the Beguine and mystic Mechtild of Magdeburg, asked God the reason for Elizabeth's short life and rapid canonization, she received this answer:

> It is right for a messenger to be quick. Elizabeth was and is a messenger whom I sent to wretched women living in castles who were so permeated with lust, so covered with arrogance,

and so constantly engulfed in vanity that they by rights should have gone into the abyss. But many a lady followed her example to the extent they could and wanted.[22]

In fact, Elizabeth's influence led a number of other women in her century, including her cousin, St. Agnes of Bohemia, to follow her example in hospital work in Germany, France and the Low Countries. Elizabeth was one of many thirteenth-century women who sought non-traditional religious lives, often involving active service in the world.

This movement appears to have started in the twelfth century and to have grown rapidly in the thirteenth, when large numbers of women became attached to already existing forms of monastic life or to the new mendicant orders. But many others lived a common life without professing formal vows or following a monastic rule. These extra-regular women included the Beguines. They often engaged in active charity and hospital work. The nature and origins of this movement has been a controversial subject, though studies in recent years have added much to our understanding of it.

This gives rise to a third series of questions: Where does Elizabeth fit into the women's religious movement of her time? What was the nature of her religious life? Was she a Beguine, a Franciscan tertiary, or something else? And what can we learn from her story about the lives of these non-traditional religious women?

These women have been the subject of considerable interest among historians during the last decades. In 1935, Herbert Grundmann was the first to write about the growth of religious fervor among women as a real movement and to insert it into the religious and social context of the yearning for evangelical poverty in the twelfth and thirteenth centuries that gave rise to the new mendicant orders. He believed that the poverty movement originated not in social protest among the poor, as some Marxist scholars had contended, but in the spiritual discontent among the nobility and rising merchant classes that led many men and women to reject worldly wealth and status in favor of the poor life of the Gospels. He saw the Beguines as arising early in the thirteenth century as the vanguard of the women's portion of the poverty movement. His view has formed the basis for most subsequent research.[23] Among the followers of this view is Goodich, who discovers a strong tendency in thirteenth-century saints, especially men and women in the mendicant orders, towards rebellion against their wealthy families and their lifestyle.[24]

While Grundmann's research is still regarded as fundamental in many ways, later scholars have been able to show that the women's movement arose earlier and was more widespread than had been thought. There is some continuity between the Beguines of the thirteenth century and twelfth-century forms of religious life for women, for instance, the Premonstratensian sisters in the twelfth century, who were originally non-cloistered and engaged in care of the sick.[25]

The uncertainty about the origins of the movement is partly due to the fact that the evidence has to be teased out from what is presented to us about individual communities, often by suspicious male clerical writers. As Jo Ann McNamara has pointed out, it is not easy to learn when the women's movement started, since so many hospices, beguinages and other women's religious houses become part of the written record only when noted by male writers or befriended by, or incorporated into some male monastic community.[26]

The social origins of the Beguines have also come under question. It is true that the wealthy Beguines are the ones most frequently mentioned by contemporaries. Many beguinages wanted to accept only women with property who could support themselves.[27] But there is evidence that women from other classes were part of the movement.[28] Scholars have found other factors as well to account for the growth of the women's movement, including a demographic imbalance that led to a surplus of women who found it impossible to marry.[29] There was also the reluctance of both the traditional monastic orders and the new mendicant movement to accept the care of women, thus causing them to devise their own forms of religious life, including the beguinages and the various forms of Franciscan and Dominican religious life for women.[30] But the rejection of wealth still played a prominent role in women's choices. The association between the abuse of wealth and the humiliating marriage market to which women were subjected may have made them more likely not only to reject the new mercantile economy and the accompanying usury but to flee marriage for the religious life as well.[31]

It was once thought that the type of religious life led by the Beguines was limited to northern Europe, but studies in the last twenty years have shown that it was actually quite common in Italy from the twelfth century on, where the women who followed this way of life were called *pinzochere* or *bizzocche*. In early thirteenth-century Rome in particular, it may have been difficult to distinguish between the nuns, who usually did not observe cloister, and the *bizzocche*, who mingled with them as they went freely about the city. This lasted until all the women adopted enclosure with the encouragement of St. Dominic.[32]

In addition to the Beguines, the *bizzocche* and the tertiaries, there were other women who undertook a non-traditional religious life: the recluses or anchoresses, who lived alone in small cells, locked away from the world. A good number of these seem to have been poorer women who had no property to bring with them to a beguinage or religious order. Some girls from Italian rural areas, including Verdiana, Giovanna of Signa, and Cristiana da Santa Croce, worked as shepherdesses, and then as servants, usually in the city (in the case of Verdiana, on a large country estate), and later took up residence as recluses in the countryside.[33]

Franciscan women were part of this religious movement. They included not only cloistered women like St. Clare and her sisters, but also women who lived in the Third Order, either "in the world" or in community, and groups of Beguines who attached themselves to the Franciscans for spiritual direction, while living their lives of active work and charitable service. This raises the question of which groups of women should be called Franciscan, and in what sense. The non-cloistered women in the Franciscan movement often have not been clearly separated from the Poor Clares on the one hand, and the Beguines and other religious women on the other. In fact, they had much in common. According to Anna Benvenuti Papi, female penitents, tertiaries, *pinzochere* and *bizzocche* in Italy, whether wealthy or not, were characterized by their essential social marginality, marked by loss of parents, widowhood, or other family disruptions.[34]

Another problem is that there is still much confusion about the nature of the Franciscan Third Order in its earliest period, before the definitive canonical approval of the Rule of Pope Nicholas IV in 1289. Formerly, historians treated the Third Order as having been founded as an original institution directly by St. Francis. Subsequent research by Meersseman and others has created a different picture: that the movement originally called the "Brothers and Sisters of Penance" arose in part out of the already-existing penitential movement. As many lay men and women became attracted to the Franciscan and Dominican teachings, the movement gradually separated into branches attached to the two orders.[35] St. Francis himself inspired many of the laity to do penance and wrote an exhortation for them to follow, which encapsulated many of the penitential ideas. Only recently have historians begun to separate Third Order from First Order history, and to deal with the question of early religious community life in the Third Order. One issue is that the origin of the Third Order Regular for women is still nebulous; these religious have not been clearly separated from the Third Order for seculars. Many times a woman without an institutional affiliation was later given dubious status as a tertiary.[36] Historians have begun digging deeper into the history of the early female Franciscan Third Order communities and their relationship to the Beguines and Italian *pinzochere*.[37]

Though thirteenth-century Franciscan women were a vital part of the religious ferment of their time, and their lives certainly demonstrate the difficulties medieval women faced in a male-dominated world, until recently, outside of St. Clare and her sisters, they have received very little attention by scholars outside the Franciscan Order compared to the interest in Beguines and mystics. Many of the sources have not been edited or discussed critically. English-speaking researchers still lack basic studies and commentaries on the sources for medieval Franciscan women; as a result, much that we have learned about medieval women has simply not been brought to bear on them.[38]

Recently, however, some women scholars have sought to show that early Franciscan women did not simply have their charism delivered to them by men; they actively contributed to the development of the Franciscan movement and its spirituality.[39] This work has been extended by Roberta McKelvie to the founder of a Franciscan congregation in the late fourteenth century, Angelina of Montegiove.[40] Nevertheless, the study of Franciscan women, as McKelvie points out, is still at an "embryonic stage of development."[41]

There were strong pressures, both internal and external, on women in religious life during Elizabeth's lifetime. Many women were undertaking to lead non-traditional religious lives and to devote themselves to active charitable service. Yet there were continuing efforts to enforce a more rigid cloister for female religious. The hierarchy thought it important that women have male direction, but male members of both the older orders and the new mendicant orders were often unwilling to provide it. At the same time, the Fourth Lateran Council had decreed that in the future all religious must adhere to an already-existing rule. In addition, women faced tensions arising from living an active life while still trying to maintain a life of poverty and prayer.

All of these pressures affected the female Franciscan movement. In order to conform various communities of *mulieres religiosae* and penitents in central Italy to the Church's new directives, Cardinal Ugolino, as papal legate in Tuscany in 1216-19, wrote a series of constitutions which these women could adopt, along with the Benedictine rule, which was also imposed on St. Clare and her sisters at this time. Together they formed the "Order of the Poor Enclosed Ladies." Later, as Pope Gregory IX, Ugolino assimilated various communities of female penitents beyond the Alps to the "Order of San Damiano," as it was now called. Thus a number of female religious communities whose origins were not Franciscan were brought under the Franciscan banner and made into enclosed nuns.[42] Another aspect of the increasing regimentation was the imposition of strict perpetual cloister on the Poor Clares, which seems to have been a kind of early preparation for the period beginning in 1298, when all nuns were to be perpetually enclosed according to Boniface VIII's bull *Periculoso*.[43] This directive, though it may have originally been intended for the traditional orders of nuns, was soon applied to the new groups of women as well.

In the late thirteenth and early fourteenth centuries, there were increasing attempts to get the friars to assume some sort of responsibility for the direction of these religious women. This attitude may have been adopted because of fears of women's independence and the possibility that they might adopt heretical thinking, fears which also helped produce the pressure towards cloister. According to Roberto Rusconi, *Periculoso* "sanctioned the definitive transformation of the feminine forms of religious life of Franciscan inspiration into monastic institutions of the traditional type."[44] Nevertheless, from the fourteenth century onward, many Franciscan women were determined to lead a non-cloistered life, and in spite of the odds, some succeeded.

Where does Elizabeth fit into this movement? This question goes much further than just the conflicting opinions about status and identity as a Franciscan. It was the common features in the lives of thirteenth-century Franciscan women like Elizabeth, Clare, and Agnes of Bohemia, the similar problems they faced and the similar choices they made, that led others to give them a common name. But in seeking their own charism, they were affected by juridical concerns of the hierarchy, as well as the broader strictures on women at the time. When we study what they were seeking, what compromises they may have been forced to make, and what they found most important in their vocation, we will discover something about the most intimate part of their lives. This tension between charism and outside pressures was also faced by St. Francis and his first male followers, of course, but their society had a quite different expectation of them as men. Thus the question of religious vocation is an important part of women's history.

Elizabeth and Methodological Questions

There have been a number of recent historical studies about Elizabeth, but there are many gaps in the treatment of her. To begin with, there are very few in-depth textual studies of the existing sources for her life. Very little work has been done on the sources since the preliminary editions at the beginning of the twentieth century, and it was only in the last few years that one of the most popular Latin lives of Elizabeth, the one by Dietrich of Apolda, received its first modern critical edition.[45] Neither this life nor the earlier one by Caesarius of Heisterbach has ever been translated into English. While one partial English translation of the documents of the canonization process was published fifty years ago, it has long been out of print.[46] Other works about Elizabeth have remained unedited until recently. One of these texts is perhaps the earliest known Franciscan life of Elizabeth, known as the Valenciennes life, written about 1250. The most important Franciscan document on Elizabeth, however, is a life whose author is commonly known as the Anonymous Franciscan. This is a late thirteenth-century life which contains eyewitness testimony from Elizabeth's canonization process, testimony which up until now has remained unknown, and which does not appear in the process as we now possess it. Among these testimonies are those of some Franciscan and Dominican friars who described Elizabeth's religious life, habit and conception of poverty.

Historical studies on Elizabeth have rarely explored the relationship between the sources. As a result, a number of basic questions about Elizabeth's life are still unresolved, including the events leading up to her choice of the religious life and the nature of that life. And the newly-discovered sources are still unexplored. A new study of the relationship between all the sources is greatly needed.

As yet, there are few studies that attempt to incorporate Elizabeth into the recent work in hagiography and women's studies. Although Elizabeth was a mystic, she left no written accounts of her visions; nor did she have a biographer or secretary, male or female, who knew her personally, or who could interpret her thought as did Mechtild of Magdeburg, Angela of Foligno and other women; even her confessor, Conrad of Marburg, did not write to any extent about her visions. Thus there is no extensive record of Elizabeth's mystical or visionary experiences that can be examined for their reflections of male and female perspectives, as scholars have done for other religious women. Yet we are fortunate to have, in addition to a brief letter by her confessor, Conrad of Marburg, eyewitness testimonies to her life by four women: Guda, Isentrude, Irmingard, and Elisabeth, who were close to her and who provide four different women's perspective on her life. I know of no studies, however, devoted to a feminist reading of this text that uses the methodology discussed above. There is a detailed study of Elizabeth's daily life based on the testimonies of these women by Raoul Manselli. However, while Manselli did compare the women's insights with that of Elizabeth's confessor, he did not use a specific methodology for recovering their viewpoint as women.47

Clearly a new approach is needed to the sources for Elizabeth's life. It should draw on the above methods which enable the historian to account for the differences between eyewitness testimony and later literary texts in the formation of the hagiographic tradition about her; and it should also try to recover something about her as an individual woman apart from the male-dominated society's construction of her. Therefore, my purpose in this study is to analyze both the traditional and the new sources for Elizabeth's life. I will especially be concerned with how these sources regard the question of her vocation within the women's religious movement of the thirteenth century. In this way, I hope to recover her voice as a woman and her personality as a saint. I will discuss the relationship between these texts, establish their place in the hagiographic tradition about Elizabeth, and analyze their significance for historians who examine her life. I will also examine how she fits into the typical pattern of women's religious lives that some historians have uncovered.

The following chapters will help fill the gap in scholarly knowledge by making it possible to study many details of Elizabeth's religious life and service to the poor for the first time, and illuminating the ways in which Elizabeth, like other thirteenth-century religious women, had to balance her religious life between poverty, prayer, service and institutional demands. The resulting picture of her will provide new insight into the lives of medieval Franciscan women and religious women in general.

Notes

[1] Rosemary Radford Ruether, *Sexism and God-Talk: Toward a Feminist Theology* (Boston: Beacon Press, 1993), p. 22.

[2] See, for example, the essays in Catherine M. Mooney, ed., *Gendered Voices: Medieval Saints and their Interpreters* (Philadelphia: University of Pennsylvania Press, 1999); another recent study is John Coakley, "Gender and the Authority of the Friars: The Significance of Holy Women for Thirteenth-Century Franciscans and Dominicans," *Church History* 60 (1991): 445-60.

[3] See the comments by Karen Scott, "Mystical Death, Bodily Death: Catherine of Siena and Raymond of Capua on the Mystic's Encounter with God," in Mooney, *Gendered Voices*, pp. 140-44.

[4] Pierre Delooz, "Towards a Sociological Study of Canonized Sainthood in the Catholic Church," in Stephen Wilson, ed, *Saints and Their Cults: Studies in Religious Sociology, Folklore and History* (Cambridge/ New York: Cambridge University Press, 1983), pp. 189-216.

[5] Donald Weinstein and Rudolph M. Bell, *Saints and Society: The Two Worlds of Western Christendom, 1000-1700* (Chicago: University of Chicago Press, 1982); Michael Goodich, *Vita Perfecta: The Ideal of Sainthood in the Thirteenth Century* (Stuttgart: Anton Hiersemann, 1982).

[6] Weinstein and Bell, *Saints and Society*, pp. 228-29.

[7] Rudolph Bell, *Holy Anorexia* (Chicago: University of Chicago Press, 1985).

[8] Caroline Walker Bynum, *Holy Feast and Holy Fast: The Religious Significance of Food to Medieval Women* (Berkeley: University of California Press, 1987).

[9] Aviad Kleinberg, *Prophets in Their Own Country: Living Saints and the Making of Sainthood in the Late Middle Ages* (Chicago:

University of Chicago Press, 1992), pp. 8-16.

[10] Karen Scott, "Mystical Death, Bodily Death," p. 144.

[11] Amy Hollywood, "Inside Out: Beatrice of Nazareth and Her Hagiographer," in Mooney, ed., *Gendered Voices*, pp. 78-98.

[12] See Ulrike Wiethaus, "Sexuality, Gender and the Body in Late Medieval Spirituality: Cases from Germany and the Netherlands," *Journal of Feminist Studies in Religion* 7 (1991): 35-52.

[13] For a summary of some of these trends, see Patrick Geary, "Saints, Scholars and Society: The Elusive Goal," in his *Living with the Dead in the Middle Ages* (Ithaca: Cornell University Press, 1994), pp. 9-29.

[14] Kleinberg, *Prophets*, p. 10.

[15] See the essays in Mooney, *Gendered Voices*; also Catherine Mooney, "The Authorial Role of Brother A in the Composition of Angela of Foligno's Revelations," in E. Ann Matter and John Coakley, eds., *Creative Women in Medieval and Early Modern Italy: A Religious and Artistic Renaissance* (Philadelphia: University of Pennsylvania Press, 1994), pp. 34-63.

[16] Anne M. Schuchman, "Literary Collaboration in the *Life* of Umiliana dei Cerchi," *Magistra: A Journal of Women's Spirituality in History* 7:2 (Winter 2001): 5-22.

[17] André Vauchez, *La sainteté en occident aux derniers siècles du moyen age, d'après les procès de canonisation et les documents hagiographiques* (Rome: École Française de Rome, 1981).

[18] Jacques Paul, "Témoignage historique et hagiographique dans le procès de canonisation de Louis d'Anjou," *Provence historique* 93-94 (1973): 305-317. Enrico Menestó made similar observations about attempts at control and the independence of some witnesses in his "The Apostolic Canonization Proceedings of Clare of Montefalco, 1318-1319," in Daniel Bornstein and Roberto Rusconi, eds., *Women and Religion in Medieval and Renaissance Italy*

(Chicago and London: University of Chicago Press, 1996), pp. 108-110.

[19] Catherine M. Mooney, "Voice, Gender and the Portrayal of Sanctity," in Catherine M. Mooney, ed., *Gendered Voices*, p. 8; see also her article in the same collection, "*Imitatio Christi or Imitatio Mariae*?: Clare of Assisi and Her Interpreters," pp. 52-77.

[20] Dyan Elliot, "Authorizing a Life: The Collaboration of Dorothea of Montau and John Marienwerder," in Mooney, *Gendered Voices*, especially pp. 186-190.

[21] Vauchez, *La sainteté en occident*, pp. 4-5.

[22] Mechthild von Magdeburg, *The Flowing Light of the Godhead*, translated and introduced by Frank Tobin, preface by Margot Schmidt (New York/Mahwah, N. J.: Paulist Press, 1998), p. 215.

[23] A recent edition is Herbert Grundmann, *Religious Movements in the Middle Ages* (Notre Dame/London: University of Notre Dame Press, 1995); for the women's movement, see especially pp. 75-152.

[24] Goodich, *Vita Perfecta*, pp. 100-123.

[25] Carol Neel, "The Origins of the Beguines," in Judith M. Bennett, Elizabeth A. Clark, Jean F. O'Barr, et al., eds., *Sisters and Workers in the Middle Ages* (Chicago and London: University of Chicago Press, 1979), pp. 240-260.

[26] Jo Ann McNamara, *Sisters in Arms: Catholic Nuns Through Two Millennia* (Cambridge, MA/ London: Harvard University Press, 1996), p. 236.

[27] See Grundmann, *Religious Movements in the Middle Ages*, pp. 148-49.

[28] For a discussion of this question and other criticisms, see Robert Lerner's introduction to Grundmann, *Religious Movements in the Middle Ages*, pp. xxiii-xxv.

[29] David Herlihy, "Women in Medieval Society," in his *The Social History of Italy and Western Europe, 700-1500* (London: Variorium Reprints, 1978), pp. ix, 3-17.

[30] Brenda Bolton, *"Mulieres sanctae," Studies in Church History* 10 (1973): 77-95.

[31] McNamara, *Sisters in Arms*, p. 235.

[32] Brenda Bolton, "Daughters of Rome: All One in Christ Jesus," in W. J. Sheils and Diana Wood, eds., *Women in the Church* (Cambridge, MA: Blackwell, 1990), pp. 101-16.

[33] Anna Benvenuti Papi, "La Serva-Patrona," in *"In castro poenitentiale:"santità e società femminile nell'Italia medioevale* (Rome: Herder Editrice e Libreria, 1990), pp. 264-303; Mario Sensi, "Anchoresses and Penitents in Thirteenth- and Fourteenth-Century Umbria," in Bornstein and Rusconi, *Women and Religion in Medieval and Renaissance Italy*, pp. 56-83.

[34] Anna Benvenuti Papi, "Mendicant Friars and Female *pinzochere* in Tuscany: From Social Marginality to Models of Sanctity," in Bornstein and Rusconi, *Women and Religion in Medieval and Renaissance Italy*, 86-87.

[35] See G. G. Meersseman, *Dossier de l'ordre de la pénitence au xiiie siècle*, 2nd edition (Fribourg: Éditions Universitaires Fribourg Suisse, 1982); among other recent works is Mariano D'Alatri, *Aetas poenitentialis: l'antico Ordine francescano della penitenza* (Rome: Istituto Storico dei Cappuccini, 1993).

[36] Papi, "Mendicant Friars and Female *pinzochere* in Tuscany," pp. 84-86.

[37] Raffaele Pazzelli, *The Franciscan Sisters: Outlines of History and Spirituality* (Steubenville, Ohio: Franciscan University, 1989); Raffaele Pazzelli and Lino Temperini, *Prime manifestazioni di vita communitarie maschile e femminile nel movimento francescano della Pentitenza (1215-1447)*, Atti del Convegno di Studi Francescani, Assisi, 30 giugno-3 luglio, 1981 (Rome: Analecta TOR, 1982); Anna

Benvenuti Papi, "Mendicant Friars and Female *pinzochere* in Tuscany," pp. 84-103.

[38] Margaret Carney, O.S.F., *The First Franciscan Woman: Clare of Assisi and Her Form of Life* (Steubenville, Ohio: Franciscan Press, 1993), p. 15.

[39] In addition to Carney's *The First Franciscan Woman*, see Ingrid J. Peterson, O.S.F, *Clare of Assisi: A Biographical Study* (Quincy, Ill.: Franciscan Press, 1993); Clara Gennaro, "Clare, Agnes and Their Earliest Followers: From the Poor Ladies of San Damiano to the Poor Clares," in Bornstein and Rusconi, *Women and Religion in Medieval and Renaissance Italy*, pp. 39-55; Catherine Mooney, "*Imitatio Christi or Imitatio Mariae?*: Clare of Assisi and Her Interpreters," in Mooney, *Gendered Voices*, 52-77.

[40] Roberta McKelvie, O.S.F., *Retrieving a Living Tradition: Angelina of Montegiove: Franciscan, Tertiary, Beguine* (St. Bonaventure, NY: Franciscan Institute, 1997).

[41] McKelvie, *Retrieving a Living Tradition*, p. 7.

[42] Roberto Rusconi, "L'espansione del francescanesimo femminile nel secolo xiii," *Movimento religioso femminile e francescanesimo nel secolo xiii* (Assisi: Società Internazionale degli Studi Francescani, 1980), pp. 277-294.

[43] See Elizabeth Makowski, *Canon Law and Cloistered Women: Periculoso and Its Commentators, 1298-1545* (Washington, D. C.: The Catholic University of America Press, 1997), p. 31, where the relevant literature is cited.

[44] Rusconi, "L'espansione del francescanesimo femminile," p. 270.

[45] *Die Vita der Heiligen Elisabeth des Dietrich von Apolda*, ed. Monika Rener (Marburg: N. G. Elwert, 1993).

[46] Nesta De Robeck, *Saint Elizabeth of Hungary: A Story of Twenty-Four Years* (Milwaukee: Bruce, 1954), pp. 155-203.

[47] Raoul Manselli, "Royal Holiness in the Daily Life of Elizabeth of Hungary: The Testimony of Her Servants," *Greyfriars Review* 11 (1997): 1-20.

Chapter I

Sources and Problems
of Interpretation

The Sources for Elizabeth's Life

We are fortunate to have a large number of sources for Elizabeth's life, though historians are not agreed in how to interpret them. In additions, the sources all have various special problems, and each needs to be considered separately.

The Canonization Process

The records of Elizabeth's canonization process, which began in 1232, less than a year after her death, and ended with her canonization in 1235, have long been considered the most valuable source for information about her, but there has been considerable controversy about the form in which the texts have come down to us.[1] A description of the stages of the canonization process will help illuminate the difficulties.

The process can be divided into four stages. The first is the preliminary stage where it was determined that the investigation of Elizabeth's sanctity should be undertaken. The surviving documents from this stage begin with a letter written by Elizabeth's confessor, Conrad of Marburg, to Pope Gregory IX shortly after August 10, 1232, in response to inquiries that the Pope's penitentiary, Raymond of Peñafort, had made about her life, evidently with a view to opening a process to examine her sanctity. Conrad described a preliminary inquest into the miracles worked at Elizabeth's tomb which he had presided over on August 10 of that year. He also included a brief summary of her life and virtues as he knew them from personal experience.[2] A summary of the depositions on the miracles taken that day also survives.[3]

The next stage, the *first examination* (the preliminary examination of 1232 was not counted in the numbering)[4] followed quickly: by mandates of October 13 and 14, 1232, the Pope appointed a commission, consisting of Archbishop Siegfried of Mainz, Abbot Raymond of Eberbach and Master Conrad of Marburg, Elizabeth's confessor, to inquire into her virtues and miracles. They were asked to hold on to the results of this investigation until the arrival of another mandate directing that they be sent to Rome.[5] This first investigation was carried out in January and February of 1233. From it we have a report containing a letter by the commissioners to the Pope, another copy of Conrad's summary of Elizabeth's life, and testimony on 106 miracles given before the commission. The commissioners stated in their letter that they had also "diligently questioned both [Elizabeth's] acquaintances and the religious and God-fearing members of her household about her way of life," but none of these depositions can be found in the existing copies of the report.[6]

The process now came to a standstill for a time. In part, the delay may have come about because of the controversy that broke out between Conrad of Marburg and fellow commission member Siegfried of Mainz. Conrad, who was appointed papal inquisitor shortly after Elizabeth's death, acted without restraint and without allowing those accused of heresy to speak or call witnesses in their defense, and Siegfried opposed his over-zealous approach. Conrad even accused some of the high German nobility of heresy. The Pope had to intervene. Then, on July 30, 1233,

Conrad was assassinated, apparently on the orders of some of the accused nobles.

Apparently no further progress was made in the investigation for about a year. But, following a visit by Elizabeth's brother-in-law Conrad to Rome in the summer of 1234, during which he spoke with the Pope about her process, Gregory IX sent a second set of mandates to Bishop Conrad of Hildesheim and the abbots of Georgenthal and Hersfeld on October 11, 1234, authorizing them to send the results of the previous investigation into Elizabeth's miracles to the Holy See, or if these were not available, to carry out a new investigation of trustworthy witnesses.[7]

The third stage was the *second examination*, held beginning on January 1, 1235. But instead of the crusade preacher and inquisitor Conrad of Marburg, the motivating force behind this stage was the powerful Teutonic order, recently established in Marburg, to which Elizabeth's brother-in-law, Landgraf Conrad belonged. In their report, the commissioners included the miracles of the first examination of 1233. They also took down testimony on 24 new miracles. None of the copies of this report contain any testimonies on Elizabeth's life.

The only surviving testimonies about Elizabeth's life known until recently are contained in a document which is usually called the *Dicta quattuor ancillarum Sancte Elisabeth*, or the "Statements of the Four Handmaids of St. Elizabeth." These four were Guda and Isentrude, who had been noble ladies of her retinue at court and who later joined her in religious life, and Irmingard and Elizabeth, women of humble birth who served with her at her hospital in Marburg. The work is an adaptation of the testimonies of these witnesses, made into a continuous narrative in rough chronological order. There are two versions, one longer and one shorter. The title goes back to Dietrich of Apolda's designation for the longer version: *Libellus de dictis quattuor ancillarum Sancte Elisabeth confectus* (Little book made out of the statements of the handmaids of St. Elizabeth). I will call the shorter one the *Dicta* and the longer the *Libellus*, although, as will become clear later, neither version is identical with the original depositions. A number of manuscripts of the *Libellus* have a prologue on Elizabeth's virtues, beginning *Ad decus et honorem*, and a conclusion.[8] These texts must have been widely circulated, judging by the number of manuscripts found.

The fourth stage is Elizabeth's canonization itself, which took place in Perugia on May 27, 1235. The documents associated with this stage include the bull of canonization, *Gloriosus in maiestate*, issued on June 1 by Gregory IX[9] and another letter written by the Pope a few days later to Queen Beatrice of Castile, beginning *Vas admirabile* (Wondrous Vessel).[10] Another document associated with the canonization is the *Processus et ordo canonizationis beate Elyzabet* (The canonization process and ceremony of Blessed Elizabeth), which the author explains was "written on account of certain detractions and calumnies." It describes the hearing of the witnesses in 1235 and the subsequent approval of the minutes of this examination by the Holy See. This is followed by a vivid description of the canonization ceremony itself, in which the author stresses the presence at the Pope's side of Landgraf Conrad. The document seems to have been written shortly after the canonization by a member of the Curia, perhaps Raymund of Peñafort, who had already taken part in the process on behalf of the Pope. The author never clearly specifies what "detractions and calumnies" his work was directed against, but Huyskens has suggested that the author's stress on the "sincere favor" the Pope gave to Elizabeth's cause may have been intended to allay suspicions that he was swayed in favor of her canonization by financial contributions made by Landgraf Conrad, a member of the new saint's family, which would have been tantamount to simony. In fact, while the writer does not try

29

at all to hide the favor the Pope showed to Conrad, he also stresses that the clergy and nobility of Germany unanimously asked for Elizabeth's canonization. Huyskens noted that the work was also perhaps intended to serve as a model for the conducting of future canonization processes.[11]

Even before Elizabeth's canonization process began, Gregory had been aware of her reputation for holiness. He had come to her aid when she was experiencing difficulties with her dower after her husband's death, by taking her and her property under the protection of the Holy See, and had corresponded with her, as described below.

One of the Pope's motives for wanting to declare Elizabeth a saint is suggested by the text of her bull of canonization. In it, he describes how, through the renown of Elizabeth's life and the miracles worked after her death, "the way to truth is pointed out to the unbelievers, and material accumulated for the confusion of the heretics." He added:

> For by the merits of the Saint who, while enclosed in the prison of the flesh, was poor in spirit, meek of mind, wept over her sins or rather the sins of others, thirsted after justice, dedicated herself to mercy, was pure of heart, truly peace-loving, and crushed by opprobrium and persecutions, these heretics see life restored to the dead, sight to the blind, hearing to the deaf, speech to the dumb, the power of walking to the sick, by the right hand of heaven. They see these vast regions of Germany which they have tried to poison by their doctrine of death exult in many ways in the embrace of heavenly doctrine.[12]

Both the Cathars and the Waldensians were active in Germany during Elizabeth's lifetime. Much of their widespread appeal was due to their claim to be living the true Christian life because of their austerity, which contrasted with the luxurious living of many clerics. Whether Conrad of Marburg's accusations against the highest members of the German nobility were true or not, they certainly give an idea of the contemporary assessment of the enormity of the problem. The Pope was aware of the need to fight heresy by positive, not just negative means. Elizabeth, a member of the aristocracy living the true Christian life, was to him a way of upholding both orthodoxy and true Christian austerity and poverty as an answer to the heretics' criticism of the Church. An example of Elizabeth's strong influence on people in this regard can be found in the depositions on the miracles. One of the witnesses of 1233 testified that she had been an adherent of the "Poor of Lyons" or the Waldensians, before returning to the Catholic faith. It seems likely that the saint's example also helped bring her back to the faith, for she later received healing through prayer to Elizabeth.[13]

In addition, the Pope seems to have wanted to hold Elizabeth up as a model for other women, at a time when they were attracted to dangerous beliefs and movements. In his letter to Beatrice of Castile, he extolled the virtues of the new saint, especially her service to the poor, and held her up as a "mirror" for Beatrice to look into and imitate.[14]

In fact, according to Caesarius of Heisterbach, "[The Pope's] devotion for her was so great that he sent special letters to the different religious orders of the Church, asking and ordering that they celebrate the feast day of St. Elizabeth, which they did."[15]

Elizabeth's cult was a genuinely popular one, as evidenced by the huge crowds of pilgrims at her tomb from the time of her death. According to Michael Goodich, who analyzed the social status of the witnesses to her miracles in the canonization process, Elizabeth was a "national" saint who appealed to all classes, but perhaps most to women and the poorer people.[16]

The great attraction Elizabeth's life held for ordinary people is indicated by the existence of at least one popular ballad about her within little more than a year after her death. A fifty-year-old woman named Matilda from the town of Beidenkopf near Marburg, who had been blind in one eye, testified before the papal commissioners that as she was on her way to Elizabeth's tomb in January 1233 hoping for a cure, "she heard people singing a song in German about the separation of a tearful Elizabeth from her husband, the Landgraf Ludwig, as he was about to leave for the Holy Land. This song moved Matilda to tears; while she was weeping, she recovered the sight in her eye."[17] The popular sympathy for Elizabeth demonstrates that the common people were attracted to a married saint whose life they could understand. Her great popularity may well also have contributed to her rapid canonization.

Other Early Sources

Outside of the canonization process, there are a few other early sources that date from Elizabeth's lifetime or shortly after her death. Pope Gregory IX wrote a letter of encouragement to her as she entered on her religious life, which still survives.[18] There is a brief letter describing her death attributed to Abbess Lutrude of Wetter, and a list of the first miracles worked at her tomb, both of which date from shortly after her death.[19]

An important early source is the *Gesta Ludovici* (The deeds of Ludwig), a chronicle of the life and reign of Ludwig IV of Thuringia, written by his chaplain, Berthold, not long after Ludwig's death in 1227, perhaps even while Elizabeth was still alive. It recorded the major events in the lives of the noble couple, including the births of their children, their travels, Ludwig's departure for the crusade, and his death. The original Latin text no longer exists, but portions of it were quoted in Dietrich of Apolda's life of Elizabeth (see below). There is also a later adaptation of the *Gesta* called the *Vita Ludovici*, or Life of Ludwig, made by the monks of Reinhardsbrunn, a monastery greatly favored by the ruling family of Thuringia, where Ludwig was buried. In fact, the monks apparently wrote their account of him as propaganda for his sainthood. The complete Latin text of this life is no longer extant, but portions of it can be found in the later chronicle of the abbey, the *Chronicle of Reinhardsbrunn*.[20] A German translation of the *Vita Ludovici* was made about 1330 by Friedrich Ködiz.[21]

Thirteenth-Century Lives of Elizabeth

There are several thirteenth-century lives of Elizabeth based on the early sources. First there is the brief life written in 1236 or 1237 by the Cistercian monk Caesarius of Heisterbach, at a suggestion made by Conrad of Marburg before his death, and later at the urging of the Teutonic Order. In his introductory letter addressed to Ulrich von Dürn, Prior of the house of the Teutonic Order in Marburg, and his brothers, Caesarius recalls how Ulrich had given a little notebook (*quaternulam*) containing a simple recounting of Elizabeth's life to Christian, a monk from Caesarius' monastery who had attended her translation in May 1236. Caesarius used it as his main source for his life.[22] From textual evidence, it is clear that this notebook was the shorter version of the handmaids' testimonies (the *Dicta*). He added a rhetorical polish to these statements and also contributed a few details from other sources. Since the Teutonic Order had taken it upon itself to promulgate Elizabeth's cult, Caesarius' life has something of an official character.

There is also another short life based on the *Dicta* and Conrad of Marburg's letter, which was found at the Austrian monastery of Zwettl. According to its editor, it was written between 1236 and 1239. It is largely a dry summary of the *Dicta*. From passages praising the Emperor Frederick II and describing his honored presence at Elizabeth's translation, we can deduce that it was probably written by one of Frederick's supporters, perhaps a courtier wanting to praise a saint close to the emperor.[23]

By far the most popular life of Elizabeth in the Middle Ages is the one completed about 1297 by a Dominican friar named Dietrich of Apolda, a native of Thuringia, who entered the order about 1247. We know that he was working on his life of Elizabeth at the same time he was writing a life of St. Dominic, a commission he received from the Minister General of his order between 1286 and 1288,[24] and that he did not finish it until 1297. Dietrich's life of Elizabeth was not the result of any commission, but it seems to have been a labor of love for him on behalf of a popular local saint, since he worked on it for close to ten years in between all his other duties. That he had an interest in women's mysticism is shown by the quotations from Mechtild of Magdeburg's *Flowing Light of the Godhead* in his biography of St. Dominic.[25]

Dietrich tells us in his prologue that he used the *Libellus* and with it Conrad of Marburg's letter. But, Dietrich says, though these sources contained the "pure and simple truth," they were not completely satisfactory because they did not provide enough details about people and places, and the information was not in any kind of order. He carried out a long search for other sources, looking at chronicles in various monasteries, questioning "very old and truthful persons," and sending letters to many places. He names among his other sources a sermon by a Dominican friar named Odo, the text of which has not been discovered.[26] He also used some of the chaplain Berthold's *Gesta Ludovici*.

There is also an account of Elizabeth's life in the *Golden Legend*, written about 1260 by the Dominican friar Jacobus de

Voragine. [27] Her inclusion in this collection is testament to her popularity and helped spread knowledge about her, since it was one of the most popular hagiographical works of the later Middle Ages and was translated into a number of languages.

There are a large number of vernacular medieval lives of Elizabeth. There are lives in German in both verse and prose, many of them based on Dietrich. [28] There are also several lives in French, most of them using the *Libellus* as a source, testifying to the wide popularity of this source in France. Among them is the thirteenth-century verse life written by the poet Rutebeuf. [29] Another was written by a monk named Robert of Cambligneul. [30] These works are not usually considered sources of reliable information about Elizabeth, but some of them do play a role in the formation of traditions found in the Franciscan biographies of her, as we will see later.

While a number of medieval lives, offices and other texts on Elizabeth from Germany and northern France have been published, no works about her from thirteenth-century Hungarian authors have been known up to now. It seems likely that the *Golden Legend* version of Elizabeth's life was current in Hungary in the fourteenth century, as evidenced by a beautifully illustrated legendary, made for the Angevin ruler Charles I of Hungary and his wife Elizabeth sometime between 1328 and 1333. The legendary is incomplete and scattered among various libraries, but the part which remains contains a number of lives of Hungarian saints of Elizabeth's Árpád dynasty (St. Stephen, St. Emeric), and saints of the House of Anjou (Louis of Toulouse), expressed entirely through images and written captions. Some of the missing leaves almost certainly contained a life of St. Elizabeth, probably based, like most of the others, on the *Legenda aurea*. [31] The earliest-known independent Hungarian treatments of Elizabeth's life are usually thought to be the late-fifteenth-century sermons by the Franciscans Pelbart of Temesvár and Oswald

Laskai.[32]   It is strange that although Elizabeth appears in early iconography in Hungary, there seem to have been almost no surviving lives, sermons or other works about her in her native land before the fifteenth century.[33] Yet a legend of Elizabeth does seem to have circulated in Hungary in the thirteenth century. The *Vita* of her niece, St. Margaret of Hungary, a nun in the Dominican convent in Veszprem from 1246-1270, says that she read the lives of her saintly ancestors, including Elizabeth.[34] This could have been the *Dicta* or *Libellus* or perhaps some other work. As I will show later, at least one thirteenth- or early fourteenth-century Hungarian author did write a life of Elizabeth.

Franciscan Sources

Lastly, there was an early tradition about Elizabeth within the Franciscan order, which, except for a few works, is largely ignored or unknown.   The source from this tradition that is probably best known and most used is the *Chronicle* of Giordano of Giano. This lively work was written around 1262 by Giordano, an Italian friar, who went on the first successful Franciscan mission to Germany beginning in 1221, and who later became the *custos* of Thuringia.[35] Other Franciscan works are less frequently consulted as sources.   One is the *Chronicle* of Fra Salimbene, written about 1284, which mentions Elizabeth several times.[36] A short life of Elizabeth of Franciscan origin from the Bibliotheca Laurenziana in Florence has been published.[37] Nor did preachers ignore Elizabeth.   Some thirteenth- and fourteenth-century Franciscan sermons about Elizabeth have also been published.[38] In addition to the Dominican sermon by friar Odo used by Dietrich, which has not been found, other early Dominican sermons about her are extant.[39]

There are two important Franciscan lives of Elizabeth that have remained unpublished until just recently: the Valenciennes Life, so named because the first complete text of it was found in a manuscript in Valenciennes,[40] and the Anonymous Franciscan, which is partly based on the Valenciennes Life. While the existence of the Valenciennes Life was only signaled in the twentieth century, the existence of the Anonymous Franciscan has been known since Franciscan authors Sedulius and Wadding first used and quoted a manuscript of it in the seventeenth century, but no complete text of it has been known until recently.[41] Historians have occasionally mentioned these works, but usually only in passing. Nevertheless, they present a tradition about Elizabeth that is worth exploring.

The Anonymous Franciscan life in particular contains many anecdotes about Elizabeth and the Franciscans. From the complete text, we learn that, according to the author, she lived next to the Franciscan convent in Marburg and had close contact with the friars during the last two and a half years of her life. Most important, this source contains testimonies by some Franciscan and Dominican friars who knew Elizabeth. These testimonies appear to have come from her canonization process, though they do not appear in the *Dicta/Libellus*. Thus the Anonymous Franciscan is potentially a very important source for early eyewitness testimony about Elizabeth. Since neither it nor the other Franciscan sources have played much part in the traditional historiography on Elizabeth, they will be discussed in later chapters.

The History of Scholarship on Elizabeth

The Bollandists began collecting material on St. Elizabeth in the seventeenth century. Their volume on the saints for November was never published, though the material has been used by other scholars.[42] Modern scholarship on Elizabeth really began in Germany in the eighteenth century with a biographical study by K. W. Justi,[43] and the publication of the *Libellus* for the first time by J. B. Mencke in 1728.[44] But these were isolated works.

It was only in the early nineteenth century that both scholarship on Elizabeth and popular devotion to her were re-inspired by the work of a young French Catholic nobleman, Charles, comte de Montalembert. During a trip to Germany in 1833, he had visited Elizabeth's church in Marburg and had become fascinated by her life. His exhaustive researches in the manuscript material in Germany and talks with German scholars resulted in a biography, *Histoire de Sainte Elizabeth de Hongrie*, first published in 1836.[45] Montalembert's work was deeply influenced by the Romantic spiritual enthusiasm and fascination with the Middle Ages, the French Catholic revival of that period, and the interest of German poets and philologists in their country's language and culture. The biography, while quite uncritical, was written in a vivid style, became immensely popular and went through numerous editions in several languages. Montalembert, influenced by the current spirit, stressed all of the legendary and romantic aspects of his heroine's life, but he did do some important work in uncovering and identifying the sources. While his work spurred the interest of scholars in Elizabeth's life, it created a rather uncritical legend for modern readers, and historians have had to spend much time reassessing the resulting image of her.

Early in the twentieth century, as part of the flurry of interest in Elizabeth occasioned by the seventh centenary of her birth in 1907, a number of German historians undertook a critical examination of the sources for her life. This interest was ecumenical; the Protestants in Germany had always admired Elizabeth for her life of charity, and Protestant scholars joined Catholic ones in the research. One German scholar, Albert Huyskens, edited both versions of the testimonies from her canonization process, the *Dicta* and the *Libellus*.[46] Another, Karl Wenck, made his own examination of the sources and the history of the canonization process, in which he strongly disputed some of Huyskens' conclusions.[47] Their work on the texts has been the foundation for historical discussion ever since. Huyskens was a Catholic and Wenck a Protestant, but both approached the material with a serious critical spirit, and engaged in extensive research to verify the historical basis for the events of Elizabeth's life.

During the earlier part of the twentieth century, most Catholic historians followed the scholarly discipline of the Bollandists, whose main concern was defending the dignity of the saints and the authentic tradition about them by firmly separating fact from legend; they excluded texts they regarded as inauthentic, especially those with a legendary flavor.[48] Jeanne Ancelet-Hustache, a Catholic historian of fine critical sense, followed this tradition. Shortly after World War II, she used the results of the previous research to write a rigorous scholarly biography of Elizabeth.[49] Her work showed the Bollandist influence in her insistence on depending almost solely on the earliest sources: that is, the *Dicta/Libellus*, Conrad's letter, the chronicle of Berthold, and a few other early documents. She considered the Franciscan tradition about Elizabeth, including the Anonymous Franciscan (then known only in a fragment), to be largely legend.

While there have been a large number of devotional lives of Elizabeth, few genuinely scholarly biographies have been written.[50] Most of the biographies and historical studies have been in German; English-language scholarship has been meager, at least until very recently. The interpretation of Elizabeth's life has been influenced not only by religious differences between Catholics and Protestants, but by other ideological pressures as well. Ulrike Wiethaus has suggested that the traditional Catholic picture of Elizabeth – the obedient, domesticated wife – played into the Nazi ideology of the 1930's and 40's, which sought to keep women in their place.[51] One of the few attempts to go beneath the traditional surface, Elisabeth Busse-Wilson's 1931 biography, took a Freudian approach. The author explored issues of the body and sexuality in Elizabeth's life, as well as her rebellion against religious conventions. It shocked the public at the time, and, as Wiethaus pointed out, it was subsequently almost ignored until the 1980's.[52]

Elizabeth and Recent Hagiographic Research

In addition, historical research on Elizabeth has been affected by recent trends of scholarly research in hagiography. Some authors of quantitative studies, such as Weinstein and Bell and Michael Goodich, largely limited themselves to including Elizabeth as part of their statistical survey.[53] André Vauchez took a statistical approach to canonization processes for medieval saints from the thirteenth century on, and analyzed Elizabeth's life as part of his picture of mendicant saints, lay saints, and royal and aristocratic saints.[54] While these works are useful for analyzing particular trends, they do not present anything like a complete view of Elizabeth even as a "constructed" saint of her time.

Bynum considered Elizabeth as an example of her theory about the compulsive relationship between medieval women and food because of her refusal to eat certain foods at her husband's table, which Bynum saw as a rejection of her husband's family.[55] Bynum did not study the sources on Elizabeth closely, however, or place the question of food in the context of the rest of her life. So there is some question about whether the pattern of food compulsion could be applied to her.

A few recent studies have discussed Elizabeth as an individual "person" rather than just as a "saint," One of these is by Anja Petrakopoulos. "The figure of Elizabeth has become an icon," she writes, "yet she had enough force to change the icon to fit her own shaping of piety." Petrakopoulos' intention was "to study not only the image of the saint but also the historical person."56 She traces in detail how the later legends dealt with the troublesome subjects of Elizabeth's sexuality, marriage and motherhood, and provides some useful insights. Nevertheless, her methodology is somewhat disappointing. She does not discuss the relationship between the sources or differentiate between the different views of the eyewitnesses, or between these and the later developments of legend .

Brigitte Stark based her study of Elizabeth on the idea that the availability of testimonies from canonization processes and other early documents affected the writing of lives of the saints from the thirteenth century on, allowing for a more individualized portrait of a saint in later works. She traces how this happened in Elizabeth's case by studying her canonization process in comparison with later works about her, including those by Rutebeuf and Dietrich of Apolda. But once again, this author does not study the sources in depth, nor does she have a methodology for treating them. This is most likely because her intention is not to separate historical events from legend, but simply to show how the portrayal of Elizabeth's individual traits developed from one work to another.57

During 1981 and 1982, a number of important studies were published for the 750th anniversary of Elizabeth's death, providing valuable insight into the Germany of her time, the ruling family of Thuringia, her place in the women's movement, and her radical conception of poverty in response to the injustices of feudal life. There was also a study of her canonization process.58 I will quote some of them in the following pages. But they did not really advance the study of the sources or methodology.

The latest feminist studies have not included much about Elizabeth, as I mentioned earlier. This is perhaps because material for the study of the relationship between a male confessor/biographer and a female saint is somewhat lacking, since her confessor, Conrad of Marburg, did not write much about her. But Jo Ann McNamara has done something to place Elizabeth in the context of the response of religious women in her time to their own marginality and how it affected their religious lives.[59]

This short survey has shown the variety of approaches to Elizabeth's life. There are a number of areas in which work remains to be done. In particular, feminist studies on the role of gender in the perception of her need to be developed and integrated with other approaches. At the same time, there are a number of unsolved questions in regard to several aspects of her life that affect the question of her religious vocation. I will turn to the study of these next.

Notes

[1] The most useful collection of Latin texts is the one published by Albert Huyskens in his *Quellenstudien zur Geschichte der hl. Elisabeth, Landgrafin von Thüringen* (Marburg: N. G. Elwert, 1908); Lino Temperini has recently reprinted Huyskens' texts of Conrad's letter, the *Dicta* and the "Canonization Process and Ceremony" in his *Santa Elisabetta d'Ungheria (1207-1231) gloria dei penitenti francescani* (Rome: Editrice Franciscanum, 2002), 439-465; my English translation of the texts will soon be published.

[2] The text of Conrad's letter was edited by Huyskens, *Quellenstudien*, 155-160.

[3] These were edited by Arthur Wyss, *Hessisches Urkundenbuch*, vol. I: *Urkundenbuch der Deutschordens-Ballei Hessen* (Leipzig, 1879), no. 28; see Huyskens, *Quellenstudien*, 16-17 for details.

[4] Huyskens, *Quellenstudien*, 243, 263.

[5] BF 1:85-86 and 86-87.

[6] The report is printed in Huyskens, *Quellenstudien*, 155. All the translations from this and other sources are mine, unless otherwise noted.

[7] Wadding, *Annales Minorum*, v. 1, p. 365; Huyskens, *Quellenstudien*, 16.

[8] See the discussion in Huyskens, *Quellenstudien*, and his edition of the *Libellus*: *Der sogennant Libellus de dictis quattuor ancillarum s. Elisabeth confectus* (Kempten and Munich: Verlag der Jos. Kösel'schen Buchhandlung, 1911).

[9] Leo Santifaller's critical text of the bull of canonization can be found in *Acht Jahrhunderte Deutscher Orden in Einzeldarstellungen*, ed. Klemens Wieser (Bad Godesburg: Verlag Wissenschaftliches Archiv, 1967), 79-81.

[10] I use the edition of Fr. Lemmens, made from the original MS.; "Zur Biographie der heiligen Elisabeth, Landgrafin von Thüringen," *Mitteilungen des historischen Vereins des Diözeses Fulda*, 4 (1901): 2-6.

[11] Huyskens, *Quellenstudien*, 25-31.

[12] Dietrich of Apolda, Die Vita der heiligen Elisabeth, 137.

[13] See Huyskens, *Quellenstudien*, 174-75 (Miracle 14, miracles of 1233).

[14] Lemmens, "Zur Biographie," 2-6.

[15] Caesarius of Heisterbach, "Die Schriften des Caesarius von Heisterbach über die heilige Elisabeth von Thüringen," ed. A. Huyskens, in *Die Wundergeschichten des Caesarius von Heisterbach*, ed. A. Hilka (Bonn, 1937): 3:386.

[16] Michael Goodich, "The Politics of Canonization in the Thirteenth Century: Lay and Mendicant Saints," in Stephen Wilson, ed., *Saints and Their Cults: Studies in Religious Sociology, Folklore and History* (Cambridge: Cambridge University Press, 1983), 172-73.

[17] This miracle is recounted in no. 84 of the deposition of 1233; Huyskens, *Quellenstudien*, 225. Verses that may be part of this song are preserved in the German version of the Life of Ludwig; see Ancelet-Hustache, *Gold Tried by Fire*, 215, 292.

[18] There are editions of two different manuscripts of this letter: they can be found in Klaus J. Heinisch, "Ein Brief Gregors IX an die hl. Elisabeth," FS 25 (1938): 379-82, and Karl Wenck, "Die heilige Elisabeth und Papst Gregor IX," *Hochland* 5 (1907-1908): 129-47.

[19] These were edited by Husykens, *Quellenstudien*, 92-94.

[20] "Cronica Reinhardsbrunnensis," ed. O. Holder-Egger, in MGH SS 30, part 1 (1896): 490-658.

[21] Heinrich Rückert, ed., Das Leben des Heiligen Ludwig, Landgrafen in Thüringen, Gehmahls der heiligen Elisabeth, nach der lateinischen Urschrift übersetzt von Friedrich Ködiz von Salfeld (Leipzig, 1851).

[22] Caesarius of Heisterbach, "Die Schriften des Caesarius von Heisterbach," 3:331-90.

[23] The life is found in Zwettl, Stiftsbibliothek, cod. 326. It was edited by Diodorus Henniges, OFM, as "Vita sanctae Elisabeth, landgraviae Thuringiae, auctore anonymo, nunc primum in lucem edita," AFH 2 (1909): 240-68; see also H. Beumann, "Bericht aus dem Umkreis Kaiser Friedrichs II. uber den Besuch am 1. Mai 1236 in Marburg," *Sankt Elisabeth*, 511.

[24] Matthias Werner, "Die Elisabeth-Vita des Dietrich von Apolda als Beispiel spätmittelalterlicher Hagiographie," *Geschichtsschreibung und Geschichtsbewusstsein im späten Mittelalter*, Vorträge und Forschungen 31, herausgegeben von H. Patze (Sigmaringen: Jan Thorbecke Verlag, 1987), 523-541.

[25] Frank Tobin, Mechtild von Magdeburg: A Medieval Mystic in Modern Eyes (Columbia, SC: Camden House 1995), 5.

[26] Dietrich of Apolda, *Die Vita der heiligen Elisabeth*, 21-22.

[27] For the date, see Giovanni Paolo Maggioni's introduction to the critical edition: Jacobus de Voragine, O. P., *Legenda aurea: edizione critica* (Tavarnuzze: SISMEL: Edizioni del Galluzzo, 1998), xiii.

[28] See, for example, Werner Stannat, Das Leben der heiligen Elisabeth in drei mittelniederdeutschen Handschriften aus Wolfenbüttel und Hannover (Marburg, 1953), for three verse lives in German, based on Dietrich.

[29] *La vie sainte Elysabel* edited, with an extensive introduction in Edmond Faral and Julia Bastin, *Oeuvres complètes de Rutebeuf* (Paris: Editions A. and J. Picard, 1960), 2:60-123, text on 101-23.

[30] *Chi commenche de Sainte Yzabiel*, edited as a supplement in Jubinal, *Oeuvres complètes de Rutebeuf* (Paris: Pannier, 1839), 2:360-412 (from Paris. Bibl. Nat. fr. 19531; 13th century, ff. 112-32v).

[31] F. Levardy, "Il Leggendario ungherese degli Angiò conservato nella Biblioteca Vaticana, nel Morgan Library e nell'Emitage," *Acta Historiae Artium Academiae Scientarum Hungariae* 9 (1963): 75-108, especially 97-99.

[32] These works are discussed in Fortunatos Boros, OFM, "Die hl. Elisabeth in der ungarischen Geschichte," FS 18 (1931): 237-39.

[33] See Boros, "Die hl. Elisabeth in der ungarischen Geschichte," 236; see also Innocenz Takács, "Die Verehung der hl. Elisabeth in Ungarn," FS 18 (1931): 252.

[34] *Vita ex Petri Ranzani, Epitomerer. Hung.*, ASS, Januarii 3:523, no. 11; see also Takacs, "Die Verehrung der hl. Elisabeth in Ungarn," 252.

[35] *Chronica Fratris Iordani*, in AF, I, especially nos. 9-10 and 25.

[36] Salimbene d'Adam, *Cronica*, ed. Giuseppe Scalia (Turnhout, 1998), 1:53 (51 in the 1966 ed.).

[37] L. Lemmens, "Zur Biographie,"14-19.

[38] See, for example Cesare Cenci, OFM, "Noterelle su Fr. Giacomo da Tresanti, lettore predicatore," AFH 86 (1993): 119-128, which contains portions of his sermons on Elizabeth.

[39] Among them is a sermon by the Dominican Peregrinus of Oppeln, given around 1300, published by Gerard de Martel, "Trois sermons inédits du xiiie siècle sur Ruth 3, 11," AFH 89 (1996): 404-410.

[40] Portions of the Valenciennes MS. were published by Ilona Király, "Egy XIII századi szent Erzsébet-legenda," *Egyetemes Philologiai Közlöny (Archivum Philologicum)* 59 (1935): 64-72.

[41] Huyskens published some passages from the Koblenz MS. and from Wadding's quotations in the notes to his edition of the *Libellus*, passim. My edition, based on the manuscripts from Koblenz and Trier, was published as: "A New Life of St. Elizabeth of Hungary: The Anonymous Franciscan," AFH 93 (2000): 29-78;

and later, with a corrected text, in my doctoral dissertation: "St. Elizabeth of Hungary and the Franciscan Tradition," (New York: Fordham University, 2000).

[42] See Huyskens, *Quellenstudien*, 31-40 for a listing of this material, found under the date of November 19, Elizabeth's feast day at the time.

[43] *Elisabeth die Heilige, Landgräfin von Thüringen* (Zürich, 1797).

[44] J. B. Mencke, ed., *"Libellus de dictis quatuor ancillarum S. Elisabethae sive examen miraculorum eius,"* in *Scriptores rerum germanicarum praecipue Saxonicarum* (Leipzig, 1728), II, 2007-2034.

[45] There are numerous editions of this work in many languages, including English. I will use the following, unless otherwise specified: *Histoire de Sainte Elisabeth de Hongrie* (Paris: Lecoffre, 1861). The work has recently been republished in France: *La vie de saint Elisabeth de Hongrie*, Preface de Guy Bedouelle, OP (Paris: Éditions du Cerf, 2005).

[46] Huyskens, *Quellenstudien* and *Libellus* (see above).

[47] Karl Wenck, "Quellenuntersuchungen und Text zur Geschichte der hl. Elisabeth. I. Über die *Dicta quattuor ancillarum sanctae Elisabeth*," *Neues Archiv der Gesellschaft für alter deutsche Geschichtskunde* 34 (1908): 427-502.

[48] See, for example, the principles enunciated by the Bollandist Hippolyte Delehaye in his *The Legends of the Saints: an Introduction to Hagiography* (London: Longmans, Green, 1907).

[49] *Sainte Elisabeth de Hongrie* (Paris: Editions Franciscaines, 1947); translated into English as *Gold Tried by Fire: St Elizabeth of Hungary* (Chicago: Franciscan Herald Press, 1963); subsequent citations will be from the English edition.

[50] Other good twentieth-century biographies are: Maria Maresch, *Elisabeth von Thüringen* (Bonn: Verlag des Buchgemeind, 1931); Ernst Wilhelm Wiess, *Elisabeth von Thüringen: die Provokation der Heiligkeit* (Esslingen: Bechtle, 1993); and Norbert Ohler, *Elisabeth von Thüringen: Furstin in Dienst der Niedrigsten* (Göttingen-Zurich: Musterschmidt-Verlag, 1984).

[51] See Ulrike Wiethaus, "Feminist Historiography as Pornography: St. Elisabeth of Thuringia in Nazi Germany," *Medieval Feminist Newsletter*, no. 24 (Fall 1997): 46-54.

[52] Elisabeth Busse-Wilson, Das Leben der Heiligen Elisabeth von Thüringen: Das Abbild einer mittelalterlichen Seele (Munich: C. H. Beck'sche Verlagsbuchhandlung, 1931).

[53] Michael Goodich, *Vita Perfecta*, passim, especially 173-77, tables throughout the text and master table on 224; Weinstein and Bell, *Saints and Society*, 203, 257.

[54] Vauchez, La sainteté en occident, 295, 317.

[55] Bynum, *Holy Feast and Holy Fast*, especially 135-36, 193, 203-304, 224.

[56] Anja Petrakopoulos, "Sanctity and Motherhood: St. Elizabeth of Thuringia," in Anneke B. Mulder-Bakker, ed., *Sanctity and Motherhood: Essays on Holy Mothers in the Middle Ages* (New York: Garland, 1995), 259.

[57] Brigitte Stark, "Elisabeth von Thüringen. Die Entdeckung individueller Züge in der Biographie einer Heiligen," in *Individuum und Individualität im Mittelalter* (Berlin/New York: W. de Gruyter, 1996), 704-21.

[58] See the studies contained in: *Elisabeth, der Deutschen Orden und ihre Kirche*; in F. Jurgensmeier, ed., *So also, Herr. . . Elisabeth von Thüringen* (1207-1231) (Frankfurt am Main: Verlag J.

Knecht, 1982); and in *Sankt Elisabeth: Fürstin, Dienerin, Heilige. Aufsatze, Dokumentation, Katalog* (Sigmaringen: Jan Thorbecke Verlag, 1981).

[59] McNamara, *Sisters in Arms*, 243-45; and "The Need to Give: Suffering and Female Sanctity in the Middle Ages," in Renate Blumenfeld-Kosinski and Timea Szell, eds., *Images of Sainthood in Medieval Europe* (Ithaca, N.Y.: Cornell University Press, 1991), 207-208.

Chapter II

The Franciscan Tradition on Elizabeth

Introduction

Until recently, historians who have sought to document the events in Elizabeth's life have relied on the canonization process and the other earliest sources and ignored later works. Dietrich of Apolda is usually considered the last source with any contact with possible eyewitness traditions.

There are other, lesser-known sources however, from the time of Elizabeth's death to the end of the thirteenth and beginning of the fourteenth century, including Salimbene and Giordano of Giano, which contain references to very early, sometimes eyewitness tradition that may help shed light on some of the difficult problems in understanding her life. Even the early sources, such as the works of Pope Gregory IX, are often as significant for what they do not say as for what they do say. Reading these sources with the method developed by feminist historians and understanding this silence can yield important information about Elizabeth and other religious women and their choices.

After examining these sources, I will trace the origins and development of the sources I have edited: the Valenciennes Life and the Anonymous Franciscan. This includes examining some traditions in Northern France and Italy which contributed to these lives.

The Early Silence

The absence of any very early tradition in the Franciscan order about Elizabeth has caused difficulties for historians. For instance, Ancelet-Hustache admitted that there might have been a historically founded tradition about Elizabeth among the Franciscans, but found it strange that stories such as the one about St. Francis giving his mantle to Elizabeth are absent from the earliest works about him, especially the biography by Thomas of Celano.[1] But the silence extends to the earliest works about Elizabeth as well.

Pope Gregory's bull of canonization and the letter to Beatrice of Castile give us the official ecclesiastical picture of Elizabeth, written by a man who was a close friend of St. Francis and canonized him; as cardinal Ugolino, he had been the protector of the Franciscan order. Therefore we might expect that if Elizabeth's religious vocation had its roots in Franciscan spirituality, it would be expressed here if anywhere. Yet though the Pope praises Elizabeth's devotion to poverty and the relief of the poor, he never mentions her connection to the Franciscans directly in these works. He describes her religious life only in the most general terms.[2]

But the historical circumstances may help explain this omission. Elizabeth's active religious life outside the cloister was controversial, and Gregory IX's attitude toward this way of life was a guarded one. In a 1241 bull, he spoke of "Not a few women [who]. . . wandering through your cities, assert falsely that they are sisters of the Order of San Damiano; and so that others might also approve of their mendacious assertions . . . they go about barefoot; wearing the habit and girdle of the nuns of that Order, and cords: they are actually called 'discalced,' or 'women with the cord,' or 'Minorite women.'"[3] Gregory also brought a number of non-cloistered women, even non-Franciscan women, into enclosed communities of the "Damianite Order," or Order of St. Clare.[4] Yet at the same time Gregory protected the "continent virgins, vowing perpetual chastity to God," who have been identified with the Beguines.[5] His aim seems to have been to discourage what he saw as a lack of discipline in the women's religious movement, for which he tended to see cloister as the norm. At any rate, he wanted a very clear distinction between cloistered Franciscan sisters and those women claiming to be Franciscan who lived, like the Beguines, without cloister or perpetual vows. He may have been unwilling to encourage other, less prudent women to identify with Elizabeth and her controversial way of life.

Yet this is not the whole story of Gregory's relationship with Elizabeth. He had some contacts, at least written ones, with her during her lifetime. According to Conrad of Marburg's letter, he put Elizabeth under Conrad's protection when she was having trouble with her in-laws over her dower.[6] At her request, he granted an indulgence on April 19, 1229 to "the hospital of St. Francis" that she had built in Marburg.[7] Most important, there is the Pope's letter to Elizabeth, which appears to have been written around the time she entered religious life. This letter may be more fruitful in regard to information about her religious vocation, and I will discuss it later when dealing with her religious life.

Some historians have sought a connection both to the Franciscans and to Gregory IX in a short life of Elizabeth known as the *Vas admirabile* life. The possible connection to Gregory stems from the fact that the life begins with the words "Wondrous vessel" – the opening phrase of the Pope's letter to Beatrice of Castile – and that it contains some traces of the typical writing style of the papal court. Father Leonard Lemmens, OFM, who published the life from a Franciscan breviary in the Biblioteca Vittorio Emmanuele in Rome, called it "the first life of St. Elizabeth."[8] Based on a passage which he believed was borrowed from this life and inserted in the Life of Gregory IX, he thought it must have pre-dated the life of Gregory, which was written

52

shortly after his death in 1241.[9] Lemmens thought that the short life of Elizabeth might be by Thomas of Celano, finding the style, thought and ideas to be similar to those in his biographies of Francis and Clare. But while this life celebrates Elizabeth's spirit of poverty, nowhere is any connection to the Franciscans mentioned. While Celano's failure to speak about Elizabeth in his lives of St. Francis is certainly explicable, the omission of all mention of the Franciscans in his life of Elizabeth would seem to be evidence against her Franciscan connection – that is, if Celano was indeed the author.

Other historians, however, have questioned the Franciscan authorship of this life. Ancelet-Hustache believes the passage Lemmens cited could just as well have been borrowed from the life of Gregory IX, and finds the argument on Celano's authorship weak.[10] Some of the manuscripts are divided into readings for the office of St. Elizabeth. It seems best to understand the *Vas admirabile* life as a more or less official short life of Elizabeth of curial authorship, intended for liturgical use. Therefore the life does not seem to be of Franciscan authorship, and, like the other early curial sources, it is silent about Elizabeth's relationship with the Franciscans.

Other Franciscan sources from later in the thirteenth century say little about this subject. Potentially one of the most authoritative is the chronicle of Fra Giordano of Giano, which describes the development of the early Franciscan order in Germany. Unfortunately the author mentions Elizabeth only briefly, saying that a lay brother named Rudeger was Elizabeth's spiritual advisor.[11] Giordano's lack of more information is surprising and disappointing, especially because he held an authoritative post in the order in Thuringia and was certainly in a position to know more details than he gives about Elizabeth's relationship with the friars.

Another surprising omission in regard to Elizabeth's Franciscan vocation can be found in the life of her by Nicole Bozon, an English Franciscan friar. Nicole wrote several Old French verse lives of women saints, including Mary Magdalen, Martha, Agnes and Lucy. He probably wrote his life of Elizabeth shortly after 1300.

Nicole seems to have made free use of his source or sources, so it is difficult to tell what they were. Louis Karl, the first to edit the life in 1910, believed that it was based on the *Libellus* and Conrad of Marburg's letter, but that Nicole apparently did not know Dietrich's life, for he made no mention of important events or people described in it.[12] Amelia Klenke, who re-edited Nicole's life in 1951, felt that it was much more likely to have been based on the *Legenda aurea*, as his other saints' lives were.[13] This seems to be more probable.

Although Nicole was a Franciscan, his life shows almost no awareness that Elizabeth had any relationship with the Franciscans. There may be one mention of the order, in the account of the young man Elizabeth prayed for, who felt he was on fire as a result of her prayers; but the two manuscripts disagree: the Cotton manuscript has Elizabeth ask that the young man join the "the Friars Preachers, whom I hold dear," while the Additional manuscript has "the Friars Minor."[14] Nicole's source, the *Legenda aurea*, does say it was the Friars Minor, a detail going back to the *Dicta/Libellus*. Therefore this was most likely what Nicole originally wrote. That Bozon as a Franciscan was largely unaware of Elizabeth's possible religious life as a Franciscan is admittedly a problem. But there is evidence that he did have access to a source for Elizabeth's life that circulated among the Franciscans, as I will explain below.

Other overlooked thirteenth-century sources, however, some of Franciscan origin, give us more details about Elizabeth and the friars.

Overlooked Franciscan Sources

A number of thirteenth-century Franciscan preachers gave sermons on Elizabeth. The famous German Franciscan preacher Berthold of Regensburg mentioned her in some passages of his vernacular sermons. He speaks of her largely as a local and popular saint, and praises her humility and piety, but says little else about her and does not describe her religious life.[15]

Another anonymous Franciscan sermon, however, contains much more information about Elizabeth. Most of it comes from the *Dicta/ Libellus*, but the author does give some additional information based on personal acquaintance with Elizabeth's confessor and her handmaid Guda. The sermon was long attributed to St. Bonaventure,[16] but the Quaracchi edition of Bonaventure's works rejected the attribution. According to Father Bihl, it is traceable to a Franciscan named Conrad of Saxony (Conrad Holzinger von Braunschweig).[17] Livarius Oliger, however, attributes the sermon to an Italian Franciscan, Servasanto da Faenza, because it is found in a series of sermons attributed to the Italian friar.[18] The question of authorship still needs further study. This sermon has been quoted from time to time by authors on Elizabeth, but some details in it about her religious life have been overlooked. If it does come from someone who had contact with the eyewitnesses, it would certainly be important.

Other sermons on St. Elizabeth can be found in the works of Giacomo da Tresanti, an Italian Franciscan preacher, active ca. 1298-1320. In a collection of his sermons for feast days and for saints,[19] there are three sermons on St. Elizabeth, which describe her as a Franciscan and reflect the opinion about her religious life current in his time. I will describe his work in more detail later.

Traditions on Elizabeth in Northern France

Northern France was the place of origin of a number of works which became sources for the Franciscan lives I am editing, the Valenciennes Life and ultimately the Anonymous Franciscan. One of these works is a liturgical office from Northern France; others are two lives in French and a version of the *Libellus* which are related to each other. Other texts which will be important in the discussion of the relationship between the sources include the short Biblioteca Laurenziana life and another series of lectionary readings, also described below.

The first of these texts is the earliest office for Elizabeth with music, *Gaudeat Hungaria*. Barbara Haggh, who recently edited this office, believes there is good reason to attribute the composition of the text to Gerard, a monk of St. Quentin-en-Isle and the music to Peter, a canon of Saint Aubert in Cambrai. These authors were active in the 1230's and 1240's, and the composition of "elegantly worded antiphons and responsories to be sung on [Elizabeth's] feast day" and the music for them were attributed to them by a contemporary writer, Henry of Brussels.[20] Since the office follows the secular, rather than the Benedictine way of celebrating the office, it was evidently not intended primarily for monastic celebration. The Cambrai origin for this office for Elizabeth is not surprising, for the relics of her heart were venerated in Cambrai Cathedral. In fact, one of the few other surviving manuscripts of the office comes from Besançon, where other relics of Elizabeth could be found in the Middle Ages.[21]

Haggh further argued for the Franciscan emphasis of *Gaudeat Hungaria*. Particular stress is given to her hospital dedicated to St. Francis in the fifth and sixth antiphons for Matins; the responsory for Vespers says that she (metaphorically) bore the stigmata of Christ. This could also be taken as a reference to the stigmata of St. Francis. The wondrous song of the birds at her death is mentioned several times, and emphasized by a melisma in the music; later authors, especially the author of the Valenciennes Life, were struck by the similarity between this event and the birds gathering together to sing at the death of St. Francis. The office shares a number of poetic features, such as the form of the verse and the rhyme schemes, with the office for St. Francis and other works composed by Julian of Speyer. This is further evidence that they all came from the same milieu.[22] The office also contains a phrase "exchanging a crown for ashes and a girdle under her breasts for a hair shirt" which is also found in the *Vas admirabile* life. It may not be possible to determine whether the author was a Franciscan, but the above details show that the author of the office was familiar with the thought of Gregory IX, or at least that of curial circles, about Elizabeth, as well as the similarities between her life and that of St. Francis. In fact, Gregory IX's letter to Elizabeth also mentions her bearing the marks (*stigmata*) of Christ.[23]

Gerard of St.-Quentin-en-Isle also has a possible connection with the *Libellus*. Huyskens attributed the *ad decus et honorem* compilation (that is, the *Libellus* with prologue and epilogue) to Gerard, based on the above report that Gerard wrote the "miracles of St. Elizabeth." Huyskens points out that the author of the *ad decus et honorem* compilation states that he was planning to write the miracles of Elizabeth, and in fact includes some of them in the epilogue (ll. 2240-45).[24] The compilation itself was clearly of northern French origin, for the first authors to use it were from that area: these include Vincent of Beauvais (1244),[25] Rutebeuf, in his French poem on Elizabeth (between 1258 and 1270),[26] and the Valenciennes life (see below). Haggh supports Huyskens in arguing that Gerard was indeed the author of the *ad decus et honorem* compilation, for some of the earliest surviving excerpts from this work are found in a supplementary service book from the Sainte-Chapelle in Paris. The fact that Gerard was associated with the Sainte-Chapelle through his writing of a chronicle about the translation of the crown of thorns, which rested in that church, seems to strengthen the case for Gerard's authorship of the compilation on Elizabeth as well.[27] It would seem very natural for Gerard, who wrote the poetic texts for the sung office, to have supplemented them with readings from a prose version of Elizabeth's life that he had in his possession, and for which he had written a prologue and epilogue.

Also important for the traditions on Elizabeth from northern France are two French verse lives. The first of these is an anonymous text in a manuscript in Brussels.[28] Since this life is based largely on Dietrich of Apolda, it was probably written at the end of the thirteenth or beginning of the fourteenth century. The second life is *Chi commenche de Sainte Ysabiel*, whose author, a religious, identifies himself in his work as Brother Robert de Cambligneul. He used several sources, including Caesarius of Heisterbach and an earlier anonymous French life.[29] He includes some of the known passages from the *Dicta/Libellus* about Elizabeth and the Franciscans, including her refuge with the friars after her expulsion and the young man who became a Franciscan after Elizabeth prayed for him. But he gives new details as well about the friars often comforting her when Master Conrad was away and their presence at her deathbed "as her life recounts to us."[30] Robert's comment that this detail came from a life of Elizabeth is especially significant, for while no other early life of her contains this detail, it does resemble an incident found in the later Anonymous Franciscan, which tells how Elizabeth summoned the friars as she lay dying to ask that her procurator Henry be allowed to join the order.[31] This suggests that Robert may have been able to draw on some of the same traditions in the Order of Friars Minor that also found their way into the Anonymous Franciscan. There is not enough evidence available about Robert himself to determine whether he was a Franciscan, though that is a possibility.

These two lives are important for another reason: both include the story of a robe and crown brought to Elizabeth by an angel.[32] As a result of this miracle, they say, Elizabeth's husband joined the crusade to give his life for Christ, and Elizabeth was freed to become a religious. The portion dealing with the robe and crown in the anonymous French life was copied very closely by Robert of Cambligneul. The story can ultimately be traced back to a Latin version appended to the text of the *Libellus* in a manuscript in Brussels.[33] This is not the last we will hear of this story; it appears in later works, including the Anonymous Franciscan.

To sum up, the various works on Elizabeth from Northern France include the rhymed office *Gaudeat Hungaria*, possibly by Gerard of St.-Quentin-en-Isle, who may also have written the prologue and conclusion later added to the *Libellus*; the story of the robe and crown in Latin, and two French vernacular lives which contain this tradition. Two of these works, *Gaudeat Hungaria* and the life by Robert of Cambligneul, contain evidence of Franciscan influence or at least knowledge of Franciscan traditions about Elizabeth. That the Franciscans had access to them is clear by their use in the Valenciennes life, which we will turn to next.

The Valenciennes Life

The first full-scale life of Elizabeth of Franciscan origin, known as the Valenciennes Life, also comes from northern France and is found in two thirteenth-century manuscripts: MS. 508 of the Bibliothèque Municipale in Valenciennes (henceforth V in references), and Cod. 864 of the Bibliothèque Municipale in Douai (henceforth D in references). The Douai MS. is mutilated at the end, but the Valenciennes MS. contains the following colophon:

Per quem sum scriptus est Gallus nomine dictus
Numquam devictus, sed semper sit benedictus.

The one by whom I was written is called Gallus by name
may he never be defeated, but always be blessed.

The "called Gallus by name" led Huyskens to believe that
the author was French (Gallic), even though it seems to refer to his
name rather than his nationality. In addition, it is not certain
whether he was the author or merely the scribe.[34]

Portions of the life are also found as readings for an office
of St. Elizabeth called *Letare Germania* contained in three
manuscripts in Cambrai. This office was edited by Barbara Haggh,
who was unable to identify the life of Elizabeth from which these
readings came, but I have identified them as coming from the
Valenciennes life.[35]

According to Huyskens, the author, a Franciscan, probably
wrote the work around 1250.[36] Ancelet-Hustache calls this
estimation of the date "too precise," but without any further
explanation.[37] Clearly, however, the author was a Franciscan friar,
and stresses anything having to do with the order. The highly
rhetorical style suggests that he had been trained in that art. The
Anonymous Franciscan, who drew on the work, describes the
author as "a learned scribe, almost the first one who was asked
and urged to write a little book about the life of the holy servant of
God Elizabeth."[38] We can presume that his reference is to the
scriba doctus of Matthew 13:51-52, who "brings out of his
storeroom things new and old." By this, he probably means that
the author used existing texts, but added his own material to
them, in same way that medieval writers frequently wrote
marginal glosses to other works. The description seems to be
accurate, for the author provides a Franciscan rhapsody on
Elizabeth's virtues of poverty and humility which amounts to a
kind of gloss on his source, the *Dicta/Libellus*. The comment by the

Anonymous Franciscan also suggests that the Valenciennes life was a commissioned work, but who commissioned it is not known.

Scholars have disagreed about whether the Valenciennes author actually relied on the *Dicta* or on the *Libellus*. Ancelet-Hustache stated that the Valenciennes life "contains no detail of the *Libellus* which is not found in the *Dicta*." [39] On the other hand, Huyskens believed the author had used the *Libellus*, based on the passages concerning the translation of Elizabeth's body and her miracles.[40] Wenck agreed that the author used the longer version.[41] In fact, there are at least three passages in the Valenciennes life that must have been taken from the prologue and epilogue to the *Ad decus et honorem* compilation because they are not in the *Dicta*; that is the miracle of the oil at Elizabeth's tomb, the raising of sixteen people from the dead, and one, which I have identified, comparing Elizabeth to St. Lawrence and Zacheus.[42]

The Valenciennes life also contains several passages from the rhymed office *Gaudeat Hungaria*.[43] It is easy to imagine that, if the original readings for *Gaudeat Hungaria* were really from the *Libellus*, as Haagh believes, the author, having come across the whole office, decided to combine the material from the *Libellus* and the office with his own reflections.

The Valenciennes life stresses Elizabeth's relations with St. Francis and his order in a number of places, yet really has no details not found in the *Libellus* or the other early sources. In this life, Elizabeth is the "mother of the friars," something the author repeats more than once.[44] He copies what the *Dicta/Libellus* tradition says about Elizabeth spinning wool for the habits of the friars. He also finds another similarity to St. Francis in the birds who sang at her death. The author makes much of the fact that the young man Elizabeth prayed for joined the Friars Minor. On the other hand, although he mentions her putting on the "gray habit,"[45] he does not directly say that this was a Franciscan habit, or compare it to that of the Franciscans.

In summary, the first life of Elizabeth written by a Franciscan draws on some traditions found in northern France, including *Gaudeat Hungaria* and the best known tradition about her, the *Dicta/Libellus*, though he does not seem to have known the Anonymous French lives. The life is important, however, because it served as the basis for more than one later Franciscan work.

The Biblioteca Laurenziana Life

The Biblioteca Laurenziana Life (Plut. XXXV, Sin. Cod. IX) was found by Father Leonard Lemmens in that library early in the twentieth century, in a manuscript that once belonged to the library of the Franciscan convent of Santa Croce in Florence. It contains lives of a number of local and Franciscan saints, including the Florentine Franciscan tertiary Umiliana dei Cerchi. Lemmens thought the short life of Elizabeth it contains was probably written by a Tuscan Franciscan in the second half of the thirteenth century. He also found what he thought was an adaptation of this life which circulated in Perugia (that is, the lectionary readings discussed below). He thought that some details which it mentions, including the miracle of the roses so famously associated with Elizabeth, could be traced back to the original documents of the canonization process; therefore he looked on it as authoritative.[46] Ancelet-Hustache, however, while not questioning the Franciscan authorship, rejected the idea that the author used the canonization process as unfounded, for Lemmens had written in 1901, before the publication of the *Dicta*, which does not contain any mention of the miracle of the roses.[47]

The Biblioteca Laurenziana Life has a number of similarities to the other Franciscan lives. Elizabeth is called "a most kind mother to the poor, infirm and afflicted," a statement similar to the one in the *Gaudeat Hungaria* office. The incident in which her prayers cause a young man to join the Friars Minor is stressed. It says that "she loved the Friars Minor deeply as the true poor of Christ," though it does not specifically say she lived in the Franciscan habit.[48] The beginning of this text (Blessed Elizabeth, daughter of the king of Hungary, brought up nobly in purple and refinements. . .)[49] is almost the same as that of the Valenciennes Life (Blessed Elizabeth, therefore, the daughter of the King of Hungary, nobly brought up in a palace and in purple. . .).[50] This suggests some connection between the two lives.

The Biblioteca Laurenziana Life contains not only a brief version of the famous miracle of the roses long associated with Elizabeth, but also a distinctive series of miracles worked by her during her lifetime. Both of these deserve further attention.

The Miracle of the Roses

The so-called "miracle of the roses" became the most famous story about Elizabeth in legend and iconography in later centuries, though it is not in the canonization process or the earliest lives of her. In the version in a fifteenth-century German life of Elizabeth, the *Vita Rhythmica*, based on the work of Johannes Rothe, Elizabeth meets her husband Ludwig while she is carrying some bread for the poor in her apron; she is afraid of his criticism of her charity, so when he asks what she is carrying, she replies, "Roses." As he looks inside her apron, the bread miraculously changes into roses.[51]

Rothe's version was long believed to be the earliest one until Lemmens found a similar fourteenth-century version in a Franciscan breviary at Montecassino.[52] The thirteenth-century version in the Biblioteca Laurenziana life, however, places the story in Elizabeth's childhood, when she was already performing acts of piety: "While she was carrying food from the kitchen, blooming flowers were found in her apron, changed by divine power."[53] Noting that this version of the story seems to be found largely in works of Franciscan origin, Ancelet-Hustache concluded that it most probably arose among the Franciscans in the late thirteenth century.[54] The Biblioteca Laurenziana life seems to be the earliest appearance of the story in works about Elizabeth. It seems likely then, that it was first attached to her life around this time, the second half of the thirteenth century.

As it happens, the same story has been associated with other saints. Perhaps the earliest is the eleventh-century Spanish saint Casilda.[55] It is not known exactly how it became attached to St. Elizabeth, but it can also be found in a life of a young Italian saint of this era who in later tradition was said to have been a Franciscan tertiary, Rose of Viterbo (d. ca. 1252).[56] In this life, as with Elizabeth, the incident is said to have taken place in her childhood:

> The said virgin was of such great piety and mercy to the poor of Christ, that one day while she was carrying bread from her parents' home to give to the poor, as she was accustomed to do, at the command of her father, who asked what she was carrying hidden in her apron, then and there she opened her apron and when it had been exposed to view with the greatest obedience, roses full of the most diverse colors appeared in her apron.[57]

At first glance, we might argue that the author of the Biblioteca Laurenziana life picked up this story from the traditions surrounding Rose and applied it to Elizabeth. Even her name, Rose, suggests a possible reason for the connection of the story to her. But the tale seems to have become attached to Rose very late. The earliest life of her, the *First Life*, which dates from shortly after her death and which exists only in a fragmentary form, does not contain it. The first work in which the story occurs, known as the

Second Life, was written in the fifteenth century, and was subsequently inserted along with the *First Life* in the acts of her canonization process, carried out in 1457.⁵⁸ Paintings showing St. Rose with roses in her apron began appearing at about this time. One of them, a fresco by Benozzo Gozzoli, was actually a retouching of a portrait of Elizabeth.⁵⁹ The story, then, occurs much earlier with Elizabeth than with Rose, in the mid-thirteenth century, and became part of the Franciscan tradition about her, including, as we will see later, the Anonymous Franciscan.

The "Miracles Source"

A second feature of the Biblioteca Laurenziana Life is its inclusion of the following set of miracles, which are absent from the earliest sources: Elizabeth miraculously catching a fish for a sick man, healing a blind boy, healing a paralyzed boy, having a vision of her dead mother, whom she frees from Purgatory by her prayers, and healing Conrad of Marburg's brother. These miracles seem to form a specific collection or series, since they, or at least some of them, are found together in other lives of Elizabeth, including a number of Franciscan origin. A passage about Elizabeth being called by Christ at her death may also form part of this series, because it occurs in a number of the same sources as well. Some of the miracles are contained in the life by Dietrich of Apolda.⁶⁰ The life of Elizabeth by Nicole Bozon contains the following: the catching of a fish, the healing of a blind boy, the cure of a paralytic and Elizabeth's releasing her dead mother from purgatory. Though this life was based on the *Legenda aurea*, both Karl and Klenke, noting this series of miracles, believed that the author had supplemented this work with some unknown source containing them.⁶¹

The miracles of Elizabeth's mother, the paralyzed boy, the catch of fish and her call by Christ are also contained in a short life, divided into nine readings, evidently for use in the breviary, beginning *"Beata Elisabeth, tam progenie quam moribus nobilissima."*[62] The miracles in this life are in a somewhat longer and more developed form.

Börner, noticing some of these miracles in Dietrich, thought they might have been taken down from oral tradition by that author.[63] At this point, it seems to be impossible to tell which is the earliest version of these stories or to reconstruct the source. These miracles may represent local Thuringian tradition picked up by Dietrich and by the Franciscans; for instance, the miracle of the fish and Elizabeth's vision of her mother occur in a short life of her contained in a chronicle by a Thuringian priest, Siegfried of Balnhusin.[64] It is possible that Nicole Bozon, although he had access to no other Franciscan tradition about Elizabeth, could have used these miracles on finding them in a Franciscan breviary.

Since the Biblioteca Laurenziana Life begins in almost the same way as the Valenciennes Life and contains a great deal of the same material, it would seem natural to suppose that the first is a condensed version of the second. In fact, the life of Umiliana dei Cerchi contained in the Biblioteca Laurenziana manuscript is a condensed version of the oldest Latin life of her by Vito da Cortona.[65] This suggests that condensation of existing material was the general practice of the compiler of this collection of lives, perhaps intended as a reference work for Franciscan preachers. But the Biblioteca Laurenziana Life also contains evidence of other material, including the miracle of the roses and the material from the "miracles source," all of which are absent from the Valenciennes Life. Therefore the author either had separate access to this material, or his work is a condensed version of some amplified version of the Valenciennes Life containing this material (see Chapter IV). The possibility of an amplified life related to the Valenciennes life will be important when we come to examine the Anonymous Franciscan in more detail.

Conclusions

From the above discussion of the sources, it is clear that there are more assertions about Elizabeth's relationship with the friars in the thirteenth- and early fourteenth-century sources than has earlier been thought. The complex relationship between these sources indicates that a literary tradition about Elizabeth was formed in Northern France and Italy in the thirteenth century, drawing on the *Dicta/Libellus*, but using other and still unknown sources as well. It is also clear that a number of Franciscans wrote about Elizabeth being connected in some way to their order.

There is undeniably a gap about Elizabeth's relations with the Franciscans in the earliest sources, however. If she was closely attached to the friars, why do the witnesses in the canonization process not say more about it? And where did the later Franciscan sources get their information? But we have yet to look at the evidence of an important new source, the Anonymous Franciscan, which will fill this gap, make the relationship between the early Franciscan sources clearer, and show how the above literary tradition about Elizabeth spread from Northern France and Italy to Germany and Hungary.

Notes

[1] Ancelet-Hustache, *Gold Tried by Fire*, p. 232.

[2] See Chapter V for a description of these works.

[3] *Ad audientiam*, Feb. 21, 1241; BF 1:290.

[4] Roberto Rusconi, "L'espansione del francescanesimo femminile nel secolo xiii," pp. 265-313.

[5] See Alfonso Pompei, "Vita comunitaria tra i pentitenti belgi," in *Prime manifestazioni*, p. 135.

[6] Huyskens, *Quellenstudien*, p. 157.

[7] Arthur Wyss, *Hessisches Urkundenbuch*, vol. 1, no. 18; cited in Bihl, "Die heilige Elisabeth," p. 265.

[8] Lemmens, "Zur Biographie," p. 6.

[9] Lemmens, "Zur Biographie," pp. 6-14.

[10] Ancelet-Hustache, *Gold Tried by Fire*, pp. 269-70, note; Huyskens, *Quellenstudien*, p. 36, note 2.

[11] *Chronica Fratris Iordani*, no. 25, in AF, 1:9-10.

[12] Louis Karl, "La vie de Ste. Elisabeth par Nicole Bozon," *Zeitschrift für Romanische Philologie* 34 (1910): 294-314.

[13] Sr. M. Amelia Klenke, ed., *Seven More Poems by Nicholas Bozon* (St. Bonaventure, NY: Franciscan Institute, 1951), p. 60.

[14] l. 160; Klenke, *Seven More Poems*, p. 66.

[15] See *Berthold von Regensburg. Vollständige Ausgabe seiner Predigten*, mit Einleitungen und Anmerkungen von Franz Pfeiffer und Joseph Strobl (Berlin: Walter de Gruyter, 1965), 1:58-59, 367; 2:239.

[16] Anonymous, "De S. Elisabeth, sermon," printed as Bonaventure's in *S. R. E. cardinalis S. Bonaventurae. . . Opera omnia* (Paris: L. Vivès, 1868), 13:623-30. It first appeared in print in Rome in 1596. For a list of the editions, see Livarius Oliger, "Servasanto da Faenza, O.F.M. e il suo '*Liber de virtutibus et vitiis*,'"*Miscellanea Francesco Ehrle*, Studi e Testi 37 (Rome, 1924), 1:167.

[17] Bihl, "Die heilige Elisabeth," p. 283.

[18] Livarius Oliger, "Servasanto da Faenza,"1:166-170.

[19] Florence, Bibl. Nat. Conv. Soppr. G. 1. 861A, 14th century; parts are printed in Cenci, "Noterelle su Fr. Giacomo da Tresanti," pp. 119-28.

[20] Barbara Haggh, Two Offices for St. Elizabeth of Hungary: *Gaudeat Hungaria* and *Letare Germania* (Ottawa: Institute of Medieval Music, 1995), p. xiv.

[21] Haggh, *Two Offices*, p. xvi.

[22] Haggh, *Two Offices*, pp. xvi-xviii.

[23] Heinisch, "Ein Brief Gregors IX an die hl. Elisabeth," 381, and Wenck, "Die heilige Elisabeth und Papst Gregor IX," insert between pp. 144 and 45.

[24] Huyskens, *Libellus*, p. 81.

[25] Vincent quotes it in the fourth volume (*Speculum historiale*) of his *Speculum Maior*, Bk. 30, ch. 136; See Huyskens, *Libellus*, p. xxv.

[26] Rutebeuf, *La vie sainte Elysabel*, in Edmond Faral and Julia Bastin, *Oeuvres complètes de Rutebeuf* (Paris: Editions A. and J. Picard, 1960), 1:60-123.

[27] Haggh, *Two Offices*, pp. xvii.

[28] Brussels, Bibliothèque Royal, MS. 10295-304, fols. 158c-165d. This life was edited by Louis Karl, "La vie de saint Elisabeth de Hongrie," *Zeitschrift für romanische Philologie* 34 (1910): 708-33.

[29] Robert of Cambligneul, *Chi commenche de Sainte Yzabiel*, Paris. Bibl. Nat. fr. 19531, 13th century, fols. 112-32v. This, the sole MS, contains 2,280 octosyllabic lines in rhyming couplets. Edition: Achille Jubinal, *Oeuvres complètes de Rutebeuf* (Paris: Pannier, 1839), 2:360-412.

[30] Robert of Cambligneul, *Chi commenche de Sainte Ysabiel*, 2:406.

[31] T 90v; K 124r.

[32] "La vie de sainte Elizabeth," 721-24 (vv. 137-382); Robert of Cambligneul, *Chi commenche de sainte Ysabiel*, 2:387, 389.

[33] Brussels, Bibliothèque Royale, Cod. 1770-1777, ca. 1300, fols. 106r-107r. The text about the angel is printed in *Catalogus codicum Hagiographicorum Bibliothecae Regiae Bruxellensis*, ed. Hagiographi Bollandiani (Bruxelles, 1886), Pars I, 1:294-96.

[34] *Libellus*, p. xxvi; *Quellenstudien*, p. 70, n. 3.

[35] Haggh, *Two Offices*, x; the readings, from Cambrai, Mediathèque Municipale 34, 35 and 91, are edited on pp. 31-41.

[36] Huyskens, *Quellenstudien*, p. 70. Huyskens did not give any reason for this dating.

[37] Ancelet-Hustache, *Gold Tried by Fire*, p. 269, note.

[38] Anonymous Franciscan, Trier MS. (henceforth T in references), 91v, lines 728-29.

[39] Ancelet-Hustache, *Gold Tried by Fire*, p. 268 note.

[40] Huyskens, *Libellus*, pp. xxvi-xxvii.

[41] Wenck, "Quellenuntersuchungen," p. 476.

[42] V 69va, D 14r, lines 228-29; V 74ra, lines 435-36; V 72rb D, 17r, lines 361-62. (All line numbers are those in the edition of the texts in my dissertation, "St. Elizabeth of Hungary and the Franciscan Tradition").

[43] See Haggh, *Two Offices*, p. xvii, for the Franciscan origin of this work.

[44] Valenciennes Life, V 65va, D 10r, line 52.

[45] Valenciennes Life, V 65va, D 10r, line 60.

[46] Lemmens, "Zur Biographie," p. 14.

[47] Ancelet-Hustache, *Gold Tried by Fire*, pp. 273-74, note.

[48] For both quotes, Lemmens, "Zur Biographie," p. 15.

[49] Fol. 326.

[50] D 9r, V 64va, line 11.

[51] Cited in Montalembert, *Histoire de Sainte Elisabeth*, 1:260.

[52] Biblioteca Cassinensis, Cod. 193; Leonard Lemmens, "Zum Rosenwunder der hl. Elisabeth von Thüringen," *Der Katholik* 82 (1902): 381-84.

[53] Lemmens, "Zur Biographie," p. 15.

[54] Ancelet-Hustache, *Gold Tried by Fire*, p. 274, note.

[55] The story is also recorded of St. Elizabeth of Portugal (1271-1336) and St. Louis of Anjou (1274-1297), both descended from Elizabeth's family. See Giuseppe Abate, *S. Rosa da Viterbo, terziaria francescana (1233-1251): Fonti storiche della vita e loro revisione critica* (Rome: Editrice "Miscellanea Francescana," 1952), p. 238.

[56] For the sources on Rose's life, see Abate, *S. Rosa da Viterbo*; he prints a critical version of the sources, which were first published in AASS, Septembris 2:414-79.

[57] Abate, *S. Rosa da Viterbo*, p. 238.

[58] A canonization process was begun in 1252 by Innocent IV, but did not come to a conclusion. The second, fifteenth-century, process, carried out under Calixtus III, was concluded in 1457 without a canonization, but later Popes recognized Rose's cult; see Abate, *S. Rosa da Viterbo*, pp. 179-84.

[59] "Rosa da Viterbo," *Bibliotheca Sanctorum* (Rome: Città Nuova Editrice, 1968), 9, col. 417-18.

[60] These are: Elizabeth catching a fish for a sick man (VI, 10), the mute paralyzed boy (VII, 6), her vision of her mother and

freeing her by her prayers from purgatory (VI, 10); Elizabeth's call by Christ (VIII, 1).

[61] Klenke, *Seven More Poems*, 60; Karl, pp. 294-95.

[62] See Lemmens, "Zur Biographie," p. 24.

[63] G. Börner, "Zur Kritik der Quellen," p. 34.

[64] The readings are found in Siegfried's Historia *universalis et compendium Historiarum*, ed. O. Holder-Egger, MGH SS, 25:700-702.

[65] My thanks to Anne Schuchman of the Department of Italian Studies at New York University, who has studied the Biblioteca Laurenziana manuscript, for lending me a microfilm of the manuscript, and for pointing out the relation between these two lives of Umiliana.

Chapter III

The Anonymous Franciscan

and His Sources

Introduction

The Anonymous Franciscan Life, so named for its likely author, an unknown Friar Minor, is a compilation from the end of the thirteenth or very beginning of the fourteenth century. It is based on a number of earlier sources, including the *Libellus* and the Valenciennes life. Though a late work, it contains authentic eyewitness testimony taken from lost records of Elizabeth's canonization process, as well as other oral or written traditions about her from the Franciscan order. This work has never been edited or studied in depth until recently. In this chapter I will examine its purpose, date, authorship and sources.

History of the Text

The text of the Anonymous Franciscan was known as far back as the early seventeenth century. The Franciscan author Henricus Sedulius quoted several passages from it in his Historia Seraphica, published in 1613. He took them from a manuscript belonging to the Friars Minor in Louvain. He described the author as "an anonymous Friar Minor, who testified that he had seen himself the things he wrote about [Elizabeth] and that he had also accepted [some] from others with certain faith."[1] Franciscan historian Luke Wadding quoted some passages from the same manuscript in his *Annales Minorum,* published in 1626.2

These mentions attracted the attention of later historians, but by then the manuscript mentioned by Sedulius and Wadding proved impossible to find. In the 1830's, Montalembert searched for it without success in various libraries in Louvain. Nevertheless, using Wadding and a German life of St. Elizabeth in a fifteenth-century manuscript from Heidelberg, which he believed was a translation of the Anonymous Franciscan, he quoted from the work as a source in his biography of Elizabeth.[3]

Around 1908, Wenck finally found a manuscript of the Latin version in Koblenz, containing approximately the final third of the life as we now know it. In the article in which he announced this discovery, Wenck proposed to publish this "very charming" source for Elizabeth's life, but the edition never appeared; perhaps because Wenck was continuing his search for other manuscripts with the rest of the life.[4] Three years later, however, Huyskens published portions of the Latin text of the Koblenz manuscript in the footnotes to his edition of the *Libellus.* In the years since then, other scholars have devoted brief discussions to the life, but lack of a complete text has made any opinion on it tenuous at best.

In 1996, I discovered an almost complete text of the Anonymous Franciscan in an overlooked manuscript belonging to the Stadtbibliothek in Trier. The manuscript had been noted by the Bollandists, but they recorded it as a different life from that by the Anonymous Franciscan.[5] Using the Koblenz and Trier manuscripts, I have been able to reconstruct the complete text of this important work. Before exploring its contents, I want to discuss what we can deduce about the author.

Description and Purpose of the Work

The life is divided into an *argumentum* (or author's foreword), a *prefacio* (preface) describing the origin of Elizabeth's name, and the life itself, which has no chapter or other divisions.

In the foreword, the author quotes from 1 John 1:1, in order to compare the eyewitness testimony he cites about Elizabeth to that given by the apostles about Jesus. He says that he is presenting "what was from the beginning, what we have heard, and what many of us, named in the following pages, present at that time, saw and heard and diligently examined with our own eyes."[6] Towards the end of the prologue, he writes, "our charity communicates to you what we have learned about our contemporary Elizabeth."[7] The "us" mentioned in the first line seems to refer to those Franciscans and other religious mentioned in the text who were eyewitnesses to Elizabeth's life, especially those who testified at the "examination" into her life frequently mentioned in the text. The author does not say that he himself was an eyewitness, though it is easy to understand how Sedulius and Wadding could have believed that he was.

The author addresses his readers as his "dearest ones"; the life was probably intended for members of his order. In fact, he skims very rapidly over Elizabeth's married life in the first few pages, in order to concentrate on her virtues as a religious. One of the major purposes of the life was not only to show Elizabeth as a saint, but also to demonstrate her closeness to the Franciscan order, both as the "mother of the friars," and as their disciple. The author stresses at every opportunity Elizabeth's Franciscan virtues of poverty and humility, and her relationship with the friars.

Authorship and Date

Nothing is known for certain about the author, except that he was a Franciscan. Because the author stresses poverty and the *usus necessaria*, it is tempting see him as a member of the Spiritual faction in the Franciscan order, though impossible to prove. Fr. Bihl, based on the excerpts published by Huyskens, surmised that the author was a German or Belgian Franciscan belonging to the province of Cologne (which included Belgium), and that he used local Franciscan traditions.[8] In a study of the cult of the medieval Hungarian saints originally published in 2000, Gábor Klaniczay put forward the idea, based on the same fragmentary text, that the author was a Polish Franciscan, because of his knowledge of Polish dynastic affairs.[9]

There is a further important piece of evidence about the author, however, which is apparent even from the incomplete text: he stresses in various ways Elizabeth's origin from the Árpáds, the Hungarian royal dynasty, and speaks at length about that side of her family, almost eclipsing that of her husband and German relatives by marriage. In the conclusion, he speaks with pride of three women, Cunegunde (d. 1292), Iolenta (1235/39-1298) and Salomeya (1211-1268), who were either born in or married into the Árpád house, entered the Poor Clares, and later became saints. The author also makes much of the devotion of Elizabeth's brother, King Béla IV of Hungary (d. 1270), both to his sister's memory, and to the Franciscans, to whom he entrusted important matters in his kingdom; he even asked to be buried with his wife in the Franciscan church dedicated to Elizabeth in Esztergom.[10] In fact, the Franciscan and Dominican orders did grow very rapidly in Hungary, as evidenced by the membership of King Béla and his wife in the Third Order, and their endowment of convents of friars and Poor Clares.[11]

There is a more definite clue to the purpose of the work in the author's recounting of how Béla's son and Elizabeth's nephew, King Stephen V (1270-72), asked that a painting of Elizabeth in a convent in Esztergom be redone to properly portray her in the Franciscan habit, with cord and sandals. The Anonymous

Franciscan, with reference to Ps. 44:1, says that he included the story "so that we might speak of testimonies about the king's daughter in the sight of kings without confusion."[12] The author seems to be indicating that his work was actually addressed to the kings of Hungary, especially to the then-reigning king of the Árpád dynasty whose descendant he was celebrating: he would not want to be embarrassed before the dynasty by the omission of something so important as King Stephen's veneration for his saintly aunt.

It is true that the dynasty that succeeded the Árpáds in Hungary, the Angevins, also made much of their descent from St. Elizabeth. In particular, Charles Robert of Naples claimed the Hungarian throne for himself in 1301, after the last of the Árpáds, Andrew III, died, precisely on the grounds that his grandmother was Stephen V's daughter Mary, and that his descent would provide him with the same royal and Christian virtues as his sainted forebears, including Elizabeth.[13] But if the Anonymous Franciscan had been written in order to support this claim, we would expect some mention of the relationship that was the cause for it; Charles' descent from Bela IV's line. But nothing of this can be detected in the work, just as there is no mention of any of the Angevin saints related to St. Elizabeth, including St. Louis of Toulouse, who was the son of her great-niece, Mary of Hungary, and Charles Robert's uncle.

It seems likely, therefore, that the Anonymous Franciscan was written by a Hungarian Franciscan both for his brothers, and with the intention of celebrating Elizabeth's life for an Árpád king of Hungary, a dynasty which gave birth to this Franciscan saint, and which had given great benefits to his order. But which king, and at what date?

Wenck believed, based on the partial text, that the work was written around 1281. But he did not discuss the question of dating in more detail.[14] More precisely, Huyskens concluded that since the latest event the author mentions is the death on December 12,

1279 of Boleslaus the Chaste, husband of Elizabeth's niece St. Cunegunde, and since the author does not mention Cunegunde's death, which occurred in 1292, the life was written between these two dates.[15] There is some difficulty with Huyskens' argument from silence, however. The author of the life also mentions Elizabeth's sister-in-law Salomeya; he does not say she is dead, though she died in 1268, well before he apparently began to write. So the failure to mention Cunegunde's death really proves nothing; the life may even have been written after 1292. There is no indication that the author of the Anonymous Franciscan knew or used the very influential life of Elizabeth by Dietrich of Apolda, which was completed in 1297. It is quite possible, however, that this work may not have become known in Hungary by the time the Anonymous Franciscan was writing.

Therefore, if we accept the hypothesis given above that the Anonymous Franciscan was writing for a king of the Árpád house, the latest date at which his life could have been written was 1301, the year in which the dynasty came to an end with the death of Andrew III. This was followed by the succession of Charles Robert of Naples and the establishment of the Angevin dynasty in Hungary. Since we know that the Anonymous Franciscan was written after 1279 (the date of the death of Boleslaus the Chaste), the royalty that the author says he is "speaking before" would have been either Ladislaus IV (1272-1290) or Andrew III (1290-1301). Therefore, considering all the above factors, we can put the date of composition of the Anonymous Franciscan sometime between 1279 and 1301.

Sources

The Anonymous Franciscan relied on a number of sources, many of which are already known or printed; others are unknown. From just the short Koblenz fragment available to him in 1911, Huyskens was able to determine that the author had used the

Valenciennes life. The Anonymous Franciscan borrowed freely from the long rhetorical passages and scriptural meditations on Elizabeth's Franciscan virtues found in this life, but did not necessarily adhere to the earlier author in matters of detail.

As mentioned in the previous chapter, the author of the Valenciennes life clearly had knowledge of the version of the *Libellus* with the prologue beginning *"ad decus et honorem,"* with its long panegyric of Elizabeth's virtues, parts of which he quotes. The Anonymous Franciscan took over these passages, as well as others from the *Dicta/Libellus* tradition that are not found in the Valenciennes Life, including Elizabeth's prayer at meeting her husband's bones, and a passage telling how Elizabeth's procurator, Brother Henry, who became a Friar Minor, sold some fish for her. So it is clear that the author had independent knowledge either of the *Dicta* or the *Libellus*, though which cannot be determined from the text, since the passages not from the Valenciennes life are common to both the *Dicta* and the *Libellus*.

There is another important detail: the Anonymous Franciscan includes the story of the dress and crown brought to Elizabeth by an angel. As we saw in Chapter III, this story is found in Latin in a very similar form in a manuscript of the *Libellus* in Brussels. The story is also found in the French vernacular life by Robert of Cambligneul, and the other anonymous French life. Given the fact that the version of the *Libellus* with the *"ad decus et honorem"* prologue was probably written in northern France, as Huyskens demonstrated, and that it seems to have had its greatest diffusion there, it is possible that the Anonymous Franciscan drew on a particular form of the *Libellus* known in France, with the story of the robe and crown, and possibly the works of the French authors who used it – or he may have had access to a work that elaborated on this story.

The Anonymous Franciscan quotes directly from Conrad of Marburg's summary of Elizabeth's life. He also had access to the "miracles source" mentioned in Chapter III.

The most important original contribution of the Anonymous Franciscan, however, is the series of eyewitness statements by Franciscans who knew Elizabeth. The author cites statements which according to him come from "the first" and the "second and last" investigations into Elizabeth's sanctity.16 This language makes it very likely that he used the actual documents of the canonization process, which speak of a "first examination" in 1233 and a "second examination" in 1235.

The Anonymous Franciscan does not limit himself, however, to the official investigations for his information. He also provides a number of other stories about Elizabeth and the Franciscans not found elsewhere, without giving any specific source, although he provides many details, including the names of the friars involved. These stories may have come from oral tradition within the Franciscan order or unknown written sources. The new material contained in the Anonymous Franciscan will be considered in the following chapters, and the specific sources he used will be discussed there.

The author evidently experienced major difficulty in compiling all this material. In the first portion, up to the death of Elizabeth's husband, he preserves the chronological order fairly well, but after this point, the narrative becomes a series of disjointed incidents in which the Franciscan material is interspersed with material from the *Libellus* and other sources without any attempt to maintain a consistent chronology. For instance, it is only after describing the beginning of Elizabeth's religious life that the author goes back to recount how she was expelled from the castle and deprived of her dower.[17]

In at least one case, confusion is introduced by a disruption of the text, apparently caused by the insertion of new material. The author mentions a lay brother named Henry, Elizabeth's procurator, who later became a Franciscan. He then goes on to quote the testimony of brother Andrew of Westphalia. He then says that this "aforesaid brother" went to Rome on Elizabeth's behalf.[18] He seems to mean Andrew, but later says that Henry was the brother who went to Rome.[19] The difficulty can be explained if the passage with the direct testimony of Brother Andrew, and perhaps the other direct testimonies and the prologue referring to them as well, were inserted into the work after the time of its original composition. In fact, these disruptions of the existing order came about after the insertion of the additional passages from the *Dicta/Libellus* tradition by the writer who adapted the Valenciennes life, since it is the sense of one of these passages, the one about Brother Henry, which is disrupted. It seems then, that the Anonymous Franciscan life may have been composed in stages, by more than one author.

The short thirteenth-century life in the Biblioteca Laurenziana provides some evidence for this. The openings of this life and the Valenciennes Life are very similar. The Biblioteca Laurenziana life, as mentioned in the previous chapter, is clearly a Franciscan source. Though very short, it contains the miracle of the roses, and the same series of miracles from the "miracles source" found in the Anonymous Franciscan. But it does not contain any of the testimonies from the canonization process, or the other Franciscan anecdotes found in the Anonymous Franciscan. It is possible, therefore, that there was a further, intermediary stage between the Valenciennes Life and the Anonymous Franciscan. This work would have contained the material in the Valenciennes life plus the miracle of the roses, the miracle of the robe and crown and the series of miracles from the "miracles source." The Biblioteca Laurenziana Life would then be a condensed version of this intermediary work. It might possibly have been written in northern France, around the area where the Valenciennes life appeared, and where the miracle of the robe and crown appeared in the form used in the French lives. The author could have combined these sources and used them in his work. The Anonymous Franciscan would have added the foreword which refers to the eyewitness testimonies, the preface, the testimonies from the canonization process and the various Franciscan anecdotes, plus the material linking Elizabeth to the royal house of Hungary.

When the various versions of the miracles in the "miracles source" are compared, it becomes apparent that the version verbally closest to that of the Anonymous Franciscan is found in the set of breviary readings known as Beata Elizabeth tam progenie, although the version in the Anonymous Franciscan is usually longer and more developed. This may mean that there was an original longer version of these miracles from which both copied, or that the Anonymous Franciscan developed these stories further on his own. The Anonymous Franciscan, therefore, used a large variety of sources in compiling the work, and may have been the last of several authors to contribute to the life.

The Influence of the Anonymous Franciscan

Although only two manuscripts of it are known so far to have survived, the Anonymous Franciscan had at least some influence on other works on Elizabeth. Some Franciscans in Germany and Hungary seem to have been acquainted with the text. As mentioned above, it served as the basis for the still-unpublished German life of Elizabeth found in a fifteenth-century manuscript in the Universitätsbibliothek in Heidelberg,[20] which was used by Montalembert for his biography of Elizabeth. This life has preserved much of the Franciscan material found in the Anonymous Franciscan, including some but not all of the new testimonies from the canonization process, such as the testimony of Brother Andrew of Westphalia and Elizabeth's Franciscan confessor, Brother Gerard. But in these cases, there are no indications in the text that these men testified at the process.[21]

The Heidelberg Life also contains much material not found in the Latin text of the Anonymous Franciscan, including an account of Elizabeth's translation, and many borrowings from the life by Dietrich of Apolda, including those on Elizabeth's persecution in her youth by her mother-in-law and the description of her husband Ludwig's virtues. In at least one passage, the author seems to have drawn independently from the *Libellus*.[22] I have not yet found any internal or external evidence to tell how long after the Anonymous Franciscan this life was written.

A possible influence of the Anonymous Franciscan is in the dissemination in Hungary of the earliest form of the miracle of the roses, which has Elizabeth as a small child meeting her father, King Andrew. Other early sources from outside Hungary mention it, but none in as developed a form as he has it (T 75v-76r, lines 51-61). The Hungarian Franciscans Pelbart of Temesvár in his *Pomerium de sanctis* (1498) and later Osvat (Oswald) Laskai (1499) in his *Biga salutis,* give the story in much the same form as the Anonymous Franciscan.[23] Pelbart and Osvat, therefore, may have used the Anonymous Franciscan as either a first- or secondhand source, thus indicating that this life was known in Hungary.

But apart from these influences, I have not yet found any evidence that the Anonymous Franciscan was widely known in the Middle Ages. As we have seen, even though Nicole Bozon was a Franciscan, and apparently wrote after the Anonymous Franciscan was composed, he shows no knowledge of it (see Chapter III).

Now that we have learned what we can about the life by the Anonymous Franciscan, I want to examine in more detail the important testimonies it contains.

The New Life and the Canonization Process

The Anonymous Franciscan is a late work, from the end of the thirteenth or beginning of the fourteenth century. Yet the author quotes a number of passages which seem to come from the official canonization records. Are these testimonies authentic?

The author describes a first and a second (and last) "inquiry about the acts of the same servant of God diligently made by great, learned and authoritative persons"[24] and says that the testimonies were put into writing,[25] although he does not explicitly use the words "canonization process." It has seldom been clearly recognized, therefore, that the Anonymous Franciscan refers to the canonization process for some of his material. Huyskens wrote that "in general, he bases himself repeatedly on the traditions of the order, which, true, in one instance can be traced back to the canonization process." (He does not say what the "one instance" is). Huyskens adds "also a detail from Berthold of Regensburg is once mentioned as a source."[26] Huyskens here identifies the Berthold that the Anonymous Franciscan calls "the German," who testified to seeing the mantle Elizabeth received from Francis in Speyer, with the famous German Franciscan preacher. Huyskens believed the testimony mentioned must date from the 1260's because Berthold of Regensburg is thought to have visited Speyer at that time. But this identification of the friar with Berthold of Regensburg is not certain. Berthold could actually have joined the order as early as 1228-1230, and so testified about Elizabeth, but there is no evidence he lived or worked in Thuringia. Our author does not specifically say the preacher Berthold who testified about Elizabeth was a Franciscan, which he most likely would have done if he knew that this friar had belonged to the Order. Therefore this supposed identification can hardly be used for dating the investigation.[27]

Bihl clearly recognized that the Anonymous Franciscan life contained testimony from an investigation, but, following

Huyskens, thought that it must have been a "private" one which took place in the 1250's or 1260's.[28] It seems very unlikely to me, however, that such an investigation into Elizabeth's life would have been made subsequent to her canonization. But scholars up to now have only had a small part of the Anonymous Franciscan, and the most detailed testimonies occur in the newly-discovered part, which makes the nature of the investigation and the author's use of it clearer.

On several occasions, our author cites evidence that he says comes from one of Elizabeth's handmaids, although testimony on these points does not occur in the process as we have it. For instance, he says that Elizabeth rejoiced at receiving a revelation that her husband's soul had been released from purgatory by her prayers. As evidence he cites one of her handmaids, though not by name (T 79r, lines 203-205). No such testimony occurs in the *Dicta/Libellus*. On other occasions, a fact is cited as coming from one witness when it comes from another in the process as we have it. The testimony about the messenger from Elizabeth's father in Hungary who was amazed to find her among her sisters spinning wool is given in the *Dicta/Libellus* by Irmingard, and by the Anonymous Franciscan as coming from Guda and Isentrude. Could this mean that the author had another, fuller version of the canonization process than the one we know?

The *Dicta/Libellus* gives the testimony of only one witness for each event, at times adding a statement that another witness corroborated it. In practice, a complete statement would have been taken for each witness about each event he or she testified to. In addition, since it was the practice to have two clerks take down each statement so that their versions could be compared for accuracy, one version might occasionally contain a detail the other clerk had not caught. If the Anonymous Franciscan possessed a fuller text, even copies of some of the original minutes, he could have chosen the statements of different witnesses or different versions of their statements to quote. The testimony about the spinning he cites as coming from Guda and Isentrude is plausible, for their testimony shows that they did remain with Elizabeth for at least a short time after they took the habit with her in Marburg, before they were removed by Master Conrad, and so could have witnessed this incident. On the other hand, the latter passage could have been a displacement of an earlier one in the *Dicta* where Isentrude also mentioned Elizabeth spinning wool for the friars, though the wording is very different. The author has given other evidence of confusion, so it is better to suspend judgment in this case.

The author cites several witnesses in the investigation by name: they are largely Friars Minor, though some are Friars Preachers: the Franciscans are Brother Gherard (*Guerardus*), said to come "from the other side of the mountains,"[29] Brother Gerard of Guerles, minister of Upper Germany,[30] and Brother Andrew of Westphalia.[31] The Dominicans who testified were named Jacobus "from the other side of the mountains," Dietrich of Malburg (in North Rhine-Westphalia), and John "from near Campania."[32] Also testifying was Brother Berthold Teutonicus, order not identified.[33] I have not yet been able to find a positive identification of any of these brothers, or any information about them, except for Gerard, who served as the minister of Upper Germany from 1246-1252. However, the numerous details given about some of these brothers might help in this.

The curial treatise on Elizabeth's canonization attributed to Raymund of Peñafort mentions that some Franciscan and Dominican friars were present at the hearings in 1235 as expert advisors to Bishop Conrad of Hildesheim.[34] The friars were used in such a capacity at a number of thirteenth-century canonization hearings; they also appear as translators, putting the examiners' questions into the vernacular for the witnesses, and their replies back into Latin.[35] In such a capacity, it would have been easy for the Franciscan consultants at Elizabeth's process to have obtained unofficial copies of the depositions, particularly those made by their brother friars, and they would most likely have been eager to preserve personal copies of these records on a matter of such interest to the order. There is also the possibility that the Hungarian royal family was able to obtain copies of these records for their saint and made them available to the author. But there is no certain way of knowing from the use of these testimonies by the Anonymous Franciscan exactly how he obtained them.

How faithfully does the author preserve these otherwise unknown traditions? One way to estimate this is by examining his fidelity to the sources which we already possess. In these cases he is generally accurate in quoting his material. In a few cases he has introduced a deliberate change into his use of the official documents connected with the process. For instance, on one occasion he softens Conrad of Marburg's description of his own behavior to the leper girl Elizabeth had taken in. Conrad had written: "I threw the leper girl out."[36] The Anonymous Franciscan changes this to "I firmly ordered that [Elizabeth] be separated from her."[37] It is therefore probable that he transcribed what he found in his documents with a fair degree of accuracy.

Given their form and content, I believe that the statements that the Anonymous Franciscan says were taken from the official investigations do come from the canonization process, which would give them considerable authority. But since they are taken out of context and might have been altered, caution should be exercised in using them.

Controversy and Answers to Objections

Even though scholars up to now have not had a complete text of the Anonymous Franciscan, the passages that were known from the Koblenz fragment have frequently been used as a basis for criticizing the accuracy of this work. Huyskens and Wenck found the life of historical interest, but since their time, with the exception of Fr. Bihl, [38] there has been little inclination, even among Franciscan scholars and those who support Elizabeth's membership in the Franciscan movement, to accept the life as important, and it is placed in the territory of legend, usually without much discussion.

The approach that historians have taken to the Anonymous Franciscan, as well as to other texts, has depended in part on their ideological approach to hagiographic works. Ancelet-Hustache fully accepted that Elizabeth was a Franciscan tertiary, based on the few statements in the *Dicta*. It is not surprising, however, given her insistence on proven pedigrees for texts, that she found the material in the Anonymous Franciscan, admittedly a late text, to be of legendary origin. She also thought that the Anonymous Franciscan's story of Elizabeth attempting to embrace a visiting Franciscan in the town square of Marburg was in shockingly bad taste. While agreeing that Elizabeth's actions portrayed in the incident fit in well with her well-known spontaneity, she finds, rather illogically, that "her supposed attitude in this incident makes the story entirely suspect."[39] The evidence presented here about the Anonymous Franciscan indicates that much of the material in it may be historically true. Yet even if this story or others in the work should prove to be legendary, this does not deprive them of all value in the eyes of present-day historians. When such stories are examined using the right methods, they can reveal much about the attitude of the writer and his contemporaries toward Elizabeth and about the society they lived in.

There have been other criticisms and objections as well, but it is best to discuss these when dealing with the specific passages of the Anonymous Franciscan in the next chapter. These critics wrote before the whole life was known, and before the extent of the testimonies, with their many details and the citing of witnesses, became apparent.

Nevertheless, the major question, which is related to Ancelet-Hustache's objection, and which has become more acute since the full extent of this new tradition has become known, is: what is the historical pedigree of these testimonies allegedly coming from the canonization process? Why, if they are authentic, were they not preserved with the rest, and why have they been absent from the major biographical tradition and even much of the Franciscan tradition on Elizabeth?

Certainly the Franciscans of the thirteenth and fourteenth century knew about Elizabeth and her relations with the order, as the traditions quoted in the previous chapter show. But these traditions are little, and frequently late. This in itself is not proof that the tradition is not genuine. The reason for the lack of a well-known Franciscan tradition about Elizabeth may lie in the eclipsing of that tradition by other factors.

According to the Franciscan chronicler Salimbene, Elizabeth "would gladly have been buried in the church of the Friars Minor, but the Friars Minor did not permit it, because at time they completely refused burials, so that they might avoid the labor, and also so that they might not have discord with [secular] clerics." Elizabeth was buried instead in the chapel of her hospital in Marburg. In another passage, Salimbene commented: "we are to be condemned and we acted in the most boorish way (which we now recognize), because we refused burial to St. Elizabeth."[40] They may well have regretted it later, when they saw how popular her cult had become. At the time, the major reasons for not accepting Elizabeth's burial, in addition to the contention between the friars and the secular clergy over burials, was probably the poverty of the friars in Germany, and perhaps the lack of specific permission for burial of anyone but the friars in Franciscan churches.[41] However it may have been, the Franciscans lost the chance to have the saint's body buried in their church, and therefore lost a good part of their identification with her and her cult. It was soon taken over by another powerful group: the Teutonic Order.

The interest of the Teutonic Order in Elizabeth's life is easy to explain. The order had become established in Marburg in 1233, and enjoyed great favor with the younger brothers of Elizabeth's dead husband – Heinrich, the new Landgraf, and Conrad. In the summer of 1234, Conrad went to Rieti to meet with Pope Gregory IX to pursue the question of Elizabeth's canonization and to ask that her hospital of St. Francis in Marburg be turned over to the Teutonic order, whose brothers were to undertake hospital work there. This request was granted, and Conrad himself joined the order in November of that year;[42] his conversion, the Pope noted in a letter to Queen Beatrice of Castile a few days after Elizabeth's canonization, was due to the influence of his saintly sister-in-law.[43] Conrad also had a role, as we have seen, in the canonization itself.

The Teutonic order now adopted Elizabeth as its patron, along with the Blessed Virgin, who had been associated with the order since its earliest days, and St. George. Like all the major military orders at this time, the Teutonic Knights were seeking to broaden their image, not wanting to be seen as just a military group. They stressed their piety, an area in which they were often thought to be deficient in comparison to the new mendicant orders, and their connection with female saints and the Blessed Virgin, who would give them an aura of spirituality. Association with popular saints like Elizabeth would also bring in more donations.[44] Elizabeth's family connection with a prominent member of the Order, Landgraf Conrad of Thuringia, would also have been welcome.

The Teutonic Knights soon took over management of Elizabeth's hospital and incorporated it into their own foundation in Marburg. The order then arranged and paid for the building of a magnificent Gothic church in Marburg to house her remains. They also dedicated a number of other churches to her.[45] In addition, as we saw in Chapter II, it was the prior of the house of the Teutonic Order in Marburg who, according to Caesarius of Heisterbach, encouraged him to write the life of St. Elizabeth and provided him with the *Dicta*. This version of the testimonies of the canonization process may have been drawn up by a member of the Teutonic order as a basis for the biography of their new saint, a kind of sketch containing the most important testimonies, to which Caesarius was to add the literary polish.

This account of the composition of the *Dicta* (already suggested by Wenck)[46] gives rise to some speculation: did the Teutonic order deliberately omit testimonies in regard to Elizabeth and the Franciscans from the *Dicta*? Certainly some indications of Elizabeth's relationship with the Franciscans are still found there. The main reason for the selection of the testimonies of Elizabeth's handmaids may have simply been their narrative quality, for these witnesses all knew Elizabeth for an extended period of time, or during the important events of her life, while other witnesses may have only been able to testify to isolated incidents. Therefore, the handmaids' statements would have made for better reading and a smoother chronology. It may not have been deliberate omission, but when it came to the choice of important testimonies to include in the *Dicta*, those of the Franciscans were of secondary importance.

So although there was a Franciscan hagiographic tradition on Elizabeth, it was not the official, public tradition about her. As we have seen, there were reasons why Gregory IX, while admiring and praising Elizabeth's spirit of charity in her work with the poor, thought it best not to stress her connection with the Franciscans.

Early memories of this connection are actually better preserved in the iconographic tradition than in written works. In Elizabeth's church in Marburg, the early art work from 1240-1250 included a series of sculptures in gold relief on her sarcophagus, in one of which she is shown taking the Franciscan habit and cord, and a series of stained glass windows, in which she is shown being crowned in heaven along with St. Francis. The two series of scenes follow a parallel plan.[47]

There is good evidence then, that the Anonymous Franciscan used authentic, early tradition about St. Elizabeth and her relationship to the Franciscan order. In the next chapters, I will demonstrate that these testimonies reflect the concerns of Elizabeth and her times, and that the Anonymous Franciscan himself added a number of comments and considerations that show how Elizabeth and her religious life were seen by a later generation of friars.

Notes

[1] Henricus Sedulius, OFM, Historia Seraphica vitae B. P. Francisci Assisiatis illustriumque virorum et feminarum qui ex tribus eius ordinis relati sunt inter sanctos (Antwerp, 1613), 591.

[2] *Annales Minorum*, an. 1229, n. 6-8, 2 (Quaracchi, 1931), 243-44, and n. 61, 179; an. 1227, n. 5, 185, n. 8, 187 and n. 11, 189; an. 1229, n. 4, 242; an. 1231, n. 42, n. 45, 306; and passim. In n. 48, 171, Wadding calls the author "A certain anonymous Minorite, the writer of a manuscript life of St Elizabeth in our library in Louvain."

[3] Montalembert, *Histoire de St. Elisabeth de Hongrie*, 1:175.

[4] Wenck, "Quellenuntersuchungen," 500-501.

[5] BHL Supplement, 1986, 287-88. The life in the Koblenz manuscript is listed as No. 2509 [a], *Vita auct. Anonymo ex Ord. S. Franc*; the Trier manuscript is listed as No. 2509 [d], *Vita. Inc. argumentum. Quod fuit ab initio.* This is the first edition of the BHL to mention either life.

[6] T 74v, lines 2-3. The line numbers are those in the edition in my dissertation: "St. Elizabeth of Hungary and the Franciscan Tradition."

[7] T 74v, lines 17-18.

[8] Bihl, "Die heilige Elisabeth," 283-84, 287.

[9] Gábor Klaniczay, *Holy Rulers and Blessed Princesses: Dynastic Cults in Medieval Central Europe*, trans. Éva Pálmai (New York: Cambridge University Press, 2002), p. 231. The Hungarian version came out before my edition of the full text of the Anonymous Franciscan was published.

[10] K 126ra, lines 805-15.

[11] Takács, "Die Verehung der hl. Elisabeth in Ungarn," 244-45.

[12] T 80r, line 243.

[13] Klaniczay, *Holy Rulers and Saintly Princesses*, 324-5.

[14] Wenck, *Quellenuntersuchungen*, 500.

[15] Huyskens, *Libellus*, xxvii.

[16] T 79v, lines 215-17.

[17] T 80v, lines 254-65, and 81v, lines 299-307.

[18] T 87v, lines 582-84.

[19] T 90v, lines 672-74.

[20] The manuscript is Pal. Germ. 105. According to Karl Bartsch, *Katalog der Handschriften der Universitätsbibliothek in Heidelberg* 1: *Die altdeutschen Handschriften* (Heidelberg: Verlag von Gustav Koester, 1887), 25-26, Professor Ernest C. Ranke prepared an edition of the Heidelberg Life in 1881, but it remained unpublished. Ranke's manuscript is in the Autographen section of the Staatsbibliothek Preußischer Kulturbesitz in Berlin.

[21] T 87v, lines 565-73, Heidelberg manuscript (H) 31v.

[22] Huyskens, *Libellus*, 30, H 15v.

[23] These works of Pelbart and Osvat are discussed by Ancelet-Hustache, *Gold Tried by Fire*, 272-73, note.

[24] T 79v, lines 216-18.

[25] T 80r, line 233.

[26] Huyskens, *Libellus*, xxvi-xxvii.

[27] For information on Berthold, see Denise Adele Kaiser, "Sin and the Vices in the *Sermones de Dominicis* by Berthold of Regensburg" (Dissertation, Columbia University, 1983).

[28] Bihl, "Die heilige Elisabeth," 284. Ancelet-Hustache misread the Anonymous Franciscan and wrote that Berthold had told of the incident in one of his sermons; *Gold Tried by Fire*, 233.

[29] T 79v, line 215.

[30] T 87r, lines 545-46.

[31] T 87v, line 565.

[32] T 80r, lines 240-41. There are several places called "Campania" in Latin, including the Champagne region in France, the region of Campania near Rome, and the German town of Kempen in North Rhine-Westphalia, Germany. It is not clear which this was meant to be.

[33] T 89r, line 622.

[34] Huyskens, *Quellenstudien*, 143.

[35] See Vauchez, *La sainteté en occident*, 53.

[36] Huyskens, *Quellenstudien*, 159.

[37] T 84v, lines 437-38.

[38] Bihl, "Die heilige Elisabeth," 283-84.

[39] Ancelet-Hustache, *Gold Tried by Fire*, 233.

[40] Salimbene d'Adam, *Cronica*, I, 452, II, 641 (translation mine). Another English translation can be found in Joseph Baird, Giuseppe Baglivi and John Robert Kane, eds., *The Chronicle of*

Salimbene de Adam (Binghampton, New York: Medieval and Renaissance Texts and Studies, 1986).

[41] In 1227 and 1233 the Franciscan brothers were granted the privilege of burial in their churches. In 1250, Innocent IV extended it to seculars. See Cesare Cenci: "De constitutionibus Praenarbonensibus," AFH 83 (1990): 90-91, note 47.

[42] For details, see Ancelet-Hustache, *Gold Tried by Fire*, 205-206.

[43] Lemmens, "Zur Biographie," 4.

[44] See Helen Nicholson, *Templars, Hospitallers and Teutonic Knights: Images of the Military Orders, 1128-1291* (Leicester/New York: Leicester University Press, 1993), 116-18.

[45] Nicholson, *Templars, Hospitallers and Teutonic Knights*, 118.

[46] Wenck, "Quellenuntersuchungen," 441-42.

[47] See Hermann Bauer, *St. Elisabeth und die Elisabethkirche zu Marburg* (Marburg: Hitzeroth, 1990), 81-83, and 78-84.

Chapter V

Elizabeth's Vocation: Choosing Poverty

Introduction

At first glance, it would seem easy to determine the driving forces and characteristic events of Elizabeth's life from the abundant sources, and thus to answer the questions: what was it that led to her attraction to poverty, and her love for the poor and for justice? Did she undergo a conversion? In what way did she grow in her understanding of the path God wanted her to follow? In reality, even the earliest sources are not always in agreement on these questions. As Chapter II has shown, they present a number of problems of interpretation. In addition, as we move from the earliest testimonies to the later lives, we discover that over time there is a change in the authors' understanding of Elizabeth's spiritual growth, the nature of her connection to the Franciscan movement and her religious life, a change that took place in response to historical conditions.

In the following two chapters, in addition to dealing with the major questions about Elizabeth's life, I will point out some of these changes, using the methodology I described in Chapter II. In this way, we will be able to better understand the reality of Elizabeth's life, as well as the concerns that motivated her later medieval biographers. This chapter will describe Elizabeth's earlier life and marriage and the growth of her love for poverty and the poor, leading to her choice of the religious life after her husband's death. In the next chapter, I will discuss Elizabeth's religious life and the gradual change in understanding of the nature of that life in the sources.

Elizabeth's Early Life in the Canonization Process

Her Marriage

Elizabeth is unusual for a medieval woman saint in that instead of remaining a virgin either alone or in a chaste marriage, as did Marie d'Oignies and others, she spent some years in a normal married life and had three children. Only a few other women saints of the thirteenth century, such as Elizabeth's aunt, St. Hedwig, duchess of Silesia (d. 1243), were married and had families, and even then, they were not praised for their family life, but their practice of poverty and austerity.[1] Elizabeth's married life, largely contrary to contemporary images of a woman saint, gave rise to different responses among the witnesses at her canonization process, to which we will turn first.

Conrad of Marburg says very little about Elizabeth's marriage. Instead, he stresses that she "lamented that she had ever been joined in marriage, and that she had not been able to end the present life in the flower of her virginity."[2] Thus he suggests that Elizabeth was bent on religious life even during her marriage; reluctance to marry was one of the most common features of medieval lives of holy women; it tended to make the idea of them being married more acceptable. That holiness required virginity or continence was something Conrad clearly believed himself. But was it really Elizabeth's belief – or simply the conventional thing Conrad expected of her?

Conrad spends a good part of his letter describing Elizabeth's charity. Even though she had always been the "consoler of the poor," he says, it was during the famine in her husband's absence in 1226 that she began to "grow in virtue" by becoming the "restorer of the starving."[3] She built a hospital at the foot of the Wartburg and served the poor there twice daily. Conrad notes that her husband approved of what she did, but this is almost his only mention of Ludwig. His account so far is along traditional ascetic lines: Elizabeth increases her virtue by her charity.

Conrad speaks only briefly about Elizabeth's mystical life -- and even this description is based more on the comments of others than on his own experience (see chapter VI). Admittedly, this is largely true of all the early sources. Isentrude, as we will see below, though she claimed to be closer to Elizabeth than anyone else, was only able to persuade her to describe one vision of hers. In fact, Isentrude recalled that Elizabeth habitually kept many of her devotional practices secret during her married life, often running ahead of her ladies to make her genuflections alone in the church.[4]

Thus the relationship between Conrad and Elizabeth differed from that of many other female mystics and their confessors/biographers in that it was not based on her visions. In other cases there was a relationship where the male cleric was a recorder, a sharer of secrets, promulgating and validating what the holy woman experienced, a relationship where men could see women as "other," more spiritual and habitually closer to God than themselves.[5] Conrad's letter is not as personal as many of these accounts written by other confessors about their penitents, though admittedly, it is too brief to contain much personal detail. On the other hand, it is possible that Elizabeth did not communicate to him much of her deepest inner life.

In contrast to Conrad's letter, a great deal of Isentrude's testimony is devoted to Elizabeth's married life. She says that Elizabeth and Ludwig lived their marriage "in a way worthy of praise. They loved each other with a wonderful affection, gently inviting and strengthening each other in the praise and service of God."[6] Isentrude adds that her husband "freely granted Blessed Elizabeth the authority to carry out all those things which pertained to the work and the honor of God, and promoting the salvation of souls."[7] This evidently refers to Elizabeth's authority for the charitable distribution of his goods, which she used to its fullest during the famine.

Isentrude describes how Elizabeth would frequently get up at night to pray, while Ludwig, concerned about her discomfort, would hold her hand, begging her to get back in bed. Perhaps because of his concern, Elizabeth then began to ask her ladies-in-waiting to wake her at night for prayer while her husband was asleep by pulling her foot. They did so, even though often enough Ludwig was only pretending to be asleep. Once Isentrude, in trying to wake her, pulled Ludwig's foot by mistake, for he had extended his leg over to his wife's side of the bed. He woke up, but "knowing her intention, bore it patiently."[8] Because of the length of her prayers, Elizabeth often fell asleep on the carpet in front of the bed. When her ladies found fault with her for this, and asked why she would not rather sleep beside her husband, she answered: "Although I cannot always pray, I can do violence to my flesh by tearing myself away from my beloved husband."[9] In all of this, there are none of the conventional statements found in many women saints' lives that would suggest that Elizabeth tried to avoid sexual relations in marriage. In fact, by waiting until her husband was asleep to begin her prayers, she seems to have tried to disturb this part of her married life as little as possible.

Isentrude apparently looked on Elizabeth's marriage as a positive help toward holiness, something about which Conrad says nothing. She never mentions any regrets Elizabeth might have had about having married, only that while married she made a vow to observe continence after her husband's death, and persuaded other women to do the same.[10]

Guda confirmed all of Isentrude's statements, and there is nothing specific from her about Elizabeth's married life. But she does confirm that the saint had the habit from childhood of trying to hide her religious devotions. For instance, while she was playing with her young companions at the Wartburg, she would run toward the castle chapel when racing another girl, and jump in on bended knee, taking the opportunity to press her lips to the floor. Or hopping on one foot, she would jump into the chapel and kiss the walls. Or after she had promised God some prayers and genuflections if she won a game, she would say to another girl: "Let's measure which one of us is taller" and then would secretly make the genuflections while taking the measurements.[11] That one should not display one's piety is a belief that goes back to the Gospel (Mtt. 6:5; Lk. 11:2-4), and we would expect a saint to display this type of behavior. This tendency of Elizabeth not to reveal her devotions is given just such an explicitly religious motivation by the additions found in the *Libellus*.[12] Guda herself does not spell out such a motivation. Perhaps Elizabeth's inner motives then and later were due just as much to a desire for privacy in her innermost thoughts, natural to someone living a very prominent public life, as they were to religious motives. But some things are even more interesting in Guda's testimony, such as her picture of Elizabeth's love of play and lively sociability as a girl, something which lives of saints rarely contain.

Isentrude's portrait of Elizabeth's married life has more support from early testimony than does Conrad's. Ludwig's chaplain Berthold, an eyewitness who was also a cleric, but not particularly concerned with advocating Elizabeth's sanctity, confirms Isentrude's testimony about the joy Elizabeth found in her love for her husband. When Ludwig returned from a journey, "is most noble wife Elizabeth, daughter of the king of Hungary, known rightly for her wonderful devotion, gloriously welcomed her beloved with a thousand kisses pressed on him with her heart and her lips."[13] This too, may be a conventional statement of what would be expected of a courtly wife, but the affection is also supported by Isentrude, a witness in support of sanctity, who felt that such sanctity went well with marriage.

Elizabeth and Conrad of Marburg

Isentrude tells us more about Elizabeth's relationship with Conrad of Marburg: she made a vow of obedience to him, reserving only the obedience she owed her husband.[14] She sometimes flagellated herself at night when her husband was asleep.

Previously, she had done this on Fridays and during Lent; now she did it more frequently under Conrad's direction. Conrad's insistence on obedience was strict. One day Elizabeth was unable to come at his command to one of his sermons because of a visit by her husband's sister, the Markgrafin of Meissen, with whom Ludwig had recently been in conflict over their territories. Elizabeth's welcome of her sister-in-law was politically important for her husband. But when Conrad heard of it, he told her he would not have charge of her any longer. When she and her ladies-in-waiting (evidently this means Guda and Isentrude) begged for forgiveness, he decided on a penance: he had them stripped to their undergarments and flagellated.[15] His attitude to Elizabeth up until her death was marked by this kind of severity. In fact, he seems to have become even more severe after her husband's death and her entrance into religious life, when he sometimes slapped her in the face for disobeying his commands.[16]

Conrad's relationship with Elizabeth has always been one of the most controversial elements of her life, and historians have often found her attachment to him hard to explain. In most ways, he was her opposite in character, and there seems to have been little sympathy between their souls. Why would Elizabeth have put up with his cruel treatment of her? We must add to this his reputation as a relentless pursuer of heretics, which has often been an embarrassment to Catholic historians. But there are some, including the Protestant Wenck, who have defended him. Wenck admitted that as an inquisitor, Conrad was "one of the darkest figures of German history," but that condemnation of him as a heretic hunter should not be carried over to his relationship with Elizabeth, since he did direct her in a way that corresponded to her total commitment to asceticism, though this may seem strange to us today. He also was prudent, and prevented her from carrying her love of poverty too far.[17]

On the other hand, Elisabeth Busse-Wilson, a student of Freudian psychoanalysis, spoke confidently of Conrad's obsession with Elizabeth, his cruelty and her obedience as a mutual sadomasochistic relationship.[18] It can be argued that such interpretations fail to take into account the medieval view of the purpose of suffering. It was a time when flagellation and other severe penances were common practice. According to Isentrude's testimony, Elizabeth on her own had previously flagellated herself on Fridays and during Lent, but did it more frequently under Conrad's direction.[19]

Today, it is more natural to think of Conrad and Elizabeth's relationship in terms of the problems of battered women subjected to men who are in positions of power over them. Ulrike Wiethaus brings out what many of Elizabeth's biographers have not admitted: while it is true that flagellation was very common as an ascetic practice and as an imposed penance in the Middle Ages, Conrad's treatment of Elizabeth went far beyond the norm considered acceptable at the time. In the Rule of St. Benedict, for instance, flagellation as a punishment was severely regulated and to be used as a last resort; Conrad was apparently not inhibited by any such considerations.[20]

But none of this really accounts for the problematic nature of Conrad and Elizabeth's relationship. What led Elizabeth to choose such a man as her confessor to begin with?

We have seen that he was not imposed on her; Wenck's idea that Ludwig chose Conrad in order to mitigate Elizabeth's desire for poverty has no foundation (see Chapter II). One of the few personal statements attributed to Elizabeth by an eyewitness makes it clear that she chose Conrad personally for her confessor and chose him because of his extreme poverty. She explained to Irmingard: "I could have promised obedience to some of the bishops or abbots who have possessions, but I thought it best to promise to Master Conrad, who does not have [any], but is a complete beggar, so that I might have no consolation in this life."[21]   Elizabeth said this to Irmingard at a later date, after she had begun her religious life, during the same conversation in which she spoke of wishing to be despised as a "sister in the world." By this time, the Pope had put

Elizabeth under his protection. But she is, I believe, also indicating why she initially chose him as her confessor during her marriage.

Conrad certainly must have been a charismatic man, as the crowds surrounding him wherever he went and the popularity of his preaching attest. It may be that Elizabeth fell under his spell, and the violent side of his personally began to show itself only later (as is often true of batterers). Perhaps at that time she was seeking in him a strong ally in her desire to practice poverty, for as much as Ludwig loved her, he could not completely share this ideal, not without renouncing his own power and rulership.

Elizabeth, the Franciscans and Poverty

Even before Elizabeth chose Conrad as her confessor, another religious influence was becoming popular throughout Europe, and would have an effect on her life. The first Franciscans made their way to Germany as early as 1221. They arrived in Eisenach, the town beneath the Wartburg, in 1225. Elizabeth was then about eighteen years old. No one knows whether she had heard of Francis or his friars before this. But she soon became involved in their work in Eisenach; we learn from Conrad that she gave them a church there.[22] The Franciscan chronicler Giordano da Giano was the one who accepted that church on behalf of the Franciscans; it was the same place where Elizabeth was later to renounce the world in the presence of the friars.[23] We learn from the *Dicta /Libellus* that Elizabeth spun wool for the habits of the Franciscans at the convent, at the same time that she began to develop a love of poverty and begging and would talk about it with her ladies. Isentrude says: "dressing herself in a shabby cloak in front of them in the palace and wrapping a plain piece of cloth around her head, she said, 'This is how I will walk when I go begging and bear misery for the love of God.'"[24]

According to Giordano, a friar named Rudeger, who was a layman when he entered the Order,"became the guardian in Halberstadt and Blessed Elizabeth's teacher of spiritual discipline;

he taught her to preserve chastity, humility and patience and to keep watch in prayer and to apply herself to works of mercy."[25]

A number of writers have spoken of Rudeger as Elizabeth's confessor, and suppose that he was later replaced by Conrad of Marburg. As we have seen, Wenck thought that though Elizabeth originally chose the Franciscan as her confessor, her husband imposed the change. It should be pointed out, however, that there is no evidence in Giordano that Rudeger was ever a priest, nor does he ever describe him as Elizabeth's confessor. Nor was it likely she could have promised obedience to him. In fact, the friars were forbidden to receive such promises of obedience from women in the First Rule of St. Francis. This prohibition is not explicitly included in the definitive Rule of 1223, but seems to be very much in its spirit. The prohibition was probably adopted as much on account of Francis' reluctance to see the friars in positions of authority as out of fear of the scandal caused by familiarity with women.[26] It is also very likely that the friars in Germany, who were small in numbers at this period, had very few priests among their number, and could not spare one to be Elizabeth's confessor. So while Elizabeth did receive spiritual advice from Rudeger and the other Franciscans, when she needed a confessor and regular spiritual director, she turned to Conrad.

The Question of Justice

If it was the Franciscans who introduced Elizabeth to a love for poverty, it was Conrad who had her official vow of obedience. Yet even here, we can trace her personal feelings about poverty and the poor in Conrad's famous *"Speisegebot"* or command to abstain from certain foods. Isentrude's testimony is important for understanding this matter, for hers is the only detailed statement we have about it. She said:

After [Elizabeth] promised obedience, the aforesaid Master Conrad directed her not to make use of any of her husband's goods about which she did not have a clear conscience. She observed this so strictly that while sitting beside her husband at table, she abstained from everything which came from offices and the profit made by officials, not using foods unless she knew that they came from her husband's own revenues and his legitimate possessions.[27]

Isentrude went on to say that it was Elizabeth's practice to make inquiries of the servants of the estate managers about the food brought in before she would eat any of it. When she found out that the food was licit, she would clap her hands merrily and say, "Good for us, now we are going to eat and drink." At banquets at court, Ludwig, who sat next to her, often secretly reassured her about the provenance of foods being served, but Elizabeth still often found herself going hungry at the rich table. Elizabeth's ladies-in-waiting joined with her in this abstention, and when they asked Ludwig whether he would be offended by it, he answered: "I would gladly do the very same thing, if I did not fear insults from the family and from others. Nevertheless, God willing, I will soon arrange my state of life differently."[28] In fact, because of this way of life, Isentrude adds, both Elizabeth and her husband bore with great patience many insults from their people.

In time, Elizabeth was able to provide for herself and her retinue out of the property assigned to her as her dower. When nothing could be found for sale, she sent messengers to ask the wealthy people who lived nearby for what was necessary, pretending that she found those things more to her liking than the foods at court. Surprisingly, though Isentrude emphasizes that Conrad's command about eating controlled Elizabeth's behavior, Conrad himself does not even mention this command in his letter.

Historians have long argued how to interpret this case of conscience. Wilhelm Maurer believed that Conrad's strict obliging of Elizabeth's conscience in the use of property was his way of allowing her to participate spiritually in the coming crusade.[29] Maria Maresch sees the refusal of illicit foods as Elizabeth and Conrad's reaction to the enormous increase in taxation needed to support the Landgraf's wars for territorial expansion, and his gradual encroachment on the lands of the Church. Ludwig was, in fact, engaged in frequent struggles with the Archbishop of Mainz over the ownership of some lands. In Maresch's view, Elizabeth felt that not only was this usurpation unlawful, but these increased taxes, which were often taken in kind and financially hurt the poor peasants, were unjust.[30] André Vauchez sees Elizabeth's action as a protest either against the injustices of the feudal regime or the rising territorial state. To him, Isentrude's statement that Elizabeth was concerned about whether the food came from her husband's "legitimate possessions" meant that she supported the traditional idea that a prince should live from his own hereditary possessions, not those of the state as a whole.[31]

The usurpation of Church lands as a motive for Elizabeth's abstention from certain foods is never mentioned directly by any of the eyewitnesses, even Conrad, who could have used it in his letter to the Pope to stress that Elizabeth was a defender of the Church. But this concern may well have been a factor influencing Elizabeth's judgment about the legitimacy of certain foods coming from these usurped lands. It may have subtly influenced the awareness of the eyewitnesses, especially Isentrude's reference to "legitimate possessions." On the other hand, Isentrude stated that the food came from the profit of the officials taking the taxes; evidently they inflated what was owed them in order to increase their own income. Then we have Irmingard's testimony about Elizabeth's motives: when describing her reluctance after her husband's death to receive sustenance from her brother-in-law, Irmingard said that Elizabeth had refused because "she did not want to receive her nourishment by theft and by taxing the poor, as was so often the practice at the courts of princes."[32] The reference to the taxes imposed on the poor is very clear, but the meaning of "theft" is less clear. It might refer to what was unjustly taken from the poor, or to Ludwig's unlawful usurpation of episcopal lands. In fact, as Maresch's analysis shows, the two questions were closely intertwined. At any rate, it is clear from Isentrude's testimony that Elizabeth's action, and Ludwig's support for it, were violently opposed by his relatives, so an important policy of the ruling family of Thuringia must have been involved.

Most historians have taken it for granted that Elizabeth practiced this abstention from certain foods because she was completely under Conrad's sway, and that her ideas of the justice of the situation were derived from his. Elisabeth Busse-Wilson, for example, believes that the motive was all on Conrad's side: he wanted to promote the interests of the Church in the struggle for control of the lands in question, and he took advantage of Elizabeth in promoting this agenda.[33] Yet they have also given Elizabeth credit for this as a saintly act, which suggests that it was her own initiative. And how do we interpret the difference between the testimonies? In particular, if the question of the legitimacy of the foods served was as important to Conrad as Isentrude states, why did he fail to speak of it? We might suppose that he did so because he wanted to play up Elizabeth's courage, superior holiness and divine inspiration, things proper to a saint, and therefore downplay the idea that he ordered it as a matter of obedience. In fact, in descriptions of female saints, particularly by medieval male writers, there is a tension between the ideas of a "good woman" -- meek, submissive, dutiful -- and a "saint": a person inspired by God, active, courageous, stronger than other people.[34] We can trace some of this in Conrad's description of Elizabeth; for instance, he never refers to the "weakness of her sex," as medieval writes frequently do when discussing women. But not only is Conrad silent about his command, he never even mentions Elizabeth's abstention from illicit food. In addition, his portrait of her stresses her asceticism rather than her concern for social justice.

The evidence does not really support the theory that the initiative was all Conrad's. We could equally well stress, as

Isentrude did, Elizabeth's personal understanding of the matter. Perhaps Elizabeth came to Conrad with this important case of conscience, and Conrad gave her a command that in his eyes would serve his purpose of training her in ascetic control (some may suspect that he also enjoyed this exercise of power). In this case, by going behind the silence of the sources, we can arrive at a different interpretation: the extreme lengths that Elizabeth went to in order to abstain from illicit foods were due to her commitment to justice, as well as a desire for strict obedience to her confessor. Nor does she fit the pattern of compulsive starvation of religious women that some historians have recently drawn, for, as Isentrude's testimony demonstrates, Elizabeth was relieved and delighted when she and her ladies could eat legitimate food -- something that fits neither the traditional ascetic pattern nor the one Bynum observed in many women.[35]

Such social concerns were not unique to Elizabeth, but were shared by a number of women of her time; this has been studied most often in those from urban backgrounds. Many Beguines from the cities and towns rejected the new mercantile economy and the marriage market that was a part of it, choosing to follow evangelical poverty instead.[36] Here the prevailing injustice was usury, regarded not only as an unlawful means of profit, but as something that hurt the poor borrower and disrupted solidarity with the poor. Jacques de Vitry's life of Marie d'Oignies, who came from a wealthy town background, tells of her determination to avoid all alms that came from "robbers and usurers."[37] Thomas of Cantimpré tells how Marie also prayed fervently for her dead mother, only to have her soul appear in a vision to tell her daughter that she was damned because she had "lived on what had been acquired by usury and unjust commerce."[38] The *Vita* of Umiliana dei Cerchi tells of her similar concern: "It is said that when her husband was close to death, she wanted to give away her dowry for the love of God, if her husband would honestly repent, and according to the precept of the priest of God, return the usurious interest he was keeping."[39] Elizabeth was concerned about the same principles as the other women, but her feudal background brought a different set of injustices to her attention.[40]

As Isentrude describes it, Elizabeth's life became more and more taken up with caring for the poor and unfortunate. When caring for the sick at her hospital, she would wipe the filth from their mouths, ears and noses, and would not even notice the smell, even though her handmaids could not bear it. She would personally visit the poorest hovels, and even tried (unsuccessfully) to milk a cow for a poor sick man. She would stand with the poorest women during religious processions. During the famine she took much out of her own mouth for the poor. When after the famine the new crop came in, she gave tools and clothes to those who could work, so they could live off the labor of their own hands. In her hospital she gave special attention to the sickest and most wretched children, who all called her "mother," and brought them playthings. She did all this with the "greatest cheerfulness of soul and face."[41]

Even though Isentrude praises Elizabeth and Ludwig's love for each other, there are signs that Elizabeth's awareness of the injustice caused by riches, and her desire for a simpler life sometimes came into conflict with her love for her husband. This tension seems to be reflected in another story that can ultimately be traced back to eyewitness testimony, for Caesarius of Heisterbach received it from Dietrich, the Archbishop of Trier, who had it from Elizabeth's husband Ludwig. According to this story, one night when they were lying awake together in bed, Elizabeth said to her husband, "I have been thinking about the good life, the life necessary to us, by which we can usefully serve God." When the Landgraf asked, "What is that life?" she continued: "I would like us to have only one plough[42] of land and two hundred sheep; you could cultivate the land with your own hands and I would milk the sheep." At these words the Landgraf, "smiling and rejoicing at her simplicity," said jokingly, "Ah! sister, if we had one plough of land and two hundred sheep, we would not be poor, but rich."[43]

Caesarius expresses a somewhat patronizing attitude towards Elizabeth's "simplicity." Elizabeth may have still been naive about some aspects of the life of the poor, but the conversation tells us more than that. Elizabeth actually did not characterize the life she wanted to live with her husband as a poor life when she spoke with him, perhaps because she was aware of how impossible it was for her him to give up his position. Therefore she expressed her ideal life of poverty in a mitigated form. Underneath it all is her realization of the spiritual dangers inherent in the rich life they were living. And Ludwig would have understood her real meaning, even if he tried to dismiss it with a joke.

Did Elizabeth Become a Tertiary during her Marriage?

As I previously mentioned, the question of if and when Elizabeth became a member of the Franciscan Third Order has been the subject of considerable controversy. It has sometimes been stated that Elizabeth became a tertiary during her marriage. In doing so, she would have become part of the growing Order of Penance—a movement that was actually wider than the Franciscan movement and its nascent Third Order.

It is true that many aspects of the way of life that Elizabeth adopted during her marriage are consonant with the life of the penitents, including her consistent turning from the world toward God as the center of her life, and her practice of the works of mercy, which are the primary marks of the penitent life.[44] It is possible that the first Franciscans who came to Eisenach around 1225 knew about the penitential fraternities in Italy inspired by St. Francis, and were acquainted with the *Memoriale Propositi*, the rule for those fraternities which originated in 1221; it was actually one of a number of such proposals for penitent life made by different groups. This rule would have been well suited to Elizabeth's married state. Could the Franciscans have given it to her as a model for her way of life?[45]

Some of the practices she adopted are in harmony with this rule: it required penitents to wear simple and unadorned garments, though this precept could be adapted to a person's state of life (Ch. 1:3). According to the additions of the *Libellus*, while her husband was away, Elizabeth, "laying aside her fine clothes, and putting a different veil on her head, conducted herself religiously, like a widow."[46] She also laid aside the silk ribbons and other ornaments which the Sisters of Penance, or Continent Sisters were not to wear, and urged other women to do so (Ch. 1:3-4).[47] At other times, Isentrude testified, she would wear coarse wool garments, such as when she went to church for purification after the births of her children.[48] The rule also required the return of unjustly acquired property (Ch 5:15). St. Francis' Letter to the Faithful, a longer version of an exhortation to the Brothers and Sisters of Penance, also strongly urges the just disposition of worldly goods, and the need to make reparation for fraudulent use of them (EpFidII 63-64). We know that the principle of justice behind this rule was a matter of conscience for Elizabeth. She persuaded others to avoid (and presumably began avoiding herself) dances and other entertainments, things that were forbidden by the *Memoriale Propositi* (Ch. 1:5).[49] Her ladies-in-waiting did some of the same things; according to Isentrude, they also refrained from unjustly acquired food.

Salvà firmly believed that Elizabeth was first professed in the Third Order Secular during her husband's lifetime, and later donning the habit, was professed again in the Third Order Regular.[50] However, there does not appear to have been any distinct Third Order Regular at this time; that is, there were not two different Third Orders, secular and regular in which she could have been professed. This also raises the question of why Elizabeth would need to be professed twice as a penitent, since this was thought to be a permanent state of life.

In 1239, after Elizabeth's death, her brother-in-law Heinrich Raspe, his wife, and some other members of the Thuringian nobility became members of the Order of Penance. We learn this from a bull sent by Gregory IX on June 27, 1239 to the Bishops of Hildesheim and Mereseburg, telling them to take into their special protection the "noble man the Landgraf of Thuringia and certain others of his land, who desire to withdraw from harmful things and be directed toward salutary things, after the example of those who are called the Brothers of Penance."[51] The following day, the Pope sent another letter to the Franciscan Provincial Minister of Saxony, ordering him to make a confessor available to Heinrich and his wife, Gertrude of Austria, according to their request, so they could begin the life of penance.[52] There is no evidence, however, that the Pope made any such provisions for Elizabeth, something that seems to have been customary when rulers were involved.

As we will see later, the evidence is much stronger for Elizabeth being professed in the Order of Penance after her husband's death, though she may have informally adopted many of the practices of the penitents during her married life. It is even possible, though far from certain, that she followed the precepts of the *Memoriale Propositi* and St. Francis' Letter to the Brothers and Sisters of Penance without any kind of profession.

To summarize the discussion so far, we have seen that there is a striking difference between the witnesses about some aspects of Elizabeth's life. Conrad, eager to present Elizabeth as someone who had a desire for the religious life from the beginning, insists on her regret about losing her virginity, something not mentioned by the other witnesses. He also seems to see her marriage as something unconnected with her holiness. On the other hand, Isentrude and the chaplain Berthold present her as a happy wife, and Isentrude forcefully states that she found marriage a help to holiness. But all the witnesses are absolutely agreed that one of the main aspects of Elizabeth's life from very early on was her desire to care for the poor and suffering. And the best evidence is that this was combined with a desire to live a life of poverty, not only in a traditional ascetic sense of renunciation, but with an eye to justice for the less fortunate. Her desire, also expressed in early testimony, is that she would have liked to live a poorer or simpler life with her husband while still in the married state.

Elizabeth's life with her husband came to an abrupt end when the news of his death in Italy arrived at the Wartburg in the fall of 1227. At that time, she had just given birth to her third child,

Gertrude. It is here that her life takes a turn that would lead to her decision for religious life – one that would also deeply influence the form that life took.

Elizabeth's Expulsion

Isentrude's account of Elizabeth's expulsion has caused perhaps the greatest controversy among historians dealing with her life. As we have seen, it is likely that Elizabeth wanted to administer her dower property, rather than receive sustenance from the common pool of family property; in the latter case, she would not have known exactly where the goods she was using had come from. But what happened after she made her desire known?

As we have seen, Wenck interpreted Isentrude's testimony to mean that Elizabeth's request was refused, and that she left the Wartburg after her husband's death because she wanted to fulfill her confessor's binding injunctions on her conscience about not eating unlawful food, but also because she was already dedicated to a life of poverty. Ancelet-Hustache and many other modern scholars follow this opinion. While Huyskens agrees that Elizabeth loved the Franciscan ideal, he was certain that she was physically expelled, not from the Wartburg, but from the castle and city where her dower properties were.

Isentrude's testimony on this question is the only detailed one we have; therefore it is vitally important. As she tells it:

> After her husband's death, Elizabeth was ejected from the castle and all the possessions of her dower by some of her husband's vassals, her husband's brother being still young. So she went into the city situated below the castle, and entered a poor building in a courtyard belonging to an innkeeper, where he kept his dishes and household goods, and in which his pigs lay, and spent that night there in great joy. In the middle of the night, when it was

time for Matins, she went to the Friars Minor in that town, asking them to sing the *"Te Deum laudamus,"* rejoicing and giving thanks to God for her tribulation.

The following day, when no rich man dared to offer her shelter, she entered the church together with her handmaids, and sat there a long time. And since her little ones had been brought from the castle in the most bitter cold, she did not know where she was to stay and where she was to lay her children's heads -- although the lordship of the town belonged to them by paternal succession. Finally, compelled by necessity, she entered the home of a priest, asking [him] to have pity on her and her expelled children.

Afterwards, she was ordered to enter the home of one of her enemies, where she was compelled to take refuge in a confined place with her whole household, although there were many buildings there. Because the host and hostess were very unpleasant to her and her people, on leaving there, she said farewell to the walls which had preserved her from the cold and rain, saying, "I would gladly thank the people, but I don't know why." And she returned again to the same dirty building where she had been at the beginning, being unable to get any other shelter.

And so, undergoing persecution from all her husband's men without cause and deprived of her property, she was forced by her poverty to send her children to different remote places, so that they might be brought up there.[53]

Isentrude continues to describe how Elizabeth had to move from one place to another, and bore many indignities, being treated as insane or a fool by the nobility. Once she met a poor sick woman who had received alms from her in the past, who pushed her in the mud, but Elizabeth only laughed at it.[54] The amount of detail that Isentrude gives indicates that she almost certainly shared this period of Elizabeth's life with her, including her expulsion from the castle, and her testimony brings out her indignation over the injustice done to Elizabeth and her children.

It should be noted that Isentrude speaks clearly about an expulsion in the physical sense not just in one place, but in several: she stresses that Elizabeth had nowhere to go, for no one dared give her shelter; at last she persuaded a priest to have pity on her and her "expelled children." She was even confined against her will for a time. There is no doubt that Isentrude is talking about an actual physical expulsion that sent Elizabeth from her dower castle in Marburg (or wherever it was) and even into hiding, and a persecution that apparently extended to anyone who might have tried to help her. The whole atmosphere of the tale is one of force and fear of violence. To reject the physical expulsion would mean rejecting the whole of Isentrude's testimony about this period of Elizabeth's life, which even Wenck did not want to do.

But is Isentrude's testimony plausible? While she gives details that demonstrate the Christian way in which Elizabeth bore with injustice and suffering, her account says nothing about the actual reasons behind the expulsion, or exactly how it came about. Nor does she name the "enemy" with whom Elizabeth was forced to stay (was she being held prisoner by one of the vassals?). It might be supposed that Isentrude is exaggerating to play up Elizabeth's sanctity, but her story is far from implausible. Women of the ruling class in the Middle Ages frequently played a part in dynastic power struggles, and Elizabeth may have suffered the effects of her own political stand. For her to undergo actual physical expulsion and imprisonment would not have been unusual.

It is important to recall here that Ludwig had given Elizabeth full power in regard to charitable distribution of his property and that she used that power to its fullest in his absence during the famine of 1226. She would undoubtedly have enjoyed the same powers when he left for the crusade a year later. Isentrude states more than once that many of the nobles were outraged at Elizabeth's stand against the injustice of the ruling family's tax policies and perhaps the unjust acquisition of territory; her actions had made it clear that this criticism extended to the officials who collected the taxes. We know that many of Ludwig's most faithful vassals had set off with him for the Holy Land.[55] After his death, Elizabeth would have been without support, and many feared that if she were free to administer her dower lands herself, she would engage in even more ruinous spending of the income of the properties and interference with the taxes.

And what of Elizabeth's brother-in-law, the new Landgraf Heinrich? He was not the inheritor of Ludwig's lands and titles, which went to Elizabeth's son, but as regent and administrator of them, he was the one most affected by her actions at the time. If she did indeed request to administer her dower property, he would have found it difficult to refuse; this was the customary law. It may have been that once she decided to settle on her property, he reconsidered, and decided, perhaps persuaded by some of Ludwig's outraged vassals, to allow them to send armed men to eject Elizabeth from her property. He may have been acting simply with a view to forcing her to come back home to the Wartburg and being able to exert some control over her. He may have been surprised when she did not return, but decided to stay in Marburg, even in poverty, knowing that she would be obliged to act against her conscience in regard to food if she did come back. If she suspected his treachery, she would have been even less likely to return.

So the version of Wenck and other scholars undoubtedly has some truth in it. I believe Wenck rejected a literal expulsion because, in spite of his admiration for Elizabeth, he fell all too easily into the traditional male attitude of seeing Elizabeth as a weak-minded woman who needed direction from men like Conrad, not one whose own actions could have aroused political opposition.

Isentrude's lack of clarity about details is not surprising. After all, the powerful ruling family of Thuringia, in the person of Elizabeth's brother-in-law Conrad, was by now, in 1235, directing her canonization process. And, if the hints Isentrude gives are accurate, Conrad's brother Heinrich was at least indirectly responsible for Elizabeth's sufferings, since he failed to help her recover her property (Isentrude offers the mitigating circumstances of his youth and perhaps lack of authority) and may have acted in complicity with those who forced her out of her home. Isentrude, a noblewoman, may also have been unwilling to say anything against Heinrich, especially since, as a long-time member of the Landgraf's household, she had probably known him well personally and did not want to accuse him directly, especially without proof. Far from exaggerating Elizabeth's sufferings, it is easy to believe that Isentrude is not even telling the worst. Her testimony is directed, however subtly, against the men of the ruling family of Thuringia, and there is evidence of some fear in her own words. She naturally would have been very cautious about what she said – but what she did say is compelling. This bit of testimony is a prime example of how we can recover women's voices and women's history from historical sources, even those written by men.

Because of her poverty, Elizabeth eventually had to relinquish custody of her children, who seem to have been taken to Kreuzburg castle, another of the Landgraf's residences. It is during the period of poverty and suffering shortly after her expulsion that we have, again from Isentrude, the only detailed eyewitness account of any of Elizabeth's visions. It is a vision that may be important for understanding the motivations for her final choice of the religious life. It was during Lent. Elizabeth had been in church, with her eyes fixed on the altar for a long time. On returning to her poor hovel, she ate a little food, but then became so weak she had to lean against the wall. Isentrude caught her in her arms. Everyone else was sent out, and Isentrude sat with her. After a time, Elizabeth, who was looking

117

towards the window, opened her eyes and began to laugh gently. After a time, she closed her eyes and wept. She continued to alternate between tears and laughter until Compline, when after a period of silence she suddenly said, "So then, Lord, You want to be with me and I want to be with You and I never want to be separated from You."[56] When she came back to herself, and Isentrude asked to whom she had been speaking, she answered:

> I saw the heavens open and sweet Jesus my Lord bending down towards me and consoling me for the many difficulties and tribulations which surrounded me, and when I saw Him, I was filled with joy and I laughed. But when he turned his face away, as if he was about to withdraw, I wept. Taking pity on me, he again turned his most serene face towards me, saying, "If you want to be with me, I will be with you."[57]

And it was then, she explained, that she had spoken as she had done. Isentrude asked her to tell her about a previous vision she had in church when the host was raised (perhaps referring to the church visit she had just made), but Elizabeth would not do so. She said: "It is better not to reveal what I saw there, but you should know that I was in the greatest joy, and I saw wonderful secrets of God."[58]

Pásztor believes that Elizabeth's primary conception of Christ, as shown by this vision, was not the suffering Christ of the Franciscans, but the Christ in glory, the Christ who is above the world, who consoles those who suffer.[59] Yet the statements that Elizabeth rejoiced in her sufferings, and accepted Christ's request to be with him, seem to suggest a close identification between herself and the suffering Christ. It was not merely an acceptance of those sufferings as being His will for her, but a desire to share His sufferings. There is a little evidence about this elsewhere in the

Dicta/Libellus: Isentrude testified that Elizabeth "bore many beatings and slaps from Master Conrad, which she had once desired to bear in memory of the blows in the face Our Lord received" during his Passion.[60] It seems very likely that this identification with the crucified Christ marked a crucial turning point for Elizabeth on her way toward complete renunciation of everything for Him.

Evidently feeling that there was no hope of dealing with her brothers-in-law, Elizabeth turned to her mother's German relatives. Isentrude reports that Elizabeth managed to make her way to her maternal aunt Mechtild, the abbess of Kitzingen, who took her to her uncle, Eckbert, the bishop of Bamberg. He suggested that she solve her problem by marrying again. Elizabeth vehemently refused, because of the vow she had previously taken to remain continent after her husband's death. The bishop then had her and her little retinue taken to his castle at Pottenstein, evidently against her will. Her ladies (probably Guda and Isentrude herself) who had taken the vow of continence with her, feared that he would try to force her to remarry and that they would have to live their life of continence alone. In trying to persuade her, her uncle apparently suggested that her vow was conditional, and therefore she might be absolved from it, but Elizabeth would never accept this. She reassured her ladies: "I did not make this vow on condition that it please my friends or provided that God did not reveal some other plan to me -- I vowed absolutely [to preserve] total continence after my husband's death." As a sign of her resolution, according to Isentrude, Elizabeth said: "If I had no other way of escaping, I would cut off my nose in secret. No one would trouble any more about me, if I were frightfully mutilated like that."

Isentrude does not say whether or not Elizabeth had now decided on the religious life. But she does report Elizabeth's cry from the heart in her grief when the bishop allowed her to meet her husband's remains when they were brought back from Italy for burial:

"Lord, I give You thanks for having mercifully consoled me by these bones of my husband which I have so much desired. However much I loved him, you know that I do not begrudge the sacrifice of himself that my beloved and I offered to You for the liberation of the Holy Land. If I could have him, I would give the whole world for him, and go begging with him forever. But I call upon You to witness that I would not want to redeem his life, even if it cost me but a single hair, if it were against your will. Now I recommend myself and him to Your grace. May Your will for us be done."[61]

After Ludwig's burial, Elizabeth was supported by his faithful vassals, who had returned from Italy with his bones, and who promised to protect her and to work to have her dower returned. At this the persecution of her seems to have abated and her uncle dropped his attempts to have her marry again. Yet the dower question was not solved right away, and, according to Isentrude, "everyone neglected her interests, and Elizabeth found herself like a beggar again, and in the same poverty."[62]

Another important piece of evidence on these questions is found in the testimony of Irmingard. Since this young woman of humble birth only joined Elizabeth after she had built her hospital in Marburg, she did not personally witness the expulsion or the way the saint was deprived of her property. But she did speak about a question that greatly interested her: what would have made a rich lady desire to live in poverty? At first, Irmingard did not have an answer. In fact, we find out from another portion of her testimony that initially this young woman from a poor background had been somewhat suspicious of Elizabeth when she came to live with her at her hospital. When Elizabeth asked Irmingard and the other poor girl Elisabeth to sit next to her at meals, Irmingard said to her, "You acquire merit for yourself through us, but you don't pay any attention to our misfortune, that we might become proud because we are eating with you and sitting beside you." Elizabeth quickly replied, using the familiar form of address: "Well, then, thou must sit in my lap," and she made Irmingard sit in her lap. Elizabeth often expressed this desire for friendship and confidence from Irmingard.

In the end, Irmingard came to another conclusion about Elizabeth's motives. This is how she described it to the papal commissioners:

> After her husband died, Blessed Elizabeth was temporarily not allowed to use her husband's property, being prevented from doing so by her husband's brother. She could have received some sustenance from her husband's brother, but she did not want to receive her nourishment by theft and by taxing the poor, as was so often the practice at the courts of princes. She chose to be abject and to earn her bread by the work of her hands like a day-laborer.[63]

Irmingard's testimony is sometimes treated as though it were in opposition to Isentrude's. It has been interpreted by Ancelet-Hustache and other historians to mean that there was no expulsion and that Elizabeth left the Wartburg voluntarily to live in poverty in Eisenach. In this case, Isentrude's statement about her being "ejected from the castle and possessions of her dower by some of her husband's vassals" would mean that Heinrich ordered the vassals to refuse to administer the revenues from her dower to her, and that she decided to leave the Wartburg so she would not be compelled to eat unjustly acquired food.

What these historians have said about the actual legal question of Elizabeth's dower is undoubtedly true. But there is no contradiction between the testimonies. Irmingard never mentions

Elizabeth leaving a castle, voluntarily or not; in fact, since she did not join Elizabeth until much later, she could not have testified from direct knowledge about the period of the expulsion. In fact, one historian, Menge, thought there was no indication that Isentrude and Irmingard were actually talking about the same event.[64] He believed that Irmingard's statement refers to the period after Ludwig's bones were buried, but before Elizabeth's dower was returned. It may have been at this point that Elizabeth was invited by her brother-in-law Heinrich to share once again in the family community revenues until the matter of the dower could be resolved, but she refused, as Irmingard said, because she did not want to be a party to injustice by sharing in the food served at court. She may also have believed that Heinrich's promises to restore her dowry were empty ones, and that his real aim was to get her to come back to her previous life and forget her scruples.

I believe then, that Irmingard was not talking about the origin of Elizabeth's life of poverty, but why she did not leave it when she was able to – something that must have been surprising to a woman like Irmingard who was raised in poverty. She probably had no direct knowledge of the events surrounding the expulsion, and because of her social position, she was probably even more hesitant to speak about the actions of particular men in power than Isentrude was. She did, however, boldly repeat Elizabeth's words about the injustices of power. Irmingard's statement appears to be a general interpretation of Elizabeth's intentions in living the life she had chosen rather than a description of a specific incident. It was Elizabeth's commitment to justice that impressed Irmingard most. In this case again, the personality of the witness and her relationship with Elizabeth contain clues to the interpretation of the passage.

It was during the time that Elizabeth was experiencing her difficulties with her dower that Pope Gregory IX put her under Master Conrad's protection, as Conrad himself states in his letter.[65] We now have another important bit of testimony supplied by the Anonymous Franciscan, the deposition of a Franciscan named Brother Andrew of Westphalia at Elizabeth's canonization process.

This testimony is out of place in the chronological order of events, for the Anonymous Franciscan puts it after the establishment of Elizabeth's hospital in Marburg, while it clearly refers to the persecution she underwent after her expulsion. This testimony and the subsequent account given by the Anonymous Franciscan show this period in a new light, with Elizabeth receiving support from the Franciscans.

The Anonymous Franciscan describes Brother Andrew as a man versed in both canon and civil law, who had served as a counselor to Frederick II before he entered the order. He "answered the investigators that at that time blessed Elizabeth had arrived at such temporal need and at such distress of total deprivation of everything that there was no one close to her left to console her." These are clearly Brother Andrew's words, but it is not as clear whether the rest of the account comes from his testimony, perhaps slightly reworded, or was obtained by the Anonymous Franciscan from other sources. It says:

> When the aforesaid Friar Minor saw the daughter of the king of Hungary and the duchess of the Thuringians and the Landgrafin not only destitute of all help [and] solace, but even exposed to uncommon abuse and oppression, after having a conversation with certain discreet brothers he diligently devised what might be done. Seeing that they were not able to protect her or defend her from her adversaries, and hoping that Master Conrad of Marburg would suffice for the relief and protection of the servant of God Elizabeth, because at that time the apostolic authority had raised him in a certain way around those parts against the heretics, they advised her that she commit herself to the guidance of the said Master Conrad and subject herself completely to his teaching. The humble daughter

gave consent without delay to the advice of the brothers, and from then on humbly obeyed him. But after the passage of a long time, Master Conrad was able neither to defend her nor to cause what was hers to be restored to her, but the most recent events for the holy servant of God went from bad to worse. The aforesaid Friar Minor . . . having urgently asked and obtained permission from his superiors, set out for the Roman curia. Immediately, divine clemency being generous to him, he asked for apostolic letters from the Lord Leo, Cardinal of the Roman See, who was his familiar friend . . . By his authority, the aforesaid brother like a faithful procurator, hastened to meet with the adversaries of the poor Elizabeth, manfully constraining them both by threats and by entreaties, in the end restoring to the poor unhappy widow what was hers.[66]

The cardinal Leo mentioned is most likely Leo Brancaleone (died c. 1230), whose titular church was Santa Croce in Gerusalemme. He was a close friend of St. Francis and a supporter of the Franciscans; he is mentioned by the early biographers of St. Francis.[67] The question of how far Andrew's testimony extends, and whether the brother who actually went to Rome was Andrew, or Henry, who subsequently became Elizabeth's procurator at the hospital, is difficult to decide because of the disruption of the text (see Chapter IV). From the description of Brother Andrew as learned in canon and civil law, it seems credible that he may have studied in Bologna, where Europe's greatest law school was located, and that he had been to Rome and was acquainted with a cardinal. But the Anonymous Franciscan also has a statement that the hermit Henry, who we learn from the *Dicta/Libellus* was the "son of the count of Wegebach,"[68] went to Rome on business for Elizabeth, though the Anonymous Franciscan himself in a later passage indicates that he did not become a Friar Minor until Elizabeth was close to death.[69] However, Henry may have actually gone on other business to Rome for Elizabeth, perhaps to request the indulgence for her hospital.

At first sight this role of the Franciscans in the recovery of Elizabeth's dower appears to conflict with other early sources, for instance the additions to the *Libellus*, which ascribe this role to Conrad of Marburg.[70] Conrad himself, however, simply said that Elizabeth had been commended to him by the Holy See without giving any details as to how this took place.[71] The friars' role as counselors and messengers in obtaining the documents appointing him seems plausible.

The Anonymous Franciscan does not tell us if these friars who aided Elizabeth were in Eisenach or in Marburg, though the sufferings the testimony mentions were those that immediately followed Elizabeth's expulsion. So they do not provide any information about where the expulsion took place. But they do confirm Isentrude's testimony that Elizabeth underwent persecution and even violence.

Elizabeth's Decision to Enter Religious Life

It is not clear at exactly what point Elizabeth's dower was restored. We do know that she spent much of Lent of 1228 in poverty after her expulsion, and that it was some time during that Lent that she made her decision to enter religious life. By now, she had returned to Thuringia with her husband's remains. Conrad tells us:

> At length, after her husband's death, when Your Holiness saw fit to recommend her to me, in her desire to attain the highest perfection, she consulted me as to whether she could acquire more merit as a recluse, or in a cloister, or in some other state. Finally she conceived of an idea, which with

many tears, she begged me to grant her, namely, to permit her to beg from door to door. When I vehemently refused this, she answered: "I will do this, for you can't stop me." And on Good Friday [March 24, 1228], when the altars were stripped, she placed her hands on the altar in one of the chapels of her city [Eisenach] where she had established the Friars Minor, and in the presence of some of the brothers, her relatives and her children, she renounced her own will, all the pomp of the world, and everything that the Savior of the world counsels us to forsake in his Gospel.[72]

Clearly, Conrad means to suggest that Elizabeth followed the evangelical counsels of poverty, chastity and obedience. Can this act be seen as entrance into the Order of Penance? Legally, a profession of continence and obedience, even while remaining in the world, put one into the penitent state, which is regarded as a religious state according to medieval theologians and canon law.[73] Elizabeth now confirmed her vow to remain continent after her husband's death; this and her vow of obedience to Conrad seem to have clearly fulfilled these conditions.

Conrad wants it understood as well that Elizabeth had completely renounced the world. He adds that though she wanted to renounce all her possessions, he did not allow her to do so, because she needed to pay her husband's debts and continue to give to the poor.[74] Even though she probably did not make a vow of poverty, Conrad wanted her to be seen as a real religious. Nevertheless, though she may have been in the penitent state, there is no indication here that she had entered any particular religious order or way of life, for she and Conrad were still in disagreement about that. He no doubt wanted her to enter a convent, while she was bent on perfect poverty, represented by begging. In fact, Conrad still considered putting her in a convent for some time afterward.

Elizabeth probably took this step before deciding on a particular form of religious life because she wanted to make her formal vow of chastity as soon as possible to prevent her uncle or anyone else trying to force her into another marriage.

Not long afterwards, according to Isentrude," at the command of Master Conrad, she moved to Marburg."[75] It was there that her religious clothing would take place. Conrad, however, says that he was reluctant to have her follow him to Marburg.[76] This is one of the strange contradictions in the sources. It is possible that Conrad did not want Elizabeth to pursue her religious life in Marburg, at least at first, but he gives no reason. Perhaps he disapproved of the step she was going to take – to live the active life there and build a hospital.

Elizabeth did not end up in Marburg right away. According to an added passage of the *Libellus*, while the hospital was being built, she went to a little village nearby called Wehrda, because "her people" in Marburg -- perhaps her old enemies the vassals -- were still persecuting her. There she built a makeshift shelter for herself and her household in an abandoned courtyard, and stayed there until a simple house of mud and branches had been built for her next to her hospital in Marburg.[77]

But Elizabeth's inner struggle was not yet over. She had already been forced to give up the care of her two older children, Hermann and Sophia. Most likely her brother-in-law was overseeing their care. In fact, it was his duty to care for little Hermann, the future ruler of Thuringia. But according to Irmingard, it was only after Elizabeth had moved to Marburg, and perhaps even some a time after she was professed, that she completely gave up the care of her youngest child, Gertrude, at that time only a year and a half old.[78] This would put us sometime towards the end of March 1229 (Gertrude was born on September 27, 1227). According to the monks of Reinhardsbrunn, before Ludwig had left for the crusade, he and Elizabeth had agreed to give their coming child to a monastery as an oblate. Now in accordance with her promise, Elizabeth gave the little girl to the convent of Altenberg. Gertrude eventually became a nun there, was elected abbess and after her death was recognized as a saint.[79] Isentrude tells us that it was only at the time she gave up her youngest child that Elizabeth was finally able to make the most difficult renunciation in regard to her children: "and because Master Conrad had persuaded her to have contempt for all things, she begged God. . . to take away her love of her children." Later she told her handmaids that God had heard her prayer: "as God is my witness, I am no longer worried about my children, I love them as I love any other neighbor. I have entrusted them to God; let him do with them what he will."[80]

Perhaps connected with this, and illustrative of Conrad's sternness on this question, is the testimony of Irmingard about a bizarre incident which up to now has been without explanation. After Elizabeth entered religious life, Conrad once ordered her to come to Altenberg, where he was to advise her about her form of life. When the nuns there heard Elizabeth was coming, they asked Conrad to give her permission to enter the cloister so that they might talk to her. Conrad answered, "Let her enter, if she wants to," though, Irmingard says, he believed she would not enter. When Elizabeth heard of his words, she confidently entered the cloister to talk to the nuns. But when Conrad heard of it, he ordered both her and Irmingard (who had opened the cloister door) to be beaten with a thick rod while Conrad himself sang the *Miserere*. After three weeks Irmingard said, she herself still had the marks of the beating, and "Blessed Elizabeth, who had been more severely beaten, had even more."[81]

According to Isentrude's testimony, Conrad had previously beat her for seemingly trivial acts of disobedience, such as failing to attend a sermon for a good reason. But why beat her after he had given her permission? Was he deliberately trying to trap her? There is a possible explanation, however, suggested by Anja Petrakopoulos: Elizabeth had been hoping to see her little daughter Gertrude, who by this time was an oblate in that convent, on pretext of visiting the nuns.[82] Hence Conrad's anger at her violating what he considered an important precept: the rejection of all earthly things.

Abandoning or sacrificing one's children for God's sake had long been considered meritorious by Christian writers, though they interpreted it in different ways. In late antiquity and the early Middle Ages, it was considered one of the things that removed women from their frail and faulty female nature and made them into men and therefore worthy of following Christ. This changed in later hagiographic works, some of them written by women, during the thirteenth and fourteenth centuries, a period when there was a new interest in the family. At this time there was a growing recognition that lay and married women could achieve holiness, as in the case of some of the Beguines and Franciscan tertiaries who were widows.[83] Now the sorrow of abandoning a child was thought to make a woman more like Mary, who had to see her own divine Son suffer and die: therefore the loss of a child or the sacrifice of maternal love made a woman more of a woman and more of a mother.[84]

Women of the princely class to which Elizabeth belonged, of course, seldom had their children by them for long. They were often sent, as Elizabeth herself was, to be married into another royal family at an early age. In many cases, the loss of children was not only accepted, but even desired. In part this may have been a real lack of maternal feeling, due to many holy women's forced marriages, and consequent dread of sex and childbirth. They also knew that having known sexual relations made them seem tainted and less holy, but they felt that their sacrifice could make up for that. Angela of Foligno said that she was consoled when her mother, husband and children died, because she had prayed for this so that she might be freed to serve God. But she also wrote that she felt great anguish over their deaths.[85]

Some recent historians have discussed Elizabeth's case. Clarissa Atkinson and Barbara Newman mention Elizabeth's "abandonment" of her children as an example of this kind of suffering love. Newman believes that Elizabeth's action was associated with guilt over her marriage. This is possible, of course;

neither, however, analyzes Conrad's role at all; nor do they speak of Isentrude's testimony which gives force and poverty as the reason for Elizabeth giving up her children. The case was certainly more complicated than an attraction to suffering. In part, this may have been because both of these writers rely on later, secondhand sources, including the *Legenda aurea* and its English translation, not the original canonization process. Because of this, they did not have a chance to compare the separate testimonies.[86]

It is true that Conrad's letter suggests that Elizabeth may have felt guilty over not remaining a virgin. His view, however, finds little support in the testimonies of the women close to her. What is most prominent in Isentrude's testimony is first, the circumstances which forced Elizabeth to send her children away, and second, the fact that it was Conrad who had this spiritual renunciation of her, and her difficulty in making it. One part of Newman and Atkinson's analysis, however, is in accordance with the evidence from the sources: Elizabeth continued to exercise her maternal nature in caring for poor children as a replacement for her own.

Summary

The testimony of the witnesses differs at a number of points. Isentrude lived the various stages of Elizabeth's life with her. Her testimony is not a written work with a clear agenda, but a collection of spontaneous memories. Nevertheless, she does have a point of view. Isentrude, who was probably married herself, describes Elizabeth's marriage as an important part of her sanctity and vocation. She lived a life of charity and mercy as Landgrafin, and showed a stubborn will when a question of justice for the poor was at stake. It was because of her conviction on this issue that she aroused the suspicion and the wrath of important officials of her husband; perhaps this can be seen as Isentrude's hint of what led to her eventual expulsion from her home. Elizabeth's prayer on meeting her husband's remains shows how strong her love for him and attachment to life with him still were. She seems to have dreamed that she might have fulfilled her wish to live a life of poverty, even of begging, and still have been able to have Ludwig with her.

In Isentrude's testimony, while Elizabeth accepted and rejoiced in her sufferings after her expulsion, asking the friars to sing the "Te Deum" in thanksgiving for them, she still continued to be concerned about her children. The period immediately after Elizabeth's expulsion was a real struggle for her. During this period, she was forced to give up her children and felt that she had left her other life completely behind. Her vision of Christ marked her final decision to follow Christ in the religious life, but even this was not the end of the struggle. She found it difficult to give up her love for her children, perhaps even after she had made a spiritual renunciation of her maternal love.

Conrad's testimony, on the other hand, suggests that Elizabeth's religious development was a straightforward one: she regretted having married, longed for the state of virginity, and was apparently only waiting for her husband's death to enter on the life she desired. He barely mentions her children, and according to Isentrude, only wanted her to renounce them. His attitude may well be due to his awareness that virginity, or at least a desire for the chaste life, was traditionally considered appropriate for a woman saint. A number of the early testimonies, however, support Isentrude's view in regard to Elizabeth's happiness in married life and her attachment to her husband. Yet the view of Conrad, a male cleric, was the privileged one; it was the one that would later be adopted by the majority of Elizabeth's medieval biographers, as we will see below.

Elizabeth's entrance into a life of poverty is an important issue. To see it as a conscious choice or an aspiration would be attractive to any biographer, medieval or modern, who wanted to stress that she was divinely inspired, but her life might been much closer to that of the involuntary poor than any biographer has yet admitted. Elizabeth lost power and status in a real way with her husband's death, and like most medieval women, was dependent on her dower as her lifeline. Loss of her status put her in the same circumstances as other poor women. She experienced the frightening reality, as Isentrude says, of not knowing where to lay her children's heads. Finally, like many other women, medieval and modern, she had to give up custody of her children because of poverty. This experience gave her a different conception of poverty, perhaps, than she might have had otherwise. In the beginning, it was not a choice: it was not poverty as an ascetic exercise, practiced comfortably in a cloister, but poverty as destitution, requiring dependence on God and others to survive. Her own experience of suffering led her to the suffering Christ, and she dedicated herself to sharing His sufferings.

She had indeed previously dreamed, as a game, of going begging from door to door, but had she seriously planned to follow such a life? Her life as a wife and mother surely would have held her back. It would have taken something from outside to cause her to make a decision, as in fact happened. Her husband was gone, and her poverty forced her to let her children go. It was only after her children were gone, as Isentrude says, and at the urging of Master Conrad, that she was able to make an act of renunciation of her special love for them.[87] She does not seem to have made the sacrifice easily, and the time it took her to make it is a measure not only of her love for her three children, but of how seriously she took this ideal of poverty as complete renunciation, and the extent to which she committed herself to it. As I have discussed above, Irmingard's statement, if it does relate to the period just before her dower was returned, shows Elizabeth making a choice to "be abject and earn her bread by the work of her hands" at this point.

This picture of Elizabeth is a far different one from the traditional picture of a medieval woman's religious vocation offered by Conrad: one based on charity as primarily an ascetic exercise for the benefit of the almsgiver. It does fit, however, the picture of sanctity that many religious women were discovering at that time. In the early Middle Ages, women used their power of inheritance and their position as heads of large convents to distribute wealth to the poor. But with their loss of power during the Gregorian reforms and afterwards, women often became the disinherited in society, and in the religious movement were attracted to a way of life where suffering and participating in the sufferings of the poor were regarded as marks of a true religious life. Jo Ann McNamara sees Elizabeth as a transitional figure between the old and new styles of charity and religious life. She belonged to the old feudal world, but participated fully as a religious in the life of the poor.[88]

Elizabeth's vision of the religious life she wanted to live continued to develop during the time after her expulsion. There is new evidence from the testimonies at the canonization process, preserved in the Anonymous Franciscan, that the Franciscans played an important part in the events that led to Elizabeth's recovery of her dower. This does not suggest that she was directly led by them to embrace the religious life, but it indicates her closeness to them and that she followed their advice.

The picture that the earliest witnesses give of Elizabeth's choice for the religious life contains a variety of viewpoints, but these tended to be solidified into a definite and more traditional picture in later works about her. It is to these works that we now turn.

Elizabeth's Early Life in Later Works

The Writings of Gregory IX

I have already discussed the silences of Gregory IX's bull of canonization and his letter to Beatrice of Castile. It is clear that Gregory, for one reason or another, did not mention Elizabeth's religious affiliation with the Franciscans. Nor does the letter he wrote to Elizabeth mention the Franciscans, at least not directly. But the letter is a valuable source for understanding how he viewed her choice of religious life, since it was written in answer to her own indication of her desire for a particular type of religious life.

"Our spirit is completely inflamed," he writes, "when we think of the purity and holiness, and the chastity of heart and body in which, with so much ardor, you desire to bear the marks (*stigmata*) of Our Lord's passion."[89] If this represents something that Gregory had heard about Elizabeth, whether perhaps in a letter from her or from the friar who went to Rome for her, it would confirm that Elizabeth saw her experience of complete dedication to Christ, reflected in her vision, as a sharing of His sufferings. Written very shortly after the canonization of St. Francis and the widespread recognition of his stigmata, the reference to her metaphorically bearing the stigmata may have been meant not only as a comparison of Elizabeth to the suffering Christ but also to St. Francis. The Pope, continuing, exhorts her:

> Sit often with Mary at the feet of the Savior, so that you may delight in the graceful words that flow from His mouth. Submit your spiritual desires to examination, do not let anything of vice be hidden in them under the veil of virtue, and immediately exclude from your mind whatever might be an obstacle to your conscience and reputation . . . . Do not cease praying, do not leave the feet of the Lord, until the southern breeze blows through the garden of your mind and inflames your soul to virtue in the face of supreme love.[90]

Here the Pope is telling Elizabeth not to leave contemplative life, typically symbolized in the Middle Ages as it is here, by Mary of Bethany, who sat at the feet of the Lord (Lk 10:38-41), or perhaps only to leave it for the active life when it has strengthened her. At the same time he counsels her against rash actions that might harm her reputation. Most likely he has in mind Elizabeth's already existing devotion to the active life and is warning her of the difficulties faced by women in such a life, especially one that would include the type of poverty Elizabeth had in mind. Openly begging, so in contrast to what was though decent for women, would certainly harm her reputation. The Pope considered this too dangerous for a woman, as he did for the wandering "Minorite women."[91]

Later, in the bull of canonization, the Pope will develop his ideas on Elizabeth's religious life. He mentions her married life only in passing. He celebrates Elizabeth above all as a lover of the poor and of poverty, beginning during her married life:

> . . . she made herself needy in many things that she might lavish in many ways her solicitude on the poor. From her most tender age, she wanted to be their protector and friend, for she knew that the reward of everlasting life, the reward of those dear to God, is acquired through the merits of the poor, so that their condition, naturally despised by the pride of the world, was a pleasure to her. For she gave many proofs of her dislike for even the legitimate pleasures which her high rank by marriage offered her. . . she weakened her delicate and tender body by her constant abstinence, succeeding in obtaining for herself the greater quantity of merit, for whatever is done voluntarily is honored with the reward of greater grace.[92]

However, amid his praise for Elizabeth's love of the poor, the Pope does not mention her refusal of unjustly acquired foods; he speaks only of her "abstinence" in the traditional sense as a form of mortification.

The Pope noted that this voluntary poverty continued after her husband's death, when, wishing to "confine herself within the yoke of obedience," she "clothed herself in the religious habit, in which she did not fail, until her last day, to celebrate within herself the mystery of the Passion of the Lord."[93] Here he once again strikes the same note as in his letter to Elizabeth: her religious life is a sharing in the Passion of Christ.

In the Pope's letter to Beatrice of Castile, we read that Elizabeth's name, which meant "satisfaction of my God," was fitting for her, since she "so often satisfied God in the persons of His poor and sick."[94] She also merited the name by serving "three dishes on the Lord's table before the Master of heaven and earth by renouncing prohibited things, keeping the precepts, and by fulfilling the counsels of the Redeemer."[95] With these words, Gregory recognizes Elizabeth as progressing through obedience from simple abstention from sin to the religious life, in which she fulfilled the evangelical counsels. When she was "suddenly stripped of the spoils of worldly ambition" after her husband's death," she put on the habit of the poor and coarse garments."[96] Again, he adds: "though she was of royal blood, having become the handmaid of the poor and needy, she emptied herself, taking on the form of a slave (Ph. 2:7) and up until her death, she obeyed the sick, pilgrims and the poor."[97]

The Pope's words give a definite picture of Elizabeth as an imitator of the sufferings of Christ. There is only a small amount of testimony in the *Dicta* and even the new witnesses found in the Anonymous Franciscan about this. Did he exaggerate this aspect of Elizabeth's life? We should keep in mind, however, that before he canonized Elizabeth, Gregory had heard about her spiritual desires from her or those close to her, and had read all the testimonies in her process, perhaps including some we no longer possess, where this idea might have been more clearly expressed.

Thirteenth-Century Lives of Elizabeth

There are other sources from the thirteenth century which speak of Elizabeth's choice of religious life. They say little about her connection to the Franciscans, but give us some information about how her earlier life and choice of a religious vocation were viewed by those of her time. Two of these are the lives by Caesarius of Heisterbach and Dietrich of Apolda.

Caesarius of Heisterbach, a Cistercian monk, clearly wrote with the monastic virtues in mind as a model for Elizabeth. He took his cues both from Isentrude's testimony and from Conrad's letter. He says that Elizabeth desired virginity from an early age: "She wanted to have St. John the Baptist, as a lover of chastity, for her apostle and to imitate him, although God's marvelous disposition ordained otherwise."[98]   And so later "when the blessed and venerable virgin Elizabeth reached marriageable age, against the desire of her heart she was betrothed and was joined in marriage to the most noble prince Ludwig."[99] Thus, according to Caesarius, Elizabeth's religious vocation was apparent from the beginning. He agrees with Isentrude that marriage is a help to spiritual growth. His emphasis is different, however, for where Isentrude had spoken of the mutual help of husband and wife, Caesarius wrote solely of a wife's influence on her husband. "Whatever good there is in men is increased and strengthened by the grace and devotion of holy women."[100] Evidently he did not see a husband's goodness as a help to Elizabeth's canonized holiness.

Caesarius describes Elizabeth's austerities during her married life: she "strove to conform herself to the passion of Christ."[101] He may have taken this phrase, which is not in the *Dicta* or *Libellus*, from Gregory's IX's letter to Elizabeth or the bull of canonization.   On the other hand, he does not include Conrad's description of her renunciation of the world in the Franciscan church in Eisenach, though he makes use of Conrad's letter elsewhere. So while largely repeating what was passed on to him by the early testimonies, in a sense he says less.

Dietrich of Apolda took a somewhat different approach in his biography of Elizabeth. The Dominican friar seems to have had in mind the needs of lay people who might see Elizabeth's married life as a model. His work, being in Latin, was most likely addressed to other clerics, who could use the information it contained in sermons destined for the laity. He makes it clear from the beginning that Elizabeth desired to marry Ludwig, and even recounts in a very suspenseful fashion the obstacles preventing their marriage, including the opposition from some of the nobles at the Thuringian court. His source for this was the additions found in the *Libellus*, which describe Elizabeth undergoing persecution during her adolescence by some counselors of her husband who wanted him to marry someone with a larger dowry; the source also says that Ludwig consoled her in these difficulties.[102] Dietrich also describes their tender love after marriage: "and so, moved by this sweetness of chaste love and mutual companionship, they could not bear to be apart from each other very much or very long. Therefore the lady frequently followed her husband through rough ways (Bar 4:26), and through great distances and through harsh, wild winds, led by sincere rather than carnal affection."[103] In stressing the theme of love and a holy marriage, Dietrich may have been inspired by the same motives as some other members of the mendicant orders concerned about pastoral matters, who wrote model sermons on the holiness of marriage and marital companionship.[104] But although he had an interest in portraying a more positive concept of married life, he did not have a more positive concept of sexuality. He tells us that Elizabeth "would flee from the delights of the flesh and therefore from a soft bed and avoided the most intimate relations with her husband, as much as she could."[105]

There is a late story included in both the *Chronicle of Reinhardsbrunn* and the interpolations to Dietrich of Apolda that shows Elizabeth experiencing a wrenching inner conflict between love for her husband and love for God. One day during the consecration of the Mass, she found herself looking with love at her husband instead of at the altar. But Christ immediately reproached her; when she glanced back at the altar, she saw in the priest's hands not a host, but the crucified Christ dripping with blood. Filled with guilt, she prostrated herself weeping on the ground; she would not go into dinner and even her husband could not get her to tell him what was wrong.[106] This story may go back to an early witness, the chaplain Berthold, but this is uncertain; it is somewhat suspect, however, because we know from Isentrude, and by implication from Conrad, and the early witness of the *Libellus* that Elizabeth did not reveal her visions. As Ancelet-Hustache commented, however, even if this story were mere legend," it would still have the merit of being touchingly symbolic."[107]

Dietrich is the only early author to picture for his readers Elizabeth's grief on hearing the news of her husband's death in Italy. She cried out:

> "He is dead, dead, and the world and everything that is sweet in the world is dead to me!" After saying this, she suddenly rose, weeping, and ran wildly through the length of the palace. And since she was out of her mind, she would have kept on running, but the wall prevented her. Those who were present approached and pulled her away from the wall to which she was clinging.[108]

Dietrich gives an analysis of some psychological depth of the feelings a woman might have in trying to balance her life between marriage and God, and presented it convincingly for lay people. This type of appeal may have been responsible for the work's popularity: There are more surviving manuscripts of Dietrich's life than any other medieval work about Elizabeth; it is also the one most translated into the German vernacular; it also served as a basis for other vernacular lives.

As a member of an order committed to poverty, Dietrich stresses Elizabeth's love for the poor and for poverty repeatedly, especially when it comes to her religious life. Repeating Conrad's description of Elizabeth's renunciation of the world, he adds: "this imitator of Christ . . . completely stripped herself and laid herself bare, so that naked, she might follow the naked one in the way of poverty and charity."[109] This description, while brief, does suggest more of the Franciscan conception of poverty as nakedness than Conrad's original description. Dietrich did not relate her choice directly, however, either to the Franciscan or his own Dominican rule and conception of poverty. In other respects, Dietrich merely repeats what the *Libellus* and Conrad's letter say about Elizabeth's decision for the religious life.

Most of the other early lives of Elizabeth say less than Dietrich about the happiness of Elizabeth's married life; but they do agree with what he says in some other respects. For instance, in the *"Vas admirabile"* life, from around 1250, Elizabeth is said to have "fled her husband's embrace," and "desiring to be joined to Christ her bridegroom, she began to turn away from intercourse with her earthly husband."[110] On the other hand, the Anonymous of Zwettl, the only early life of Elizabeth which was possibly not by a cleric, but by someone close to the emperor Frederick, says: "she engaged in intense prayer as much as she could, without offense to the marriage debt."[111]

Many medieval biographers of Elizabeth were clearly seeking for a definite conversion in her life, in the sense of a turning point, a decision for a complete dedication to God in religious life. They were looking for an event that could be placed in her marriage rather than afterwards. This is exemplified by both the Latin and French vernacular versions of the story of the robe and crown brought to Elizabeth by an angel.[112]

The Latin version tells how Elizabeth's husband met a knight from "lands beyond the Alps." He was anxious to see Elizabeth, about whose holiness he had heard so much, and made Ludwig promise that he would be able to see her. When they arrived at the castle, dinner was prepared for the guest. Ludwig sent for Elizabeth, who was praying in her chamber in poor clothes (evidently she had sold or given away all her rich garments to benefit the poor). She replied to her husband, after a long string of biblical quotations about wifely obedience, that the humble clothes she was wearing were not fitting, but nevertheless she would come soon. She then prayed to God that she might be clothed so that no scandal might be caused to her husband. As soon as she had finished her prayer:

. . .behold the angel of the Lord descended from heaven, and bearing in his hands a divinely made gown and a gold crown surrounded with various precious stones, he spoke to her, saying, "O bride of the heavenly king and friend of the saints, Jesus, the Son of God, whom you have loved with all your heart, all your mind, and all your strength, sends you with loving greetings this wondrous garment and this gold crown. Put on then, as soon as possible this garment of gladness and crown [yourself] with this crown of glory, so that in the sight of people you may appear like an angel of the Lord and as is fitting for the daughter of a king, you will be crowned with the crown transmitted to you by the Son of the eternal king.[113]

The guests were filled with awe when Elizabeth appeared in these heavenly garments. When they were gone:

The Landgraf, calling the venerable duchess aside, asked her from where or from whom such a marvelous garment and such a wondrous crown had been transmitted to her. To which she answered, "My lord Landgraf, know that these gifts were transmitted to me from heaven, by an angel from the Son of God, who in all my troubles and necessities has graciously consented to aid me through His ineffable mercy. I give thanks to Him for his indescribable goodness. Experiencing Him in childhood as a sweet guide, in adolescence as a commander sweeter still, and in maturity as the sweetest lover, I have experienced Him today as the most intimate spouse, a most faithful counselor, the most kind protector and the most prompt and generous giver." At these words, divinely inspired, the Landgraf said to her: "My lady Landgrafin, through whose grace and prayers I hope to be saved, because God is with you, so that my sins might not require me to be separated from you in eternity, behold, I promise before God that for the salvation of my soul I shall undertake to go, signed with the cross, to lands overseas."[114]

The incident in the Brussels manuscript ends here without recounting the important following event: Ludwig's death. But by referring to her as the "Bride of Christ," the angel is clearly announcing to Elizabeth a religious vocation. Later, when she speaks to Ludwig, she refers to Jesus as her "lover" and "spouse." Even without the conclusion where Ludwig conveniently dies so that Elizabeth will be free to pursue the religious life, the Latin text clearly shows the desire to place the development of a definite religious vocation for Elizabeth as the bride of Christ as far back in her life as possible.

But the two French versions do connect the incident directly with Ludwig's death. In the anonymous French life, the angel says that God sent the robe to "his sweetest friend" -- language that echoes that of the love poetry of the trouvères.[115] Elizabeth tells her wondering husband that such presents are a reward for those who serve God. He says he wishes to do so as well, and goes on crusade, where he dies.[116] Robert of Cambligneuil, who used the anonymous French life as his source, says that the angel told Elizabeth that this crown and robe would make her his "*amie*," his love. He repeats what his source says about Ludwig's crusade very closely.[117]

It is instructive to compare these accounts with a similar incident in Dietrich. It tells how Elizabeth and Ludwig unexpectedly received a visit from some of her father's magnates who had come from Hungary. Ludwig told his wife that he was sorry there was no time to get her new finery for the occasion. Elizabeth replied that it was not important, "for I do not put any glory in clothes." Nevertheless, when Elizabeth appeared before her guests, they saw her arrayed in attire of heavenly beauty. When Ludwig expressed amazement, Elizabeth replied, laughing, "The Lord knows how to do such things when he wills."[118] In Dietrich, this story is presented as merely another event (though a miraculous one) in the daily lives of Elizabeth and her husband, rather than a conversion story where Elizabeth is freed to serve God. This was appropriate for Dietrich, who made a point of describing their marriage in terms that lay and married people could be interested in. He emphasizes their companionship, even playfulness, rather than wifely obedience, and does not see this event as a religious conversion, though there is at least a hint that God will eventually be able to do more for Elizabeth than her husband can. The author of the anonymous French life, who was actually following Dietrich, did not use his version of this story, however. He chose to substitute the other version, perhaps because it more clearly supplied a conversion story.

The *Golden Legend*, by the Dominican Jacobus de Voragine, written about 1260, is another part of the later development of Elizabeth's legend. Much of this collection is made up of the lives of the traditional saints: Biblical figures, apostles and often legendary martyrs from the early Church. Elizabeth is one of only four contemporary saints whose lives are told in the collection. All of these are from the mendicant orders, the others being St. Dominic, St. Francis and the Dominican Peter Martyr. Jacobus, then, recognized not only the traditional mode of sanctity but also the newer type represented by the penitential movement, the mendicant orders and the Beguines.[119] Elizabeth herself is a departure from the other women Jacobus includes. She is the only contemporary woman, and one of very few who were married; the vast majority of the others were virgins or lived in non-sexual "spiritual marriages" with their husbands.[120]

Jacobus says that he is following what was "contained in her legend."[121] By "legend" the author evidently means the *Dicta*, which he uses as his major source, though he removes the names of the testifying handmaids. He also used Conrad's letter, and some of the miracles from the canonization process of 1235.[122]

Jacobus is uncomfortable with the fact that Elizabeth was a wife. He insists, as Caesarius did, that Elizabeth "was compelled to enter the state of marriage, because she was urged to do this by her father's command."[123] Yet he does include her prayer over her husband's bones. He mentions Elizabeth's refusal to eat certain foods at her husband's table, but treats it more as an act of temperance or abstinence than a protest against injustice. His treatment so far follows traditional ascetic lines, but the Dominican author also stressed Elizabeth's devotion to poverty:

> Though in a position of the highest dignity, she desired the state of poverty above all else, so that she might make return to Christ for his poverty and so that there would be nothing belonging to the world in her. Sometimes, when she was alone with her handmaids, she would put on poor clothing, cover her head with a shabby kerchief, and say to them: "This is how I will go about when I have come to the state of poverty."[124]

Jacobus says that Elizabeth herself persuaded her husband to go to the Holy Land where he died (something not found in the original statements of the canonization process). His account of the expulsion is particularly revealing:

> As soon as the news of her husband's death spread throughout Thuringia, she was denounced by some of her husband's vassals as wasteful and a spendthrift and was shamefully and totally ejected.

This was so that her patience might be brought to light, and so that she might obtain the poverty she had long desired.[125]

Jacobus sees Elizabeth's expulsion both as a trial of her patience, and as a means of fulfilling her desire for poverty, though, unlike modern historians, he does not see it as a choice of her own making.

The Thirteenth-Century Franciscan Sources

The Franciscan sources on Elizabeth present her earlier life in a "Franciscan" way, and one that also expresses the particular concerns of the period at which they were writing. This is certainly true of the Anonymous Franciscan and also of the Valenciennes life, the only previous Franciscan source to address her early life in detail.

The opening lines of the Anonymous Franciscan, as I have mentioned, hint at Elizabeth's resemblance to Christ through comparison of the witnesses to her life to those of the life of Jesus. The author portrays Elizabeth's Christlike nature from a Franciscan standpoint, through her poverty and her love for the poor. He emphasizes these things throughout her life, beginning when she was a very young child in her father's palace in Hungary: "She would frequently give some gifts of charity to the poor gathered in front of the palace that was the home of the king, where she obliged those accepting, because they were in her debt for the gift, when they prayed, to say the Lord's Prayer or the Hail Mary for her."[126] Later on, the author adds: "she used to frequent the kitchens of the royal place, so that she might provide delicacies not for herself, but for the poor."[127] When the kitchen workers complained, her father, King Andrew, heard about it. One day he came upon her as she was bringing some food for the poor in her apron, and asked her what she was carrying. When she answered "Roses," he asked to see, and her apron was indeed full of roses. Seeing the miracle, the king "decreed that his beloved daughter Elizabeth might have general liberty in the future to give generously to Christ's poor."[128]

For the Anonymous Franciscan, Elizabeth's vocation started very early. She loved the Apostle John for his virginity. "But in her youthful years, deceived by the enticements of her parents, she contracted betrothal with the illustrious man the Landgraf, duke of the Thuringians. But later, when she vehemently regretted this, overcome by the salutary warnings of many people, who pricked her conscience about her betrothal, almost preferring to die, she gave tearful consent to the marriage."[129] [He may have been trying to reconcile statements in the Dicta with those of Conrad and other biographers]. The author leaves out many of the comments in the *Dicta/Libellus* about the happiness of Elizabeth's marriage. Like a number of other medieval biographers of Elizabeth, he evidently wanted to stress her religious vocation and expressed distrust of married life as anything that could contribute to sanctity.

According to the Anonymous Franciscan, however, this was a time when her love for poverty and Christ's sufferings did grow. He borrows from the Valenciennes life: "On rogation days, dressed in wool and barefoot, following the procession of the cross, she gloried in the cross of Our Lord Jesus Christ; the world was crucified to her and she to the world (cf. Gal. 6, 14)."[130] But he increases the emphasis on Elizabeth's identification with the poor. Where the Valenciennes life, borrowing largely from the *Dicta*, had simply said that "in the stations of preaching, so that with the apostle she might be made the scum of all (1 Cor. 4:13), she always placed herself among the poorest women," the Anonymous Franciscan has: "in the stations of preaching, along with her lesser ones, she, the least of all, always placed herself among the poorest women."[131] The "lesser" and "least" clearly associate her with Franciscan minority.

Her love for the Franciscans grew as well. "She was a special mother to the Friars Minor; in her time they gathered together in her city under her castle, the Wartburg in Eisenach, and due to her benefits, as it is said, they grew abundantly in buildings and in necessities for their use, according to what will appear in the following [pages]."[132] Here the author seems to have confused the convents in Eisenach and Marburg; it was the latter to which much of the later discussion of her benefits most likely refers.

The Anonymous Franciscan omits one early indication of Elizabeth's desire to lead a life of poverty found in the testimonies: Isentrude's description of how she would put on poor clothes and speak of the time when she would go begging. Perhaps this is because it was a prophecy of Elizabeth that was not literally fulfilled, since she did not actually go begging as a religious. The *Libellus* had suggested that Elizabeth was "like a prophet of her future misery," for she did have to beg after her expulsion.[133] The Valenciennes life mentions this incident of dressing as a beggar out of its chronological place, at the end of the life, and as an example of Elizabeth's humility, rather than a prophecy.[134]

But Elizabeth was soon freed to live the religious life. The Anonymous Franciscan describes, in much the same terms as the Brussels manuscript of the *Libellus*, how Elizabeth was too poorly dressed to appear before the nobleman visiting her and her husband, and prayed for help. He then continues:

> Scarcely had she completed this prayer, when *behold the angel of the Lord stood nearby* (cf. Luke 2:9) and brought a gown of wonderful workmanship, and in addition a gold crown adorned with most precious jewels, and said to her with a most joyful face, "O bride of the King of Heaven, Jesus the son of God whom you love with all your heart lovingly greets you and sends you this gown and this gold crown. Therefore put on this gown of joy and this crown of glory, so that as befits the glory of a king's daughter and such a noble duchess, these things may be yours in honor and eternal glory."[135]

147

Hearing about this angelic visit, Ludwig exclaims, "Truly, this Lord is good, and now I want to become his servant," and takes the cross.[136] In reality, Ludwig had first taken the crusade cross in 1224, and did not depart right away because of the delaying tactics of Frederick II. He received the cross a second time from Bishop Conrad of Hildesheim in 1227, and departed soon afterwards. This makes the idea that he took the cross as the sudden result of a miracle very doubtful.[137] It is only in regard to Elizabeth's heartfelt anguish over his bones, brought back from Italy, that the Anonymous Franciscan gives some idea of the depth of her married love.[138] He passes quickly, however, to her seeking of perfection through the religious life.

The Anonymous Franciscan does not add much new about Elizabeth's expulsion from the Wartburg. In fact, he does not narrate it until after he describes her clothing and her habit, which, judging from the attention he gave them, were the most important features of her life. He does not add anything of his own about the expulsion, but simply repeats what Isentrude stated. He does not relate Elizabeth's leaving the Wartburg to her decision for poverty, but, following the Valenciennes life, highlights it as an example of her patience.[139]

There is a clear increase in the emphasis on Elizabeth as a Franciscan from the Valenciennes life to the Anonymous Franciscan. In part this is no doubt due to the increasing desire of the Franciscans to claim Elizabeth, now a popular saint, as one of their own; this has been shown by the Anonymous Franciscan's treatment of her earlier life. It is also due, however, to the previously unknown testimonies from the canonization process that the Anonymous Franciscan had at his disposal, as will be shown in the following chapter.

Conclusion

Studying the development of Elizabeth's legend from the earliest testimonies to the later biographies is an important means for recovering her individual story as a woman of her time, and learning how it was gradually elaborated to form a more typical and traditional instance of female sanctity and choice of a religious vocation.

Both the earliest evidence from the canonization process and the later biographies show considerable difference in how they describe the growth of Elizabeth's religious vocation. Her confessor and her clerical biographers tend to stress her early recognition of her religious vocation during her marriage. Some of the later writers like Caesarius of Heisterbach and Jacobus of Voragine declare that she was actually devoted to chastity from her childhood and married unwillingly. Others, like the Latin writer of the miracle of the robe and crown, and his French followers, evidently attempted to supply a decision for religious life, during her marriage, a definite indication of Elizabeth as the bride of Christ which they thought the earliest sources lacked. But the testimony of Isentrude, the woman closest to Elizabeth, suggests that she experienced a difficult struggle before she was able to make a decision that would bind her to the religious life, and that only after adversity had deprived her of her beloved husband and children.

The earliest female witnesses, Isentrude and Irmingard, stress that Elizabeth's interest in poverty was closely bound to her belief in justice for the poor. Conrad, on the other hand, stressed more ascetic motives for her choice of poverty. Isentrude and Irmingard's clear statements about Elizabeth's refusing food that was unjustly acquired and her motives for doing so -- that she refused to participate in injustice -- tend to disappear in later recountings by Jacobus de Voragine and Pope Gregory IX. But all the witnesses are agreed that Elizabeth had not only a deep personal devotion to relieving the miseries of the poor, but a belief in poverty as a desirable and holy way of life.

There is evidence then, that Elizabeth's life was being rewritten from the beginning to be more in tune with the medieval, particularly clerical, expectation of a female saint – someone who was always dedicated to virginity and would have shunned marriage if she could, someone who desired to live a life of personal asceticism. The existence of other testimonies about Elizabeth from those who knew her is all the more striking because they do not meet these expectations.

It is instructive to compare the varying images we get of Elizabeth's life and vocation to the portrayal of her aunt, St. Hedwig (c. 1178-1243), for whom we possess only one image, that of her anonymous clerical biographer who wrote about 1300, based on her canonization process, and of the bull of canonization by Clement IV (1267). The actual testimonies at her canonization process are lost.[140] Hedwig was brought up at the Benedictine monastery of Kitzingen, married Duke Henry I of Silesia and became the mother of seven children. Her biographer and the bull of canonization insist that she did everything she could to restrict sexual activity in her marriage. After studying what happened to Elizabeth's image, we might wonder whether the earliest witnesses told a different story, and whether her life and view of marriage might have been as distorted as Elizabeth's was in later biographies.

The desire to find a dramatic or at least recognizable moment of conversion in the lives of female saints, Bynum believes, is typical of male medieval writers who wanted to see women's religious lives in the same way they viewed and described theirs: with conversion as a sudden crisis, a dramatic event involving the escape from normal roles and structures into a radically different way of life, or, in anthropological terms, a plunge from the high status of worldly life to the low status of religious submission. Bynum, however, believes that this model is not typical of women. And indeed none of the earliest witnesses directly describes a definite conversion in Elizabeth's life. Even the primary male witness, Conrad, tends to see her life as a continuous desire for the religious life, though she was not able to fulfill it right away.

The most detailed description of Elizabeth's life by a woman, Isentrude's, gives even more clearly the impression of a constant, everyday struggle to live and overcome obstacles, something which, according to Bynum, is very typical of how medieval religious women described themselves. What for men is a single crisis is the permanent state of women's lives.[141] Being expelled from the castle and dower lands, and being plunged into poverty was certainly a catastrophic event in Elizabeth's life and a change from high to low status, but it is described by Isentrude as merely the most difficult of the obstacles she had to overcome. It eventually led to her decision for the religious life, but this decision could be seen as the result of a long maturation period, rather than a sudden crisis. Isentrude's description of Elizabeth's struggles in managing her dower lands in such a way that she could get enough to eat without violating her conscience while living at court shows an awareness of how power structures made it difficult for Elizabeth to escape from her restricted role as a woman, even while she nominally held some power. Her life of poverty was in a way simply a continuation of this struggle.

On the other hand, the later biographers who made use of the robe and crown story, including the Anonymous Franciscan, saw a very clear need to provide such a conversion story, thus adhering closely to the typical male pattern.

Elizabeth's decision for a particular type of religious life was closely bound up with her own individual experience. She knew that injustices to the poor were caused by the rich, and made an effort not to add to these injustices by her decision in conscience not to eat unjustly extorted foods. She expressed a desire for a simpler life with her husband, one that would not involve such injustices. Her basic views on poverty were in line with those views expressed by St. Francis: "If we had possessions, we would need arms for our protection. For disputes and lawsuits usually arise out of them, and, because of this, love of God and neighbor are greatly impeded."[142] Elizabeth's ideas were also in line with the general ideas of the poverty movement of the time. Guilt over possessions led many to embrace voluntary poverty. Unlike many, however, Elizabeth felt that these ideals could perhaps be lived in married life; in the end she devoted herself to these ideals in the religious life.

Nothing in the testimonies we have seen suggests what role the Franciscans might have played in these decisions, but since Elizabeth was acquainted with the Franciscans, and certainly must have been aware of the religious movements of her time, it is natural to expect that the Franciscans had an influence on her, especially since, as we have seen, they did advise her in her difficulties.

With her expulsion from the castle and lands of her dower (whether in Marburg or Eisenach), Elizabeth had an experience of involuntary poverty and the real lot of the poor, one which seems to have affected her deeply and to have given her conception of poverty a strong and individual quality. In beginning her religious life, Elizabeth met with opposition from her confessor, Conrad of Marburg, who did not want her to live a life of extreme poverty and begging. Pope Gregory IX seems to have had similar concerns. How Elizabeth actually lived her religious life will be the subject of the next chapter.

Notes

[1] See André Vauchez, "Lay People's Sanctity in Western Europe: Evolution of a Pattern (Twelfth and Thirteenth Centuries)," in *Images of Sainthood in Medieval Europe*, pp. 21-32.

[2] Huyskens, *Quellenstudien*, p. 156.

[3] Huyskens, Quellenstudien, p. 157.

[4] Huyskens, *Quellenstudien*, p. 114.

[5] John Coakley, "Gender and the Authority of the Friars," pp. 445-60.

[6] Huyskens, *Quellenstudien*, p. 121.

[7] Huyskens, *Quellenstudien*, p. 121.

[8] Huyskens, *Quellenstudien*, p. 116.

[9] Huyskens, *Quellenstudien*, p, 117.

[10] Huyskens, *Quellenstudien*, pp. 114-15, 117.

[11] Huyskens, *Quellenstudien*, p. 112.

[12] Huyskens, *Libellus*, p. 37.

[13] "Cronica Reinhardsbrunnensis," ed. O. Holder-Egger, MGH SS, 30:606.

[14] Huyskens, *Quellenstudien*, p. 115.

[15] Huyskens, *Quellenstudien*, pp. 118-19.

[16] Huyskens, *Quellenstudien*, p. 127.

[17] Wenck, "Die heilige Elisabeth," p. 14; also see especially pp. 14-16.

[18] Busse-Wilson, *Das Leben der hl. Elisabeth von Thüringen*, pp. 227-35.

[19] Huyskens, *Quellenstudien*, p. 115.

[20] Ulrike Wiethaus, "Naming and Un-naming Violence against Women: German Historiography and the Cult of St. Elisabeth of Thuringia," *Medievalism and the Academy*, ed. Leslie J. Workman, Kathleen Verduin and David D. Metzger (Cambridge: D.S. Brewer, 1999), 1:187-208.

[21] Huyskens, *Quellenstudien*, p. 135.

[22] Huyskens, *Quellenstudien*, p. 157.

[23] *Chronica fratris Iordani*, no. 41, in AF 1:13.

[24] *Dicta*, Huyskens, *Quellenstudien*, p. 120.

[25] *Chronica Fratris Iordani*, no. 25, in AF, 1:9-10.

[26] First Rule of 1221, ch. XII; in *Die Opuscula des hl. Franziskus von Assisi*, ed. Esser, p. 388.

[27] Huyskens, *Quellenstudien*, p. 115.

[28] Huyskens, *Quellenstudien*, p. 115.

[29] Wilhelm Maurer, "Zum Verstandnis der hl. Elisabeth von Thüringen," pp. 16-64.

[30] Maresch, *Elisabeth von Thüringen*, pp. 160-62.

[31] André Vauchez, "Charité et pauvreté chez Sainte Elisabeth de Thuringe, d'après les actes du procès de canonisation," in Michel Mollat, ed., *Études sur l'histoire de la pauvreté* (Paris: Publications de la Sorbonne, 1974), 1:163-73.

[32] Huyskens, *Quellenstudien*, p. 129.

[33] Elisabeth Busse-Wilson, *Das Leben der heiligen Elisabeth*, p. 126.

[34] See Elizabeth Petroff, *Consolation of the Blessed* (New York: Alta Gaia Society, 1979), pp. 1-13.

[35] Bynum, *Holy Feast*, pp. 135-36, and 224.

[36] McNamara, *Sisters in Arms*, p. 235.

[37] Jacques de Vitry, *The Life of Marie d'Oignies*, in *Two Lives of Marie d'Oignies*, p. 88.

[38] Thomas of Cantimpré, *Supplement to the Life of Marie d'Oignies*, in *Two Lives of Marie d'Oignies*, p. 232.

[39] "De B. Aemiliana seu Humiliana," AASS Mai 4:387.

[40] For this concern of women, see also Jo Ann McNamara, "The Need to Give: Suffering and Female Sanctity in the Middle Ages," p. 210.

[41] Huyskens, *Quellenstudien*, p. 121.

[42] Latin *aratrium*; the English version, a carucate, measures from 60 to 160 acres.

[43] Caesarius, "Die Schriften des Caesarius von Heisterbach," 354. This is one of several mentions in the early

sources of Elizabeth and Ludwig using "brother" and "sister" in addressing each other.

[44] Pazzelli, *The Franciscan Sisters*, p. 203.

[45] It is edited, along with some of these other rules, in Meersemann, *Dossier de l'ordre de la pénitence au xiiie siècle*, pp. 39-81.

[46] Huyskens, *Libellus*, p. 23.

[47] Huyskens, *Quellenstudien*, p. 117.

[48] Huyskens, *Quellenstudien*, pp. 117-18.

[49] Huyskens, *Quellenstudien*, p. 117.

[50] Salva, "Exordia Tertii Ordinis Regularis," p. 154.

[51] BF 1:271.

[52] BF 1:272.

[53] Huyskens, *Quellenstudien*, pp. 121-22.

[54] Huyskens, *Quellenstudien*, pp. 122.

[55] They are listed in "Cronica Reinhardsbrunnensis," p. 611.

[56] Huyskens, *Quellenstudien*, p. 123.

[57] Huyskens, *Quellenstudien*, p. 123.

[58] Huyskens, *Quellenstudien*, p. 123.

[59] Pásztor, "Sant'Elisabetta," p. 93.

[60] Huyskens, *Quellunstudien*, p. 127.

[61] Huyskens, *Quellenstudien*, p. 124.

[62] Huyskens, *Quellenstudien*, p. 125.

[63] Huyskens, *Quellenstudien*, p. 129.

[64] Menge, "Zur Elisabethforschung," p. 309.

[65] Huyskens, *Quellenstudien*, p. 157.

[66] T 88r-88v, lines 567-90.

[67] 2 Celano, 119, in Armstrong, Hellmann and Short, *Francis of Assisi: Early Documents*, 2:326; and the *Legend of Perugia*, 92, ibid., p. 224.

[68] Huyskens, *Quellenstudien*, p. 129.

[69] T 90v; K 124ra-rb.

[70] Huyskens, *Libellus*, p. 46.

[71] Huyskens, *Quellenstudien*, p. 156.

[72] Huyskens, *Quellenstudien*, p. 157.

[73] This is the conclusion of Mariano d'Alatri in the introduction to his *Aetas penitentialis: l'antico ordine francescano della penitenza* (Rome: Istituto Storico dei Cappuccini, 1993), pp. 14-15.

[74] Huyskens *Quellenstudien*, p. 158.

[75] Huyskens, *Quellenstudien*, p. 125.

[76] Huyskens, *Quellenstudien*, p. 158.

[77] Huyskens, *Libellus*, p. 41-43.

[78] Huyskens, *Libellus*, p. 74.

[79] According to an interpolation in Dietrich IV, 1; *Die Vita*, pp. 61-62.

[80] Huyskens, *Quellenstudien*, p. 126.

[81] Huyskens, *Quellenstudien*, pp. 135-36.

[82] Anja Petrakopoulos, "Sanctity and Motherhood," p. 284.

[83] Clarissa Atkinson, *The Oldest Vocation: Christian Motherhood in the Middle Ages* (Ithaca: Cornell University Press, 1991), pp. 164-65.

[84] Barbara Newman, "Crueel Corage: Child Sacrifice and the Maternal Martyr in Hagiography and Romance," in her *From Virile Woman to Woman-Christ: Studies in Medieval Religion and Literature* (Philadelphia: University of Pennsylvania Press, 1995), pp. 76-107; Elizabeth is treated on pp. 86-87 and 94.

[85] Angela of Foligno, "Memoriale," 1:1 and 1:3, in *Angela of Foligno, Complete Works*, translated, with an Introduction by Paul Lachance, O.F.M., Preface by Romana Guarnieri (New York/Mahwah, N. J.: Paulist Press, 1993), pp. 126, 143.

[86] Atkinson, *The Oldest Vocation*, pp. 165-69; Newman, "Crueel Corage," p. 87.

[87] Huyskens, *Quellenstudien*, p. 126.

[88] McNamara, "Suffering and the Need to Give," pp. 207-208.

[89] Heinisch, "Ein Brief Gregors IX an die hl. Elisabeth," p. 381, and Wenck, "Die heilige Elisabeth und Papst Gregor IX," insert between pp. 144-45.

[90] Heinisch, "Ein Brief Gregors IX," pp. 381-82, and Karl Wenck, "Die heilige Elisabeth und Papst Gregor IX," insert between pp.144-45.

[91] See Chapter III, p. 87.

[92] Santifaller, "Zur Originalüberlieferung," p. 80.

[93] Santifaller, "Zur Originalüberlieferung," p. 80.

[94] Lemmens, "Zur Biographie," p. 3.

[95] Lemmens, "Zur Biographie," p. 3.

[96] Lemmens, "Zur Biographie," p. 4.

[97] Lemmens, "Zur Biographie," 3-4.

[98] Caesarius, "Die Schriften des Caesarius von

Heisterbach," p. 350 (no. 3).

[99] Caesarius, "Die Schriften des Caesarius von Heisterbach," p. 353 (no. 5).

[100] Caesarius, "Die Schriften des Caesarius von Heisterbach," p. 354 (no. 5).

[101] Caesarius, "Die Schriften des Caesarius von Heisterbach," p. 357 (no. 8).

[102] Huyskens, *Libellus*, p. 15.

[103] Dietrich, *Die Vita der heiligen Elisabeth*, p. 34.

[104] See the sermons by Humbert of Romans and Gilbert of Tournai in David D'Avray, "Marriage Sermons in 'ad status' Collections of the Central Middle Ages," *Archives d'histoire doctrinale et littéraire du moyen âge* 47 (1980): 71-119.

[105] Dietrich, II, 2, *Die Vita*, p. 35.

[106] Ködiz, II, 6, pp. 23-24; *Cronica Reinhardsbrunnensis*, 603; interpolation in Dietrich of Apolda, III, 3, in *Die Vita*, pp. 54-55.

[107] Ancelet-Hustache, *Gold Tried by Fire*, pp. 80-81.

[108] Dietrich, 4:6; *Die Vita*, pp. 70-71.

[109] Dietrich, *Die Vita*, p. 88.

[110] Lemmens, "Zur Biographie," p. 9.

[111] Anonymous of Zwettl, "Vita sanctae Elisabeth," p. 253.

[112] See Chapter III for a description of the sources for this story.

[113] *Catalogus codicum Hagiographicorum Bibliothecae Regiae Bruxellensis*, 1:295-96.

[114] *Catalogus codicum Hagiographicorum BibliothecaeRegiae Bruxellensis*, 1:96.

[115] Karl, "La vie de sainte Elizabeth," 722 (v. 285). The section in the robe and crown occupies vv. 137-382 (pp. 721-24).

[116] Karl, "La vie de sainte Elizabeth," p. 724.

[117] *Chi commenche de sainte Ysabiel*, pp. 387, 389.

[118] Dietrich II, 9; *Die Vita der heiligen Elisabeth*, pp. 42-43.

[119] See André Vauchez, "Jacques de Voragine et les saints du xiiie siècle dans la *Légende Dorée*," in *Legenda aurea: Sept Siècles de diffusion*, Actes du colloque international, l'Université du Québec à Montreal, 11-12 mai 1983 (Montreal: Editions Bellarmin/ Paris: Librairie J. Vrin, 1986), pp. 27-56.

[120] This is discussed in Dyan Elliot, *Spiritual Marriage: Sexual Abstinence in Medieval Wedlock* (Princeton: Princeton University Press, 1993), pp. 173-74.

[121] Jacobus de Voragine, *Legenda aurea*, 2:1156.

[122] The sources are discussed in André Vauchez, "Jacques de Voragine et les saints du xiiie siècle," pp. 41-47.

[123] Jacobus de Voragine, *Legenda aurea*, 2:1158.

[124] Jacobus de Voragine, *Legenda aurea*, 2:1161.

[125] Jacobus de Voragine, *Legenda aurea*, 2:1164.

[126] T 75v, lines 41-44.

[127] T 75v, lines 48-49.

[128] T 76r, lines 60-61.

[129] T 76r, lines 66-70.

[130] T 76v, lines 80-82.

[131] T 76v, lines 82-84. Valenciennes, V 65rb., lines 49-50.

[132] T 76v, lines 85-88.

[133] Huyskens, *Libellus*, p. 31.

[134] V 73ra, lines 393-94.

[135] T 78r-78v, lines 162-67.

[136] T 78v, lines 182-83.

[137] Ancelet-Hustache, *Gold Tried by Fire*, p. 128.

[138] T 79r, lines 191-199.

[139] T 81v, lines 306-308.

[140] Robert Folz, *Les saintes reines du moyen âge en occident (vie-xiiie siècles)* (Bruxelles: Societé des Bollandistes, 1992), pp. 129-39.

[141] Caroline Walker Bynum, "Women's Stories, Women's Symbols: A Critique of Victor Turner's Theory of Liminality," in her *Fragmentation and Redemption: Essays on Gender and the Human Body in Medieval Religion* (New York: Zone Books, 1992), pp. 27-51.

[142] Legend of the Three Companions IX, 35, in Armstrong, Hellmann and Short, *Francis of Assisi, Early Documents*, 2:89.

Chapter VI

Elizabeth's Vocation:

Living The Franciscan Life

Introduction

As we saw in the previous chapter, Elizabeth desired an unconventional form of religious life, but she experienced difficulties in living it as she had hoped. The earliest witnesses, Irmingard and Elisabeth, described in detail the way they lived this religious life with Elizabeth in her hospital in Marburg. Now we have other testimonies from the canonization process in the Anonymous Franciscan to add to them. These early witnesses show us Elizabeth's religious life as lived by her and her sisters, and also how it was viewed by the friars who lived in close contact with them. The way this religious life was viewed by later writers changed over time, however, and was made to conform more closely to the expectations of a later generation, in the same way her decision for the religious life was.

In the first part of this chapter, I will discuss how the earliest witnesses viewed Elizabeth's religious life. I will then discuss how it was viewed by the authors of the thirteenth-century lives, and how this view was shaped by their concerns and those of their time. Next I will consider how Elizabeth's religious vocation and relationship to the friars is portrayed in the late thirteenth- and early fourteenth-century Franciscan sources: the chronicle of Salimbene, the Franciscan sermons and the Anonymous Franciscan himself as a later commentator on the early testimonies. These works show how the Franciscans viewed her religious life in response to the changing times.

Elizabeth's Religious Life in the Canonization Process

The information given in the *Dicta/Libellus* about the type of religious life Elizabeth led is scattered throughout the testimonies of the various witnesses; it is revealed incidentally in discussion of her holiness and her charity. The largest amount of testimony is devoted either to her clothing and profession or the habit she wore. There is also new evidence from the testimonies in the Anonymous Franciscan about her conception of poverty and the nature of her sisterhood as well. Through analysis of these testimonies, we can gain a clearer picture of Elizabeth's religious life.

Elizabeth's Profession and Habit

According to Isentrude, after Elizabeth recovered her dower, she moved to Marburg, and "there she put on a gray tunic, an inexpensive and humble habit."[1] Guda testified more specifically: "Blessed Elizabeth was professed, putting on the gray habit from the hand of Master Conrad. And at that time Guda herself put on the gray tunic with her, solemnizing with the habit the vow of chastity which she had made into Master Conrad's hands several years previously."[2] Guda thus clearly refers to a religious profession, with a specific form of clothing, and in her case, a vow of virginity, whereas Elizabeth was solemnizing her vow of continence. It was shortly after this that Conrad ordered Isentrude and Guda to leave Elizabeth, fearing that they would remind her of her way of life in the world, so Isentrude's testimony stops there. Irmingard gives us an even clearer description of what Elizabeth's habit looked like: "She lengthened her gray cloak, which was short, with cloth of other colors. In a similar way, she also mended the torn sleeves of her tunic with other colors of cloth."[3]

The only description in the *Dicta/Libellus* of her religious vocation and the reason why she had chosen it that is attributed to Elizabeth herself comes from the testimony of Irmingard, who said that the saint had told her: "The life of the sisters in the world is the most despised, and if there were a more despised life, I would have chosen it."[4] The expression "sisters in the world" seems to refer to non-cloistered female religious in general. Elizabeth realized that this choice of life was controversial and disdained by many people. Conrad says little about the type of religious life she led, but does refer to her as "Sister Elizabeth."[5]

This is where the new testimonies from the Anonymous Franciscan supply more details. His account has caused some difficulties, so I will quote it in full:

> We have also found and read then in certain statements that this blessed woman, renouncing the world completely after her husband's death, humbly had herself tonsured in the house of the Friars Minor, barefoot, girding herself with a cord for a belt. Soon she also asked that a little house be built next to the church of the brothers, in which she was guided by the wholesome advice of the Friars Minor, placing herself completely under their teaching and discipline; up until the end, she walked with them in the house of God in perfect harmony. It was said at that time that these things took place near a certain castle called the Wartburg in the monastery of St. Catherine, of the order of the Cistercian Ladies. Certain people also testified at that time that Brother Burchard, the guardian of the Friars Minor of Hesse, in the presence of Brother Henry, called Placido, of the same order, happily tonsured her, as his dearest daughter and spiritual friend, and clothed her after her husband's death,

with Master Conrad celebrating Mass at that time in
the place [i.e. convent or church of the friars]. [6]

This is one of several passages of the Anonymous
Franciscan that have caused controversy. Gieben, who knew this
passage only from the citation in Sedulius, rejected the statement
that Brother Burchard clothed Elizabeth, since as *custos* of Hesse,
he would have had no authority in Thuringia, where her
renunciation of the world took place; this was proof to Gieben that
the Anonymous Franciscan had no historical value.[7]

What really happened was that in describing the place of
Elizabeth's clothing, the Anonymous Franciscan borrowed from
different sources, including the more complete version of the
testimonies he possessed. In doing this, he confused three different
occasions: Elizabeth's vow to preserve continence if she survived
her husband, which took place in St. Catherine's monastery in
Eisenach during her marriage, as recounted by Isentrude;[8] her
renunciation of the world after her husband's death, which took
place in the Franciscan church in Eisenach in March of 1228, as
recounted by Conrad of Marburg;[9] and her profession and clothing
in Marburg, which Isentrude says took place "more than a year"
after her husband's death, thus in the late fall of 1228 or early in
1229.[10]   What is unique to the Anonymous Franciscan is the
statement that "certain people also testified" that Brother Burchard
clothed Elizabeth in a Franciscan friary. It is the last statement
which has caused the controversy.

The objection raised by Gieben is not relevant, for the
presence of the *custos* of Hesse would have been perfectly natural
for Elizabeth's *clothing*, which according to Isentrude and
Irmingard took place in Marburg in Hesse and not in Eisenach, as
Gieben thought.[11] We do not know to whom we should attribute
the testimony the Anonymous Franciscan cites about Elizabeth's
clothing, but since the other statements the author mentions come
from the canonization process, it is reasonable to think that this one

does too. The one notable difference between these testimonies and those of the handmaids is that Guda testified that Conrad himself clothed Elizabeth. This question might be cleared up if the full testimonies quoted in the Anonymous Franciscan ever become available.

The Anonymous Franciscan adds other new testimonies from the canonization process about Elizabeth's life and her habit; one indicates its Franciscan character:

> When questioned about these things, her faithful friend, brother Gherard called "from beyond the mountains," of the order of Friars Minor, a contemporary of blessed Elizabeth, in the second and last inquiry about the acts of the same servant of God. . . answered that she was of such profound humility that after her husband's death she commonly went about in a shabby tunic, patched, especially in the sleeves, girded with a quite rough cord, covered with a mantle with many patches and lengthened with cloth of another color, like another abbess Clare of the cloistered sisters.[12]

The Anonymous Franciscan says that three Dominican friars, as well as several other religious and lay people also testified about Elizabeth's habit. The nature of the habit Elizabeth wore seems to have been very important to those who testified at the canonization process as a sign of penitence. Although the Anonymous Franciscan cites a number of witnesses in regard to her habit, none of them said anything about any rule that Elizabeth followed; nor does the author himself say anything about this.

The Franciscan Convent in Marburg

As we have seen, the Anonymous Franciscan supposes the existence of a Franciscan convent in Marburg. He says that Elizabeth was clothed in the habit and tonsured "in the house of the friars," implying, without explicitly stating, that this took place in Marburg. He cites testimonies from the canonization process that explicitly say that a number of friars, including the guardian of Hesse, were present. He adds that Elizabeth built her house next to the church of the friars. Many of the other statements in this life, which are original to this author and which will be discussed below, refer to the relations of Elizabeth and the friars in Marburg, indicating the presence of a Franciscan foundation there.

The very existence of a Franciscan convent in Marburg in Elizabeth's lifetime has been the subject of debate. Maurer contended that there is no proof that there was such a convent; statements in the later Franciscan tradition that there was are simply "legendary embellishments." Maurer uses this conclusion to support his contention that Elizabeth could not have been a Franciscan tertiary.[13] Huyskens, however, supported the idea that there was a Franciscan convent in Marburg during Elizabeth's lifetime, and that she perhaps took part in its foundation.[14]

The earliest known document to refer to a Franciscan friary in Marburg is an indulgence granted in 1235 by Siegfried, Archbishop of Mainz, for those aiding the Franciscans in building their church in the city, which they had begun in 1233.[15] The question is whether this was the *first* convent of the friars in Marburg. No official early document referring to a convent before 1233 has been found. Until now, the only evidence for this is from the late fifteenth-century *Landeschronik* of Wigand von Gerstenberg, who wrote that in Marburg in 1229 "there was a little church and convent; there were three or four barefoot friars in it. Next to the little cloister, she [Elizabeth] built a hospital."[16] Maurer refused to accept this late evidence as trustworthy.[17]

However, there is another early statement that has been largely overlooked: the Franciscan chronicler Salimbene, who wrote about 1284, says that the friars refused burial in their church to Elizabeth (see Chapter IV); this seems to indicate there was a Minorite church in Marburg at the time of her death in 1231.

There is another reason for believing that the fine convent being built in 1235 was not the first place the friars lived in Marburg. The Franciscan missionaries in Germany were not at first in a position where they could build their own convents. Often they made do with already-existing churches on the outskirts of town. For instance, when Giordano of Giano and his companions arrived in Erfurt in November 1224, they stayed at first in a leprosarium outside the city walls; later they moved to the deserted church of the Holy Spirit, which had formerly belonged to the Augustinian nuns. The description of how they accepted this location gives the feel of these early German "places" of the friars: when asked by the man who served as their procurator in the town whether they wanted a cloister built, Giordano, who had never seen such a thing in the order, replied: "I don't know what a cloister is: just build us a house near the water so we can go down to it and wash our feet."[18] Six years later, the townspeople built them a convent. This was the case in other countries as well: as the order gained in popularity and resources, newer and larger convents were often built inside the city walls.[19]

If Elizabeth built her hospital near the "place" of the friars, as the Anonymous Franciscan indicates, then this "place" must have been outside the city walls, for that was where her hospital was built. Like others too, the original friary in Marburg was probably centered on an already-existing chapel or church; the friars may have stayed in an unused building nearby, or had a small house built for them. The Anonymous Franciscan describes it as "the place where the friars were received" or the "house of the friars," which suggests a small or temporary residence; he avoids using the word "convent."[20] We do not know the exact date of its foundation; but it is possible that Elizabeth was responsible for bringing the friars to her dower lands in Marburg, as she was for bringing them to Eisenach. Battes believed that it was possible that Elizabeth gave the friars a piece of her widow's estate in Marburg as early as 1224 or 1225, but that at any rate they were very

167

probably already established there during her stay in Marburg between 1228/29 and 1231.[21]

The information given in the Anonymous Franciscan that Elizabeth's house and the Franciscan convent were close together conforms with the details given in other, later sources like Wigand Gerstenberg's chronicle, which also gives a reason for the building of a new convent: it says under the year 1233: "shortly thereafter he [Landgraf Conrad] took the chapel and St. Elizabeth's dwelling away from the barefoot brothers and allowed them to build a larger and better church in Marburg, where they still live."[22] This is the same year that the friars began building the convent mentioned in the indulgence of the bishop of Mainz.[23] The move, then, took place at the time that the Teutonic Order was expanding its own buildings around the site of Elizabeth's hospital, and the Franciscans were clearly in the way. This is another way in which early memories of the connection between Elizabeth and the Franciscans were lost.

Elizabeth's Religious Life and Conception of Poverty

Elizabeth and her sisters now began to serve the sick at the new hospital. This period, from the end of the twelfth to the end of the thirteenth century, marked a new phase in the development of hospitals in Europe. Most of the earlier hospital foundations had been attached to monasteries; in the thirteenth century, the number of hospitals founded by confraternities in cities and towns grew rapidly in Italy and Germany, including the hospitals of the Order of the Holy Spirit. Men and women often both served at the same hospital, domiciled separately to preserve chastity. It was also the time when the military orders, which dedicated themselves to serving the sick as well as to fighting, established a number of hospitals in Germany, especially the Order of the Hospital of St. John of Jerusalem and the Teutonic Order.[24] Women also took part in the hospital work in these orders. In the Order of the Hospital, married women could nurse the sick and take the habit of the order on the death of their husbands; in the Teutonic Order, the noblewomen were called *consorores,* and the lay sisters who did heavy work were called *conversae.* The women's branch of the Premonstratensian order not only ran their own hospices but tended the sick in their own homes. Many Beguines also dedicated themselves to the sick in hospices they maintained in their communities.[25] Or they could go where the sick were. Marie d'Oignies and her husband John, after agreeing to a chaste marriage, gave all their property to a leprosarium in Willambroux near Nivelles and served the patients there "for the sake of the Lord."[26] This service to the poor was very much a part of the apostolic movement and its devotion to poverty and serving the poor.

Judging from the few early documents dealing with Elizabeth's hospital, it seems to have been much like most of the hospitals run by confraternities in Germany in the thirteenth century. The *custos* or *magister* of the hospital was a layman named Hermann, whose wife Irmentrude also served the sick there. Both men and women tended the patients. There were lay brothers (the *conversus* named Henry, who was Elizabeth's procurator, may have been one of these).[27] Then there were the handmaids, Irmingard and Elisabeth, who served the sick with Elizabeth. Many confraternity hospitals staffed by both men and women followed the Augustinian rule, but nothing is said about this in the sources for Elizabeth's hospital.[28]

After establishing her hospital, Elizabeth gathered poor patients there, and gave to them and the other poor of the locality the remainder of the money that she had received as indemnity for her dower. One of the handmaids, Elisabeth, describes the scene vividly:

> On the night of the day when the 500 marks
> were generously given as alms, there was a clear
> and shining moon, and when the stronger of the

169

poor people had left, many of the weaker and the sick remained lying next to the fence enclosing the hospital and in the corners of the courtyard. When Blessed Elizabeth entered the courtyard and saw them, she said to those with her, "Look, the weaker ones have remained; let us give them something more." And she ordered that six Cologne deniers be given to each one, and she did not want the children to be given less. Afterwards, she had loaves of bread brought and distributed to them. When this was done, she said: "We want to make their joy complete, so let fires be lit for them." And for a long while she had fires prepared, and the feet and nails of many were washed and anointed with oil. And the poor people began to sing and to enjoy themselves. When she heard this, Blessed Elizabeth said: "You see, I told you that we must make people happy." And she herself rejoiced with those who were rejoicing.[29]

We have many moving testimonies about Elizabeth's service of the sick at the hospital. She clearly acted as a kind of head nurse, taking all the most difficult cases herself. She directed the other women in the hospital work. She also visited the poor in their homes to tend to them.

Irmingard testified that in addition to working at the hospital, Elizabeth spun wool on commission for local convents, and evidently handled the cash herself:

> She got food in return for spinning wool sent to her from the monastery in Altenburg, as many people know, for a price less than was owed. She also offered money on the altar which she had acquired by the work of her hands. And Irmingard said that very often when she was sick, lying in bed,

she spun wool; indeed she did not know how to spin flax. At times Irmingard took the distaff from her hands, so that she might spare herself. But so that she might not be completely idle, she pulled off wool for future work and spreading it out, prepared it with her hands.[30]

When Elizabeth received gifts in kind, she gave them to her procurator, Brother Henry, to sell for her.[31] Another example of Elizabeth using money also came from the *Dicta*, where she tells one of the handmaids: "I have some money in my purse, which many be useful for comforting that poor little woman and her child, go and take it to them."[32]

Though Conrad continued to direct Elizabeth while she was living in Marburg, he was very frequently absent from the city on preaching tours. Nonetheless, he provides some information about her hospital service. He tells how she placed the "most wretched and despised" of the sick next to her at her table. When Conrad criticized her for this, "she answered that she received from them a singular grace and humility. Like an undoubtedly very prudent woman, recalling to me her past life, she said that it was necessary for her in this way to treat contraries by contraries."[33] Conrad saw that Elizabeth "wanted to make [spiritual] progress," and described the steps he took to help her achieve it. He sent all the unnecessary members of her household away, except for a lay brother and two women: a girl of humble birth and a harsh widow who was deaf. He believed that being with the poor girl would increase her humility, and the harshness of the widow would stimulate her to patience.[34]

Conrad recounts how, for "the greater exercise [of perfection]" Elizabeth took in a paralyzed orphan boy and cared for him, carrying him many times each night for the necessities of nature and washing his soiled clothes. She did the same for a young leper girl, without Conrad's knowledge, and performed "all the services of humanity" for her, washing her, feeding her and even humiliating herself by kneeling to take off her shoes. When he found out about it, he says, "I was afraid that she would be infected by the disease, and – may God forgive me! – I punished her very severely."[35] He also threw the leper girl out. Elizabeth later undertook to cure a young boy of scabies, and succeeded due to her medical skill.

And yet, says Conrad, Elizabeth was attracted to contemplation and practiced it to an astonishing degree.

> In spite of these works of the active life, I say before God that I have rarely seen a more contemplative woman. For some men and women religious frequently saw her as she was coming from her secret prayers, with her face wondrously radiant, as though sunbeams were coming from her eyes. Indeed, very often when she was sent into ecstasy of soul, for a very long time afterwards she ate very little or no food.[36]

It is noteworthy that after her husband's death and the beginning of her life in poverty, we hear very little from the witnesses about Elizabeth fasting, though we do hear that she ate poor food (according to the *Libellus*, if she ate insipid meals, it was because she was a poor cook).[37] We do hear from Conrad that she frequently could not eat after a vision, but this is about all that is mentioned by any witness about Elizabeth fasting during the last part of her life. Irmingard even tells us that she consulted a doctor about her way of life, afraid that her deprivations might be hurting her, but this seems to be deprivation due to poverty.[38]

The new testimonies in the Anonymous Franciscan add to this picture by showing an Elizabeth who was seeking for the most perfect form of religious life. Once again relying on an official deposition, the author describes a conversation the saint had with her Franciscan confessor Brother Gerard of Guerles, later the provincial minister of Upper Germany, "about the inestimable treasure of precious poverty":

> The saint answered, like one who was no longer in the world, "Since it is a question about holy poverty for me, I desire with all my heart that in the crossroads outside the walls there should be a cell for me of muddy straw and earth and that in front of the little door or window, there might be a linen thread fixed on which is to be hung a small vessel in which passersby would place alms by which I should be sustained. . . as it is customary to do for poor lepers." And after saying these things in a vehement spirit, she was wondrously carried away and elevated above herself, and her slight body suddenly fell as though unconscious into the most devout arms of the said minister, her sweetest father. At last, coming back to herself, she began to breathe a little, praising and blessing the King of Heaven. The same minister, when asked where this saint was, answered that she was in the hospital of St. Francis in Marburg.[39]

The testimony quoted earlier from Conrad tells us that Elizabeth was determined to live a life of begging if she could, and the joy she expresses here at the thought of living on alms harmonizes with that statement. Even though the active life she had chosen and vigorously followed would not have been consistent with life as a recluse, for Elizabeth the life of a recluse totally dependent on alms, totally dependent on the care of God and others, as the lepers were, was the highest life of all, because it was perfect poverty. As we have seen, many recluses in Italy started out being among the "involuntary poor." And yet Elizabeth had not chosen to live that life. Or it may be that she was still uncertain about her path and was still aspiring to that higher life.

Her ideas had deepened in many ways since she had play-acted at begging for alms with her ladies-in-waiting at court. She had experienced real involuntary poverty on being expelled from the Wartburg, and knew what having no one but God to turn to was like. It is not surprising that Elizabeth is represented as falling into ecstasy at the close of this speech. For many other women, including Clare, a life of complete and hidden poverty often led to more seclusion and to the heights of contemplation.

Elizabeth and her Sisters

We learn only a little from the *Dicta/Libellus* about the other women who lived with Elizabeth. Isentrude and Guda, Elizabeth's noble ladies-in-waiting had made a vow of continence with her and later received the gray habit with her. However, they did not stay with her for long after this, for Master Conrad sent them away, and they were apparently no longer part of the community. As we have seen, Conrad himself says that he left with her only a young woman of very low birth and a widow, but nothing in his statement indicates that these women were part of a religious community. In the testimonies as they are arranged in the *Dicta/Libelllus*, the four women who testified about Elizabeth are referred to as her *ancillae* or handmaids. Indeed, all four of these women -- Isentrude and Guda, and the other two, Irmingard and Elisabeth, who were of humble birth -- served Elizabeth at one time or another, but "handmaids" is a strange term to apply to the two noblewomen. Historians treating Elizabeth have not really discussed this title or its meaning.

The Latin word *ancilla* was commonly used in the Middle Ages to refer to a female chattel slave, and it did not lose this meaning even after the introduction of the less restrictive serfdom.[40] At the same time, it had a clear Biblical precedent in the words of the Virgin Mary to the angel Gabriel, *Ecce ancilla Domini* (Behold the handmaid of the Lord), in which she agreed to do God's will in becoming the mother of God (Luke 1:38). A number of medieval religious women, including some who were wealthy and noble, chose this name to express their desire to be absolutely abject in their humility and obedience to God. For instance, Marie d'Oignies, who came from a wealthy middle-class background, is described as a handmaid by her biographers, Jacques de Vitry and Thomas of Cantimpré (though it is not clear if this is her own designation for herself).[41] At the same time, like Elizabeth, Marie is described as having a handmaid or servant of her own, named Clementia. Elizabeth's niece, St. Margaret of Hungary (1243-1270), a Dominican and contemplative, carried out the lowliest kitchen duties at her royal monastery of Veszprem, where she lived from her childhood on, rejecting all offers of marriage. She said of herself: "I would like to be a handmaid of the poor rather than the daughter of a king, for I would be better able to serve God."[42] Dauphine of Languedoc, the wife of St. Elzéar, and a Franciscan tertiary, would wash dishes and do the housework at the hospice where she lived. A witness said of her: "she, a lady, for many years in the hospice of her house took on herself the lowly and servantlike tasks. . .in all things and for all things she acted like a servant girl."[43]

It was probably as a religious title that Elizabeth and those who wore the habit with her applied the word "handmaid" to themselves as an expression of poverty and humble service. They lived together in the same house, and Elizabeth shared equally in the lowliest tasks. Irmingard tells how the saint would wash the earthenware dishes and utensils they used, and often sent the others off on errands so they would not prevent her from doing so. When they returned they would find her hard at work washing the dishes.[44] Their common life and common meals were like those of the Beguines.

Of the side of their religious life that pertains to worship or common prayer, we hear almost nothing, though the handmaid Elisabeth describes an incident in which she and St. Elizabeth were together at Mass in a chapel in the town of Wehrda a short distance from Marburg.[45] But at least some informal kind of community life is described in the testimonies; perhaps if we had the complete testimonies that were given at the canonization process, we would learn more about this.

Irmingard recalled how Elizabeth did not want to be called "Lady" by her handmaids, who were of very humble birth, but wanted them to use the familiar singular "Thou," or simply "Elizabeth." She would even have them sit next to her and eat from the same dish, a sign of familiarity.[46] Clearly Elizabeth did not treat her handmaids as servants, but as friends and sisters on the same level with her.

The handmaid Elisabeth shared Irmingard's fascination with the details of Elizabeth's solidarity with the poor, as her account of the distribution of Elizabeth's dower money to the poor shows. She gives another lengthy account of the way the saint cared for a poor pregnant woman while she was staying in Wehrda by arranging shelter for her in a shed next to her house, and caring for her for four weeks after the birth. When the woman was ready to leave, Elizabeth gave her some flour, bacon and lard, money and new clothes, and had her handmaid Elisabeth remove her fur sleeves to wrap the child in. The woman's husband also received some shoes (there is no explanation for where he was during her pregnancy). Very early the next morning, the woman and her husband left secretly, abandoning the child in the house where she had stayed. When the handmaid Elisabeth entered the house and found the child alone, she went to tell the saint, who called on the city magistrate to look for the parents, but to no avail. The handmaid Elisabeth begged the saint to pray for the return of the child's mother. "For she was afraid of Master Conrad, for he would be disturbed at this kind of thing." But the saint replied calmly, "I am not able to ask for anything else from God, except that His will be done." Shortly afterwards, however, the baby's father did return and confess, indicating that he had been unable to go on, and had returned as if by force. The mother confessed the same when she was found and begged forgiveness. The bystanders insisted that the woman be punished by having the clothes Elizabeth had given her taken away, since such things should not be used "by someone with a bad reputation." Elizabeth said, "Do what you think is right." The clothes were taken away, but Elizabeth, taking pity on the woman, immediately gave her some other clothes.[47] The story gives a vivid impression of Elizabeth's compassion for the neglectful mother others despised.

Like Irmingard, Elisabeth was amazed that the saint wanted to have a close relationship with her handmaids; she recalls how she always called them "dear" or "friend" and her "very merry words." But it was evidently hard for the handmaid Elisabeth to achieve the same intimacy, for she always continued to call the saint "my lady" until the day of her death.[48]

The only other sister or companion of Elizabeth named in the *Dicta/Libellus*, apart from the "four handmaids" themselves, is a girl named Hildegund, whose hair was cut and who joined the sisters. She was probably of lowly birth as well; her sister was one of the sick cared for at the hospital.[49] The Anonymous Franciscan, however, quotes the testimony of Brother Gherard, which gives us a more detailed idea of this sisterhood:

> The same brother also firmly declared that he also saw a certain other noblewoman, a relative of the Roman Emperor Frederick, with whom he had a conversation for one whole day over many things pertaining to salvation, [and] who, following the life of blessed Elizabeth in a cord and habit as abject as it was humble, walking barefoot, actually asked for the alms necessary for herself from the Friars Minor just as faithfully as she did humbly. The same brother declared that he saw a large number of other very noble women living in a completely similar way, with whom he had many

salutary conversations and visits about these and other matters.[50]

Were these women in fact part of Elizabeth's community at the hospital? We cannot be sure that Gherard saw these women in the same place as Elizabeth, but the fact that he associates other noblewomen with Elizabeth's way of life is important for its indication that this witness, at least, saw Elizabeth as part of, or even the leader of, an established way of life for women. Perhaps the most fascinating information given is that at least one of these women used to beg from the friars. Begging was an early ideal of the Franciscan way of life, but it was generally prohibited for women. St. Clare and her sisters were not able to rely on it; they had to have property to support themselves, though in the early days, the friars would beg for food for them.

Summary

The testimonies in the Anonymous Franciscan clearly establish that Elizabeth did embrace the religious life with a religious profession and clothing. She lived in close contact with the Franciscan friars in their convent in Marburg, and she wore a poor gray habit like theirs. She also lived in a religious community with several other women, who were not just servants, as has sometimes been supposed, but were treated by Elizabeth as sisters and equals.

Elizabeth's service to the poor and her own life of poverty were marked in a number of ways by her experience of destitution after her expulsion. This is evident in her treatment of the poor woman who had abandoned her child. Elizabeth was much more compassionate toward her than anyone else was, perhaps because having been forced to give up her own children, she could more readily understood that woman's feelings. Elizabeth's own attitude toward charity could be summed up by her words, "We must make people happy,"[51] and her rejoicing in the community she shared with the poor. Like St. Francis, she saw poverty as a way to a Christian society truly made up of brothers and sisters. But this society should be defined clearly. Vauchez, for instance, sees Elizabeth's protest against the society of her time as a purely personal and moral one: while she had a clear conception of injustice, she did not make any effort to change feudal society at large.[52] It is true that Elizabeth's means were not political, but personal, and her aim was not to start a revolution in feudal society. The society of brothers and sisters she sought was on the level of a personal community, a bond formed between herself and others that completely bypassed social barriers, as we can also see in her relationship with the handmaids of humble birth. This concern for lowering social barriers does not occur in Jacques de Vitry's life of Marie d'Oignies. Jacques himself seems little interested in Marie's relationship to her handmaid Clementia, so we do not know whether she may have had something of the same relationship to Marie as Elizabeth's handmaids did to her. In Elizabeth's case, we probably would not have known about it if the handmaids themselves had not testified in such detail to it.

There is also a marked difference in attitude between Conrad and Elizabeth in regard to her works of charity in the active life. Conrad, whose approach was one of complete rejection of "the world," including all loves except God, saw Elizabeth's work with the poor as her progress in personal perfection, which seemed to be more important to him than the poor themselves. He is a representative of an older view of charity as a way for the almsgiver to obtain merit. (Irmingard's accusation that Elizabeth was "gaining merit" for herself at the expense of her handmaids is almost a caricature of Conrad's attitude.) There is no strict dichotomy between Elizabeth and Conrad, however. According to Conrad, Elizabeth found that the poor could cure her pride. She received grace and humility from them, so in a way this was an ascetic exercise. Her humility, however, was not only "humiliation," as Conrad saw it; it was a desire to share her life with the humble by becoming one of them.

Yet for Elizabeth, asceticism seems to have always acted as a kind of substitute for the poor life she wanted to live. Under Conrad's direction, she had practiced flagellation frequently during her married life, but after she began to live in poverty, we hear no more from the handmaids about her flagellating herself, but we do hear about the blows Conrad imposed on her as punishment. Conrad's emphasis on complete renunciation was shared by Elizabeth, though in a different way, because for Elizabeth renunciation and her mystical experiences were closely related.

Brother Gerard's description of Elizabeth's ecstasy gives us for the first time something that relates her to other religious women -- a friar or other male cleric who witnesses and communicates a woman's mystical experience, something which Conrad does not really give us. But the account of this experience harmonizes with what we know about Elizabeth's ecstasies from Isentrude's testimony. For instance, in both this incident and the one described by Isentrude, the ecstasy comes upon Elizabeth unexpectedly, and the witness has to catch her when she falls. In this case, she evidently did not share the content of her experience, but the exterior signs, such as her obvious emotional reactions, are the same. Brother Gerard's account shows the Franciscan's interest in Elizabeth's concept of poverty, the one thing all the Franciscan witnesses seem to remember most.

Much about Elizabeth's life as described above resembles the way of life of the Beguines and other hospital sisters who were not cloistered and who lived in close contact with the poor. Like the Beguines, Elizabeth also spun wool to make her living. But not all the women in the religious movement of the time, though they chose poverty and renunciation for themselves, engaged in manual labor or nursing. For instance, while she did give to the poor, Umiliana dei Cerchi preferred to remain a recluse shut away in her room living on the begrudging allowance her male relatives permitted her. One reason she may not have considered manual labor as an option may have been her pride in her family's lineage.[53]

Robert Folz has contrasted Elizabeth's attitude toward the poor to that of her aunt, St. Hedwig. After the birth of her seventh child, Hedwig and her husband, the duke of monastery of Trzebnica. Studying the sources, Folz concludes that Hedwig showed many of the same characteristics as Elizabeth: her humility and love of the poor. But she did not have the experience that Elizabeth did of being left on her own to live like the poor, nor did she identify herself as completely with them. Her charity was often exercised at a distance. Folz concluded that Elizabeth, along with St. Francis, "was the artisan of the 'Revolution of Charity' which opened the thirteenth century," that is, the revolutionary change of identification with the poor.[54] The contrast between Elizabeth and Hedwig is the more striking because they came from the same family and same feudal background, one which had a more ancient concept of the religious life. But, as in the case of Umiliana dei Cerchi, not all women were able to make the transition to a new understanding of life with the poor as Elizabeth did.

Elizabeth's Religious Life in the First Biographies

The thirteenth-century lives of Elizabeth add little to what is said in the early testimonies. When Caesarius of Heisterbach describes Elizabeth's assumption of the religious life, he tells only of her clothing in Marburg, where "having scorned the delights and joys of this world, she put on a very low and despised gray habit."[55] He says that in her hospital Elizabeth "satisfied Christ in his members like Martha, and was satisfied by the word of divine preaching, like Mary,"[56] confirming what Conrad says about Elizabeth's combination of the active and contemplative life. He also repeats what Irmingard said about her patched habit. Other than this, Caesarius adds little or nothing beyond what we can glean from the testimonies. In his sermon for the translation of St. Elizabeth, however, he adds that Elizabeth "honored her handmaids in the place of sisters," and even called them *domine*, ladies.[57] From his testimony too, it seems that Elizabeth's companions were sisters rather than servants.

A more specific statement about the kind of religious life Elizabeth led comes from the Zwettl life, probably written by someone close to the Emperor Frederick II. It says that Elizabeth "put on the gray habit of the Friars Minor," and that she "loved the poverty of the Sisters Minor."[58] It is not clear whether the last statement refers to the Poor Clares, or is just a general description of Franciscan women.

Dietrich of Apolda gives a description of Elizabeth's habit that echoes some of the themes we saw in the testimonies from the canonization process. He describes Elizabeth herself as an *ancilla*, or handmaid:

> . . .she began to establish a hospice, where she placed the sick members of Christ, in whom she aided Christ the Lord himself; and so that she might also make herself suited for serving them unencumbered, rejecting the importance and pomp of secular garments, the king's daughter humiliated her body as, for example, the handmaid of Christ showed herself a servant woman.[59]

In the *Golden Legend*, Jacobus de Voragine also describes how Elizabeth entered the religious life. He stresses her observance of the evangelical counsels:

> Now, so that she might not lose the hundredfold fruit which is given to those who preserve evangelical perfection and are transferred from the left hand of misery to the right hand of glory, [Elizabeth] put on a religious habit, that is,

humble and abject gray garments. She preserved perpetual continence, after her husband's death, kept perfect obedience, and embraced voluntary poverty. She also wanted to go begging from door to door, but Master Conrad would not permit it.[60]

Jacobus does not mention Elizabeth's words in the *Dicta* about being one of the "sisters in the world," though he quotes part of the sentence that contains it. His only mention of the Franciscans is in the story about the young man for whom Elizabeth prayed, and who became a Friar Minor, which is also in the *Dicta*.

The Franciscan Sources

In addition to these traditional lives, there are other works of Franciscan origin from the thirteenth and early fourteenth centuries, which speak of Elizabeth's relations to the order. What they have to say reveals much about the contemporary conception of female Franciscan religious life.

The first undoubtedly Franciscan life of Elizabeth is the Valenciennes life. But while the author makes several references to Elizabeth as "the mother of the friars," a title later adopted by the Anonymous Franciscan, he says little else that would specifically relate her life to that of the Franciscans. He celebrates Elizabeth's poverty and humility and in her religious life compares her to both Martha and Mary.[61] He never says that she wore the Franciscan habit or embraced the Franciscan religious life. But he does have this passage calling on the Friars Minor to celebrate her:

> We read of blessed Francis that in his lifetime he preached to the birds, so that those winged beings of heaven and birds given wings through contemplation might be made preachers. We also read of this holy widow that the birds, having gathered together after her death in the same way, seemed to be celebrating the services for the

dead, just as she was similar to those who, by preaching [and] flying, were obliged to be saddened about her death. He was the father of the Friars Minor, she was their mother, as she said. He watched over them like a father, she nourished them like a mother. Therefore let the Friars Minor as a whole mourn their mother and with various lamentations, in a way, with different melodies, let them deplore her loss.[62]

Other Franciscan sources are more specific. Salimbene writes of Elizabeth: "This saint, after her husband's death, lived under the obedience of the Friars Minor, and was always devoted to them."[63] The anonymous Franciscan sermon long attributed to Bonaventure, probably from the end of the thirteenth century, says of Elizabeth:

A sign of her perfect humility was the cord and habit of the [Friars] Minor, which she adopted as best she could, as I myself have heard from her confessor and from her handmaid, who was brought up with her from her youth. . . . Many noble women, following her example, did penance and entered religious life.[64]

This is perhaps the most explicit early example of Elizabeth's religious life being described as penitential. It also agrees with the testimony of Brother Gherard, who said that a number of noble women followed Elizabeth in her way of life.

Neither of these authors mentions the Third Order in connection with Elizabeth. But in the sermon by the Italian Franciscan Giacomo da Tresanti, from about 1300, we find the following:

[Elizabeth] intermingled the gray of virtue and of modesty, the color which she also assumed in her bodily dress out of reverence for Blessed Francis, whose very special daughter she was and a docile disciple of the Friars Minor also. It is also said by some people that she belonged to the Third Order of Blessed Francis.[65]

At the end of the thirteenth or beginning of the fourteenth century, then, we find a Franciscan writer speaking for the first time of the Third Order in connection with Elizabeth. Like Salimbene, Tresanti stresses Elizabeth's religious life and her obedience to the Franciscans, while keeping this separate from the question of her membership in the Third Order. The first Franciscan writer I have found who makes a definite statement that Elizabeth belonged to the Third Order is Arnaud de Serrant or Samatan, in the *Chronicle of the Twenty-Four Generals of the Order of Minors (1209-1374)*, probably written in the last quarter of the fourteenth century. He says of Elizabeth: "But after her husband's death, entering the Order of Penance under the third rule of Blessed Francis, wearing the cord and mantle, she bore fruits worthy of penance."[66]

What does this progression from "mother of the friars" to Franciscan tertiary mean? Gieben believed that it was merely that a legendary Franciscan tradition continuously grew in its exaggerated expressions, like those in the mistaken imagination of the Anonymous Franciscan, and made a Franciscan tertiary of Elizabeth in spite of the lack of evidence in the earliest sources.[67] But while Gieben complained about the lack of critical study of the sources on Elizabeth, his interpretation of the Anonymous Franciscan was based on a fragmentary text, and he did not examine the historical context.

If we look at the texts rather as indicating a development in the understanding of female Franciscan life during the earliest decades of its development, they make much more sense. The later writers begin with a more precise understanding of the Third

Order and, in particular, religious women in the Third Order in the juridical sense. That is, after the Third Order became a religious institute with a proper rule, approved by Nicholas IV in 1289, which was later followed by a number of groups of women, including those who were inspired by Elizabeth's example, who professed this rule, Franciscan writers were able to look back and recognize the germ of what was to become the life of religious in the Third Order in the life of Elizabeth and her sisters.

During Elizabeth's lifetime, the rule of the Brothers and Sisters of Penance of 1221 existed, but was clearly intended for those living "in the world." Many of these early tertiaries went far in their austerities and lived as recluses or in semi-religious communities. Umiliana dei Cerchi, and other early tertiaries in Florence are examples of this.[68] But this was a type of life not actually provided for in the existing rule for the penitents. It is clear that the author of the *Chronicle of the Twenty-Four Generals* actually read into the evidence the situation of a later time when female religious of the Third Order lived under the clearly defined Rule of 1289. Further back, in the early fourteenth century, there is some confusion in the writers as to whether Elizabeth formally belonged to the Third Order or not. This was at the point when the Rule of 1289 had just been established. Before this, Fra Salimbene and others reflected the understanding of female Franciscan life current in their time when, apart from St. Clare and those women in the "Order of San Damiano," the women religious of the Franciscan movement really had no clear formal structure or rule to which they could lay claim. To those of the time the Franciscan habit, or something resembling it, and obedience to the friars, or close spiritual relations with them, were the clear signs of a woman's Franciscan identity. Gieben was, therefore, right to deny that Elizabeth belonged to the "Third Order," in the sense of her being a Third Order religious, because this state did not exist in a juridical sense before 1289. It is equally clear, however, that later

Franciscans could recognize in Elizabeth the essential nature of the Third Order. This is especially true of the Anonymous Franciscan.

Elizabeth's Religious Life in The New Life

The Anonymous Franciscan speaks at greater length than any other source about Elizabeth's relationship with the Franciscans. He portrays her as a Franciscan in her habit and her way of life with her sisters, as both a teacher and mother of the friars, and at the same time their disciple. The author describes how she was formed spiritually by her love of St. Francis and her relationship to the friars, and procured both material and spiritual benefits for the friars in the convent in Marburg. To him she was a Christlike figure and an imitator of the Franciscan virtues of poverty and love for the poor.

The Anonymous Franciscan quotes extensively from early eyewitness testimony not found elsewhere and adds his own comments, thus giving us a glimpse into the way a friar of the next generation thought about Elizabeth's vocation, as compared to those early testimonies. He also shows how the friars of that later generation, reflecting on Elizabeth's relationship with their brothers, derived spiritual meaning from it for themselves. When compared to other works from the same period, the Anonymous Franciscan shows a similar understanding of the nature of female Franciscan life as it applied to Elizabeth.

Elizabeth's Profession and Habit:

The Anonymous Franciscan himself gives a number of details about the form of Elizabeth's habit, based on the early testimonies. For him, it was an important sign of her vocation.

> Indeed, so that after her husband's death, she might not lose the hundredfold fruit given to those who preserve evangelical perfection . . . she put on the religious habit with three or four of her

handmaids, that is, humble and abject gray garments, embracing perfect continence and voluntary poverty. For so despised was her habit that she wore a gray mantle, lengthened with cloth of another color, and she also had the sleeves of the tunic mended with cloth of another color. For she said that if she ever found a poorer life and habit than that of her sisters, she would rather obey those poor religious than many more excellent ones concerned with earthly possessions.[69]

This last statement by the Anonymous Franciscan and attributed to Elizabeth, that if she found a poorer habit than hers she would adopt it, may in fact be an adaptation of Irmingard's statement about choosing the habit and way of life of the "sisters in the world" because they were the most despised.

The Anonymous Franciscan's strongest statement about the Franciscan nature of Elizabeth's habit does not come from the contemporary witnesses he quotes, but from a story which he tells, without a specific source, concerning Elizabeth's nephew, King Stephen V of Hungary, and what happened when he visited a cloister of religious in the Hungarian city of Esztergom:

And when he had been sitting for a very short while in chapter with the brothers of that place and saw in that same place, along with various other pictures of the saints, a picture of blessed Elizabeth depicted with shoes and without a cord, he ordered the prior of that place to have that image of St. Elizabeth with shoes and without a cord effaced without delay, and to hasten to have it painted with the cord and the habit of the Friars Minor, the cord and habit which she wore while she lived, and the habit in which she deserved to obtain the title of sanctity.[70]

The Anonymous Franciscan also places a special emphasis on the approval by St. Francis and Pope Gregory IX of Elizabeth's way of life. He says, again without a specific source, that when Francis and Gregory were speaking about Elizabeth's virtues, Gregory, who was still a cardinal then, removed the mantle from Francis's shoulders, and told him to send it to Elizabeth as a fitting token of her spirit of poverty and humility. Elizabeth wore this mantle until her death, the author says, and it was later preserved by the Teutonic Order; brother Berthold "Teutonicus" testified at the canonization process that he himself had seen it and held it in Weissenberg in the diocese of Speyer.[71]

Elizabeth's Sisters and Her Religious Life

The Anonymous Franciscan states definitely a number of times that Elizabeth lived with others in a religious community. In his description of Elizabeth's vision, for example, he calls the women with her not only her "handmaids" but her "sisters," even though this took place before her renunciation of the world or her clothing.[72] Later on, she called her handmaids and those women who remained with her at her hospital her "sisters."[73] He too uses the term "handmaid" not only for the sisters, but for Elizabeth herself.[74]

However, unlike any other early Franciscan source, the Anonymous Franciscan relates Elizabeth's life a number of times to that of Clare and her sisters. For instance, he says that Elizabeth was "always obedient to [the friars] like one of the enclosed sisters of Assisi," reinforcing the idea that her habit and her relationship to the friars were like Clare's.[75] He concludes his life with mention of some of Elizabeth's female relatives by blood or marriage, who were also her spiritual daughters: her nieces Iolenta and Cunegunde and her sister-in-law Salomeya, who, as he said, followed her example – and were all Poor Clares. On this occasion, however, the author calls them "the order of sisters of the blessed poor man St. Francis."[76] He clearly wishes to stress the similarity between their lives and Elizabeth's. But the general nature of the terms he uses suggests that he does not see a clear distinction between Poor Clares and religious women of the Third Order. This is also evident in another story he recounts, probably from oral tradition in the order:

> And since at her time there were not yet anywhere on that side of the Alps any sisters of St. Clare, [Elizabeth] once said "I am more certain about myself than about anything else, that if God, the creator of all, had seen fit to create me a man, I would have worked faithfully with all my strength to give myself back to him as a Friar Minor. But I protest before angels and men that in this vale of misery, I desire nothing else to be made of me, a miserable sinner, except what the will of divine clemency will think it fitting to arrange."[77]

The Anonymous Franciscan recalled these statements, no doubt, because they exalted the Franciscan order, and would be an example to the friars; nevertheless the reference to Elizabeth desiring a life more like the friars seems to be accurate, for we know that she was attracted to a life of begging, as several statements in the *Dicta /Libellus* and Conrad's letter tell us; this was something she could have done as a friar, but not as a woman.

This is a case where the Anonymous Franciscan's source and his own comments seem to diverge. The author himself shows little understanding of the frustration exhibited by Elizabeth's remark; he thought she wanted to be a Poor Clare, though this is not the obvious meaning of her words: Elizabeth was actually speaking of her desire to be a friar. This makes his reporting of the remark all the more striking and believable. While the author frequently refers to Elizabeth's habit as being similar to that of the Poor Clares, he is well aware that she is not a Poor Clare. Clearly he is uncertain about what terminology to use for the various groups of Franciscan women.

The Anonymous Franciscan follows the Valenciennes life in describing Elizabeth's love of prayer and her vision after her expulsion: "She who in the palace was Martha through her works of charity, became Mary in her humble dwelling through sweetness of contemplation."[78] He also followed the Valenciennes life in addressing Elizabeth with the words: "For you have always chosen the ecstasy of contemplation, although you perfected the service of Martha."[79] Both these Franciscan authors clearly admire the balance between these two elements in Elizabeth's religious life, a balance that was important to the Franciscans as an order in which the active and contemplative lives were combined. But we can see at the same time something that he does not mention: the tension and difficulty that balancing these two aspects of religious life caused Elizabeth. This is evident from the contrast between the statements he attributes to her and his own comments on them. Another reason she thought about becoming a recluse was surely the ability to practice contemplation, but her devotion to the service of the poor meant that the pure contemplative life would be impossible for her.

Elizabeth and the Friars

The Anonymous Franciscan portrays Elizabeth as being on intimate terms with the friars in Marburg. He describes how she visited the friars and "begged for the pasturage of devotion" from them.[80] He also shows Elizabeth as attaching a high value to the vocation of a Friar Minor. Speaking to the friars about her son, Hermann, the future Landgraf, she said, "I would rather have my son a true Friar Minor than to have him King and Emperor of the whole world."[81]

The Anonymous Franciscan says that "the man of all honesty and prudence, brother Gerard, called of Guerles, minister of Upper Germany of the order of Friars Minor," was "the father and special confessor of blessed Elizabeth and was more intimate with her and had more influence over her than anyone after Master Conrad."[82] This passage raises questions about Elizabeth's relationship with Conrad of Marburg, who has been traditionally seen as completely dominating her. Nonetheless, the additional role given to the Franciscan confessor here is not implausible. From Conrad's own statements, and those of other witnesses, it is clear that during Elizabeth's Marburg period Conrad was frequently absent on preaching tours, for he was one of the main crusade preachers in Germany at the time.[83] Gerard may have been substituting for him in his absence. The Anonymous Franciscan is careful not to push Conrad aside in favor of the Franciscan. Nevertheless, since we cannot be sure from the text whether his statement about Brother Gerard being the most influential person in Elizabeth's life next to Conrad comes from the witness Gerard himself or is the author's, it should be accepted with some caution.

According to the Anonymous Franciscan, Elizabeth not only received spiritual direction from the friars, she also gave them advice about matters of discipline at the convent. The Anonymous Franciscan recounts, without naming a source, that one day Elizabeth visited the friars at their convent and had a spiritual conversation with them, during which she spoke eloquently about "the honey-sweet Jesus." One of the friars started to leave, but when called back by the three other brothers present, rudely refused to return. At this, Elizabeth said, "Dismiss him, my dearest brothers, because in truth he is not our brother, nor is he to be a true Friar Minor."[84] The "Anonymous Franciscan adds that Elizabeth's words were prophetic, for very shortly afterward this man left the order.

Such stories were very frequent in the accounts of the relationship between other religious women and friars. The men found that even though they as clerics had authority, the women were in some ways spiritually superior, and were able to make prophetic utterances. This filled a lack they may have felt in themselves, and at the same time reinforced the idea of the woman as Other. Frequently in these stories, the women know by revelation the friars' spiritual status. For instance, the Franciscan tertiary Margaret of Cortona (1247-1297) answered the anxious question of a Friar Minor over how often he should receive communion by consulting with Christ about it, and was able to know when priests were spiritually unworthy.[85] Yet Elizabeth's particular relationship with the friars means that her intervention had even more authority, if she was indeed responsible for bringing the friars to Marburg and they were living on land obtained from her family. In the case of Margaret of Cortona, one of the reasons for Fra Giunta Bevegnati to write a life of her was to increase the prestige of the order through the holiness of a woman attached to it. Something similar could be said in Elizabeth's case.

Elizabeth was clearly not living in absolute poverty without money, and therefore she had the resources to aid the friars in a material way. The Anonymous Franciscan recounts how Elizabeth supplied the brothers with various things such as cloth for their habits and food. Elizabeth was the "mother of the Friars Minor," as the author repeats several times.[86] She also served as their procurator and benefactor, at a time when the compromise solution to the question of ownership among the Franciscans was first regulated by the papal decree *Quo elongati*, issued by Gregory IX in 1230. This decision regulated the means by which the friars had the use of convents, churches and other property through third parties. This decision is not mentioned directly by the Anonymous Franciscan, who seems to have been an advocate of strict poverty. This whole account, however, does show to what extent all the early friars, both before and after *Quo elongati*, were dependent on those like Elizabeth with the means to provide for their material needs, though she, like them, was deeply concerned for poverty.

Elizabeth as "Strong Woman" and "Another Christ"

The Anonymous Franciscan speaks of Elizabeth several times as the "strong woman" of Proverbs 31 (*mulier fortis* in the Vulgate). This Biblical passage had been established by Gregory IX as the Epistle for Elizabeth's feast day Mass.[87] When telling the story of Berthold, the worldly young nobleman whom Elizabeth converted by her prayers and who became a Friar Minor, the author rejoices: "Thus the strong woman won for God souls that the devil tried to seize."[88] But for the Anonymous Franciscan, Elizabeth's greatest strength lay paradoxically in her lowliness, as he explains in quoting the other half of this verse when describing Elizabeth's death: "Therefore, the poor little simplicity of the Friars Minor lamented, not undeservedly, having despaired of recovering a mother so very pious and humble, rather than such a noble provider."[89]

The final passage about Elizabeth in the Anonymous Franciscan fittingly rounds out the author's treatment of her as another Christ, as well as the "strong woman." He tells how Brother Dietrich "Teutonicus" and his companion received a shock when they arrived in Marburg on business for the order:

> As they wandered about the main square, inquiring where their brothers were lodging, Elizabeth, the loving mother of the Friars Minor, came across them, and seemed about to run into the most chaste arms of the aforesaid brother, but the modest simplicity of the brother prevented it. She went about the square like a procurator, mercifully providing for the Friars Minor and the other poor people. What then, will you see in the Sunamite, but the dancers of the camps, that is, the good of total piety, total charity – great good indeed (cf. Cant. 7:1). Then the people who were present, when they saw what had happened, laughing and leading

them to the place of the brothers, like strangers and pilgrims (Heb. 11:13; 1 Pet. 2:11), said to them: "Now you know who it was and what kind of woman it was who touched you" (cf. Luke 7:39). And it happened as they were talking, and *telling what had happened on the way* (Luke 24:35), behold, the king's daughter and noble duchess Elizabeth came in the door, carrying wine to drink for the brothers under her poor patched mantle. She *stood in the midst of them* (Luke 24:36) and humbly prostrating herself before them, offered to perform the service of washing, which the King of Kings and Lord of Lords consecrated with his sacred hands on rising from table after supper with his disciples. The brothers were not able to bear this; instead they gently reproved her because she had acted in such a simple manner towards the brothers in the middle of the main square of her own city. That *strong woman,* (Prov. 31:10) *full of graces* (cf. Luke 1:28), answered: "May God pardon me for this and I beg your pardon as well, for when I saw the brothers from far away so worn out from their journey, I was filled with such joy, as I wanted to minister to them, that my outward appearance was not able in a way to hide the overflowing superabundance of my interior joy."[90]

The style of this story is unusual for the Anonymous Franciscan. Apart from the various passages he quotes from the Valenciennes life, he rarely uses Biblical quotations in the narrative parts of his life, but this passage is a complicated mosaic of Biblical allusions. This is not merely a bit of narrative, but a story that was clearly of meaning for the author and the fruit of much meditation on its Biblical significance. The author himself may have elaborated it from oral tradition within the order, or it may have been copied from an unknown written source.

This tale of Elizabeth and the Franciscans is representative of the difficulties their relations with the female penitents caused the friars; they were often seen as a cause of scandal to the laity or a threat to chastity. The author hints at this through the quotation from the warning given to Christ by the Pharisee about the sinful woman who touched him and washed his feet with her hair: "If this man were a prophet, he would know who touched him and what kind of woman she is" (Luke 7:39). This play on the Biblical quotation is humorous: clearly the brothers are not prophets, but the people of Marburg know Elizabeth and what kind of woman she is – not a sinful woman, but a saint. The author continues subtly to turn the narrative to Elizabeth's advantage through the use of biblical allusions and quotations. Like the apostles, the visiting Franciscans at first fail to recognize Elizabeth's Christlike nature, but when she "stands in the midst of them" as the risen Christ stood among the disciples after their return from Emmaus, and comes carrying wine (a Eucharistic symbol) and offering to wash their feet as Christ did, it becomes clear to the reader. This passage corresponds to the one in the foreword to the life, in which Elizabeth was compared to Christ.

Through the use of Eucharistic symbols and language, Elizabeth is compared to Christ both in providing food and serving the friars as Christ served his disciples. The friars, as they meditated on the story over time, saw the relationship as providential and a sign of God's care for them. This connection between Elizabeth and Christ as givers of nourishment to the friars is a more fitting example of Bynum's theory about the medieval view of women as nurturing figures, related to the life-giving flesh

196

of the Eucharist, than the actual examples Bynum used in speaking about Elizabeth.[91] But this association seems to exist largely in the minds of the male writers about Elizabeth, as was also true of many of the women Bynum spoke of. The Anonymous Franciscan and the author of the Valenciennes life both tend to speak about Elizabeth's motherhood in relation to food she supplied to others, especially the friars: she "nourished them like a mother";[92] on the other hand the testimony of the women who lived with Elizabeth frequently mention her motherly actions, but do not associate them solely with the supplying of food, but rather with an actual maternal or quasi-maternal relationship, such as her concern for her own children, as we saw in Isentrude's testimony, or her tenderness toward the children of the poor.[93]

Although the Anonymous Franciscan refers to Elizabeth as Christ, he is far from masculinizing her. This relatively brief passage contains references to her as the "strong woman" of Proverbs, as the Bride in the Song of Songs, and as the Virgin Mary. The story is the epitome of the Anonymous Franciscan's multilayered approach to Elizabeth. Unlike St. Clare's biographer, he does not shrink from seeing Elizabeth as Christ, even as he compares her to Mary.[94]

This story also reveals something about Elizabeth's relations with the townspeople of Marburg. Although Brother Dietrich and his companion may have been shocked that Elizabeth would act with uninhibited affection toward them in public, the townspeople were amused and seemed to take it in stride. The reason was undoubtedly that, while she had suffered opposition from the noblemen who had been her husband's officials, Elizabeth was still known to the townspeople of Marburg as their "lady." She was accepted, and because of this veneration for her, the relationship of her and her sisters with the friars was accepted as well.

Throughout the later Middle Ages, authentic-sounding and detailed stories like this were often invented in hagiography, perhaps in response to the authentic details found in canonization processes from the thirteenth century on.[95] This story, which at least in its core elements is startlingly lifelike in its description of the friars' social embarrassment and Elizabeth's spontaneous personality, may be one of these, or it may be a true detail from Elizabeth's life. But in either case, through meditation and interpretation in the Franciscan community, it became meaningful for the friars reflecting on their relationship with Elizabeth and the sisters.

Summary

The Anonymous Franciscan supplies us with a wealth of material about Elizabeth's life in Marburg, and her relationship with the Franciscans there. He also gives us an abundance of firsthand testimonies about Elizabeth's devotion to poverty in her religious life. At the same time, the author often displays confusion and uncertainty in his attempts to name Elizabeth's form of life. Nevertheless, the early testimonies he quotes allow us to gain a much clearer picture of Elizabeth as a religious.

Elizabeth's case was similar to that of other women living new forms of religious life, such as the Beguines in many areas of Germany, who were directed and aided in their way of life by the Franciscans and Dominicans. The relationship was one of mutual aid. Elizabeth not only received help from the friars, but was their benefactress as well. In this, she was like the women of female penitent communities in Italy, who helped support the friars by their alms.[96] In the end, the Friars Minor lost any claim they might have had to direct and organize her cult. Nevertheless, the benefits she had given them had succeeded in helping to establish the friars in Marburg.

The connection between convent and hospital that we see in Marburg is typical of the very earliest years of the Franciscan order, when Francis himself and his brothers served the lepers, and of the early convents which were built on the periphery of the cities among the poorer citizens and more recent immigrants. As yet, they had perhaps made little impact on the citizens. Thus it is not surprising that the people in the central marketplace from whom Brother Dietrich and his companion asked for directions to the place "where their brothers were lodging" apparently had difficulty supplying it, because they lived on the outskirts of town. Here in Marburg, as was frequently the case in other urban areas, the friars later moved into the center of the city, into a larger, more elaborate convent with their own church. This location served to bring them into the mainstream of urban life among the merchants and more prosperous citizens to whom the Franciscans soon began to direct their ministry.[97] What Elizabeth shared with the Franciscans was the very beginning of their ministry in Marburg, with its early fervor for poverty.

The complicated development of Elizabeth's vocation, which took place in the stages evidenced by the various testimonies, proved difficult for the Anonymous Franciscan to track. There was a beginning in her vow to remain continent after her husband's death; later came her renunciation of the world, a step which she seems to have decided on sometime during her wanderings after her expulsion, and which she acted on quickly and decisively in Eisenach in order to prevent any further talk of remarriage; finally, there was her profession and clothing in Marburg. The Anonymous Franciscan did his best to make sense of all this by combining her various resolutions and the different steps she took into one event. Perhaps this was due again to the need to find a clear conversion in Elizabeth's life. This attempt to regularize or make clear the sometimes complicated facts is significant, for we frequently find the same process in Elizabeth's modern biographers in their attempts to make sense of her expulsion in relation to her vocation (see Chapter II). They made her decision for the religious life simpler than it really was, doing away with Elizabeth's uncertainty and struggles. And it is the uncertainty that is important for understanding Elizabeth, as I will show later.

On the whole, the Anonymous Franciscan seems to be in some confusion about where Elizabeth belonged in the Franciscan family. Expanding freely on the statements of an early witness who compared Elizabeth's habit to that of St. Clare's, the author several times attaches Elizabeth to the Poor Clares; he clearly thinks this would have been her true vocation if this option had been available to her. Yet the information he presents about the way Elizabeth lived does not always harmonize with this belief, for Elizabeth lived an active life, not an enclosed life as Clare did. (There are indications, in fact, that St. Clare herself did not live an enclosed life at first, though later Franciscan authors tend to portray her as living this way from the beginning).[98] The Anonymous Franciscan has provided his particular interpretation of the records. Yet this interpretation does not destroy evidence that shows Elizabeth hesitating and struggling for a way of life for herself – should she be a recluse, or a hospital sister, or live a life of begging?

Similar statements might be made about the author's treatment of Elizabeth's Franciscan poverty. Living at a time when the controversy over the Spirituals was growing more intense, he himself was enthusiastic for the friars' early life of poverty – for instance, he carefully preserves the primitive word "place" instead of "convent" for the residences of the friars. He presents Elizabeth as an example of true Franciscan poverty – barefoot, living in the lowliest way, serving the poor. Yet he preserves statements from the earliest sources that show that Elizabeth used money and did not completely renounce her property. In fact, Elizabeth would have been unable to preserve complete poverty because she was engaged in hospital work, which required keeping some property for administration (also, as we learn from Conrad's letter, she had to keep some property to pay her husband's debts.) Once again, this detail seems alien to the author's purpose, although he includes it; I believe this is evidence for the authenticity of the details. Above all, the Anonymous Franciscan shows that the Franciscan community of his time actively meditated on Elizabeth's role in regard to the friars in both Eisenach and Marburg. To them, she was a reminder of the Franciscan virtues of poverty, humility and minority, and like Francis himself, "another Christ."

Working as a compiler as well as a commentator, the Anonymous Franciscan presents us with original details as well as layers of commentary on them. All of these contribute to our knowledge of how Elizabeth's contemporaries saw her, as well as how the Franciscan understanding of her life had developed by the late thirteenth century.

Comparison of the Franciscan Sources

We have seen something of how the Anonymous Franciscan treated the various statements he found in his sources about Elizabeth's Franciscan vocation, and how he designated her form of religious life. When we compare his portrait of Elizabeth with that of the other Franciscan writers from the same period, we can see that the Anonymous Franciscan shares a number of their concerns. Like our author, they hesitate about where to put Elizabeth in the Franciscan family and how to describe her relationship to the friars.

The Anonymous Franciscan says that "according to certain statements" Elizabeth "was guided by the wholesome advice of the Friars Minor, placing herself completely under their teaching and discipline."[99] This is probably not a direct quotation from any early testimony; the author describes it as coming from "certain statements"; it could have ultimately come from statements at the canonization process, or oral tradition from other intimates of the saint, or some unknown source. However, the wording is probably that of the Anonymous Franciscan. Later he says that she was "always obedient to them [i.e. the friars] like one of the enclosed sisters of Assisi."[100] This second case is clearly the author's own comment on Brother Gherard's testimony.

These statements of the Anonymous Franciscan are quite consistent with other late thirteenth- and early fourteenth-century Franciscan sources. For instance, Salimbene says that after her husband's death, Elizabeth "lived under the obedience of the Friars Minor, and was always devoted to them."[101] Giacomo da Tresanti says that she was "a very special daughter" of St. Francis" and "a docile disciple of the Friars Minor also."[102] In the Anonymous Franciscan, these statements do not replace the idea of Elizabeth as "mother of the friars," which he took over from the Valenciennes Life, which expressed the earliest Franciscan view of Elizabeth. But the emphasis on obedience does indicate that a new concern had arisen. At a period when there was growing suspicion about the freedom many religious women had, and more pressure towards having them cloistered, culminating in the bull *Periculoso* in 1298, the obedience of women to the friars became especially important.

The accounts of the Franciscan writers from this period are also consistent in their description of Elizabeth's habit. The Anonymous Franciscan, as mentioned above, quotes contemporary testimonies from the canonization process about Elizabeth's cord and habit: she wore them "like another abbess Clare of the cloistered sisters."[103] His own comments agree with this assessment in comparing her to St. Clare, but in describing how King Stephen asked to have Elizabeth painted in the cord and habit of the Friars Minor he seems to be making a more general statement connecting Elizabeth to the friars and the Franciscan movement as a whole, rather than specifically the Poor Clares.

Once again, other contemporary accounts are comparable. The anonymous sermon by a Friar Minor says: "A sign of her perfect humility was the cord and habit of the [Friars] Minors, which she adopted as best she could."[104] Giacomo da Tresanti, in saying that Elizabeth wore a gray habit out of reverence for St. Francis, attributes to her a very general connection to the

Franciscan order. Yet he adds, which the Anonymous Franciscan does not, that it is "said by some that she belonged to the Third Order."[105]

It is impossible to know whether there was any direct connection or influence between the Anonymous Franciscan and these other authors. Clearly they are from the same historical milieu and share the same concerns. Yet the Anonymous Franciscan is more inclined to see Elizabeth as a proto-Poor Clare rather than an early example of a religious of the Third Order, as was beginning to become more general about this time. In fact, the Anonymous Franciscan never mentions the Third Order at all.

This tendency becomes even clearer when we compare the Anonymous Franciscan with the Heidelberg life, which is itself a fourteenth-century or later adaptation of the Anonymous Franciscan. Rather than putting Elizabeth among the women of the Third Order, it connects her even more strongly to the order of St. Clare, on the hints given by the Anonymous Franciscan. It has Elizabeth saying that she wanted "with all her heart" to enter Clare's order, but was unable to do so.[106]

The Anonymous Franciscan, therefore, describes Elizabeth's Franciscan vocation in much the same terms as other writers of his time. At the end of the thirteenth century and looking back to Franciscan origins, these writers seem confused or uncertain about how to describe Elizabeth's place in the Franciscan movement. Some tried to assign her an identity as a Poor Clare, or someone who would have been a Poor Clare if she could; others began to identify her as a member of the Third Order, which had just received its definitive juridical structure and rule. The Anonymous Franciscan tends to believe she was like a Poor Clare, though aware that her life did not respond to the cloistered ideal. He does not provide any alternative possibility, such as the Third Order. Apart from these passages, however, he is largely content with describing Elizabeth's vocation as the earliest witnesses described it. So there were two different traditions within the order in regard to Elizabeth's place in the Franciscan family; the tradition of the Third Order became the predominant one in the later fourteenth century when the juridical status of the Franciscan tertiaries became more certain and the way Elizabeth's life fit into the idea of the Third Order was recognized.

Conclusion

This chapter has shown that there is much more detail than has usually been thought about Elizabeth's religious vocation, her group of sisters, and her relationship to the Franciscans in all the available sources, including both the traditional sources and the little-used Franciscan sources. These last sources show Elizabeth interacting with the friars at their convent in Marburg, and the Franciscans playing a role in her clothing and profession. We also find testimony suggesting that Elizabeth lived both as a Beguine and as a Franciscan. The newly-discovered testimonies in the Anonymous Franciscan fill in details about this sisterhood, which seems to have been larger than thought, and to have included noblewomen as well as poor women. The thirteenth-century biographers of Elizabeth, Caesarius and Dietrich, preserve the first, rather general, descriptions of her religious life found in the testimonies. Even the Franciscan Valenciennes life adds little to this picture. They shared the uncertainty of the time over the saint's religious vocation, the uncertainty which Elizabeth herself felt.

We find little in the early testimonies about some aspects of religious women's lives that were usually given great prominence in the biographies of them written by men, such as extreme fasting and other ascetic practices, visions and revelations. Brother Gerard, Conrad and other witnesses do speak about Elizabeth as an ecstatic and contemplative, but Elizabeth herself seems not to have stressed this aspect of her life. The women who shared their lives with her give a more detailed picture focusing not just on visions or the external form of habit, but on the struggles and events of daily life.

The early testimonies also tell us more about Elizabeth's conception of poverty, one that was consonant with the ideals of St. Francis but at the same time reflected her own personal experience of poverty, both involuntary and voluntary. We can see the way she was torn between a desire for absolute poverty as a recluse and the demands of charitable service. In her understanding of serving the poor, she showed a strong difference from her confessor Conrad, who thought of charity more as an ascetic exercise.

Elizabeth's place in the growth of the women's religious movement of the thirteenth century seems to have been, as McNamara has said, a transitional one. She faced problems of poverty that arose both in the feudal and the urban worlds. She fought the injustices of the feudal system of taxation, but eventually broke free of an aristocratic mode of piety and serving the poor, one that other women, like her aunt, St. Hedwig, were content to preserve. The women's religious movement had largely grown in an urban atmosphere, where status became increasingly dependent on money as well as lineage, and where the pressure of the guilt of sudden riches and usurious practices had given an urgency to the renunciation of wealth for God and turning to the poor to seek social unity. The Franciscans played a part in this movement.

Michel Mollat argues that the friars, especially the Franciscans, had a new approach to the problems of the poor: Francis saw the humanity of the poor and did not regard them only as the instrument for the salvation of the wealthy through the distribution of alms, but as brothers and sisters in Christ. Mollat believes that the friars were a success in the cities because the order was based on a fraternal, not a hierarchical model. This was the idea on which the comunes or town governments and the communal fraternities had been based for the past century, and which brought rich and poor together to experience both political community and common religious ties.[107] Elizabeth was from a feudal background, but given the urbanization of northern Germany in her time, she must have been able to recognize a changing world. In the urban setting in Marburg, she expressed the idea of social unity by calling her servants "ladies" and asking them to address her familiarly.

The later accounts that the Anonymous Franciscan added to the earlier testimonies demonstrate a different set of concerns. They show Elizabeth displaying some of the traits common to the friars' biographies of holy women. Elizabeth was regarded as holy because of her prophetic utterances about the state of their souls; she was a mother who nourished them and represented Christ to them. The early testimony of Brother Gerard about Elizabeth's visions shows the typical confessor's interest in this aspect of women's holiness. Sometimes startling utterances attributed to Elizabeth stand out from this picture. One of these is her quoted statement about wanting to be a Friar Minor herself; she felt that she was equal to the work they did, but also painfully aware of the reality of her life as a woman in a male-dominated world.

The Anonymous Franciscan, along with the other Franciscan writers at the end of the thirteenth century, had difficulty in determining Elizabeth's place in the Franciscan movement. This can be explained by the uncertain juridical status of Elizabeth and the other Franciscan women of her time. It was only toward the end of the thirteenth century and the promulgation of the Third Order Rule of Nicholas IV that there was a juridical position against which Elizabeth's experience could be measured. This is why references to her as a tertiary appear at this time, although her life was not formally structured according to a rule like that of the later tertiaries. The comments of the Franciscan sources show a desire to make that life more institutionally certain than it really was.

These later Franciscan writers also displayed other contemporary concerns. Their descriptions of Elizabeth's ties to the order, written at a time when the earlier freedom of movement of religious women was giving way to cloister, stress her obedience to the friars. At the same time, this study has shown that both the early testimonies by the Franciscans at Elizabeth's canonization process and the comments by later Franciscan writers demonstrate a real appreciation for her Franciscan virtues and a true example of the "loving care and solicitude" that Francis wanted his brothers to have toward Clare and the other women in the Franciscan movement.

Other women were soon to imitate Elizabeth's life of poverty and loving service. Her example played an important role in the development of what was to eventually become the Third Order Regular. The next chapter will be devoted to an examination of how these women also attempted to balance poverty and service to the poor.

Notes

[1] Huyskens, *Quellenstudien*, p. 125.

[2] Huyskens, *Quellenstudien*, p. 114. The *Libellus* has "two years"; Huyskens, *Libellus*, p. 16.

[3] Huyskens, *Quellenstudien*, p. 130.

[4] Huyskens, *Quellenstudien*, p. 135.

[5] Huyskens, *Quellenstudien*, p. 157.

[6] T 80v; lines 255-66.

[7] Gieben, "I patroni," pp. 240-41.

[8] Huyskens, *Quellenstudien*, pp. 114-15.

[9] Huyskens, *Quellenstudien*, p. 157.

[10] Huyskens, *Quellenstudien*, p. 114.

[11] Huyskens, *Quellenstudien*, p. 124.

[12] T 79v, lines 214-25.

[13] Maurer, "Zum Verstandnis," p. 54.

[14] Huyskens, *Quellenstudien*, p. 121 (Isentrude's testi-mony), and pp. 57, 95-104.

[15] Battes, "Das Vordringen der Franziskaner in Hessen und die Entwicklung der einzelnen Konvente bis zur Reformation," FS 18 (1931): 315; John B. Freed, *The Friars and German Society in the Thirteenth Century* (Cambridge: Mediaeval Academy of America, 1977), pp. 195, 198.

[16] Wigand Gerstenberg, *Landeschronik*, in, *Chroniken von Hessen und Waldeck*, ed. Hermann Dietmar, Vol. 1. *Die Chroniken des Wigand Gerstenberg von Frankenberg* (Marburg, N. G. Elwert, 1909); 189; (reprinted ibid, 1989). Dietmar believed that this report came from local Marburg tradition.

[17] Maurer,"Zum Verstandnis," p. 54.

[18] *Cronica Fratris Iordani,* no. 43, AF 1:13.

[19] For Germany, see Freed, *The Friars and German Society,* p. 34. This phenomenon was first noted by Jacques Le Goff in his "Apostolat mendiant et fait urbain dans la France médiévale: l'implantation des ordres mendiants," *Annales: Economies, sociétés, civilisations* 23 (1968): 335-52.

[20] T 92v; line 768; T 86v, lines 512-13.

[21] Battes, "Das Vordringen," pp. 314-15.

[22] Wigand von Gerstenberg, *Landeschronik,* p. 201.

[23] See Battes, "Das Vordringen," p. 314.

24 See Werner Mortiz, "Das Hospital der heiligen Elisabeth in seinen Verhaltnis zum Hospitalwesen des fruhen 13. Jahrhunderts," in *Sankt Elisabeth*, pp. 101-116.

25 See McNamara, *Sisters in Arms*, pp. 252-57.

26 Jacques de Vitry, "The Life of Marie d'Oignies," in *Two Lives of Marie D'Oignies*, p. 56.

27 The brothers are mentioned in a document by Gregory IX of March 30, 1231; see Huyskens, *Quellenstudien*, p. 100.

28 See Moritz, "Das Hospital der heiligen Elisabeth," pp. 108-109.

29 Huyskens, *Quellenstudien*, p. 133.

30 Testimony of Irmingard in Huyskens, *Quellenstudien*, p. 129.

31 Huyskens, *Quellenstudien*, pp. 129-30.

32 Testimony of the handmaid Elisabeth in Huyskens, *Quellenstudien*, p. 134.

33 Huyskens, *Quellenstudien*, p. 158.

34 Huyskens, *Quellenstudien*, p. 158. Should these two women be identified with Elisabeth and Irmingard? It seems unlikely. Elisabeth would show herself, as we see later, afraid of Conrad, and evidently disliked him. But Irmingard and Elisabeth continued to be with Elizabeth until the end of her life, so Elizabeth could not have been attended by these harsh women alone.

35 Huyskens, *Quellenstudien*, pp. 158-59.

36 Huyskens, *Quellenstudien*, p. 159.

37 Huyskens, *Libellus*, p. 52.

38 Huyskens, *Quellenstudien*, p. 136.

39 T 87r-87v, lines 548-58.

[40] According to Susan Mosher Stuard, "Ancillary Evidence for the Decline of Medieval Slavery," *Past and Present* no. 149 (1995): 3-28, this is true of Mediterranean Europe throughout the later Middle Ages.

[41] Jacques de Vitry, "The Life of Marie of Oignies," in *Two Lives of Marie d'Oignies*, p. 59; and Thomas of Cantrimpré, "Supplement to the Life of Marie d'Oignies," p. 241.

[42] Franknoì, *Monumenta romana*, 261; quoted in Michael Goodich, "Ancilla Dei: The Servant as Saint in the Late Middle Ages," in Suzanne Wemple and Julius Kirschner, *Women of the Medieval World: Studies in Honor of John H. Mundy* (Oxford: Basil Blackwell, 1985), p. 134.

[43] Jacques Cambell, *Enquête pour le procès de canonisation de Dauphine de Puimichel, comtesse d'Ariano* (Turin, 1978), pp. 48, 326; quoted in Goodich, "Ancilla Dei," p. 135.

[44] Huyskens, *Quellenstudien*, pp. 136-37.

[45] Huyskens, *Quellenstudien*, pp. 133-34.

[46] Huyskens, *Quellenstudien*, p. 136.

[47] Huyskens, *Quellenstudien*, pp. 133-34.

[48] Huyskens, *Quellenstudien*, p. 138.

[49] Huyskens, *Quellenstudien*, pp. 132-33.

[50] T 79v-80r, lines 225-32.

[51] Huyskens, *Quellenstudien*, p. 133.

[52] Vauchez, "Pauvreté et charité," pp. 172-73.

[53] This is the suggestion of Anna Benvenuti Papi, "Mendicant Friars and Female Pinzochere in Tuscany," in Bornstein and Rusconi, *Women and Religion in Medieval and Renaissance Italy*, p. 92.

[54] Folz, *Les saintes reines du moyen âge en occident*, p. 167.

[55] Caesarius, "Die Schriften des Caesarius von Heister-bach," p. 366.

[56] Caesarius, "Die Schriften des Caesarius von Heister-bach," p. 367.

[57] Caesarius "Die Schriften des Caesarius von Heisterbach," p. 383.

[58] Anonymous of Zwettl, "Vita sanctae Elisabeth," pp. 256, 257, 268.

[59] Dietrich, *Vita der heiligen Elizabeth*, VI, 4, pp. 89-90.

[60] Jacobus de Voragine, *Legenda aurea*, p. 1165.

[61] V 67vb, D 12v, lines 160-62.

[62] V 72ra-b, D 16v-17r, lines 349-56.

[63] Salimbene d'Adam, *Cronica*, ed. Giuseppe Scalia (Turnhout: Brepolis, 1998), 1:53 (51 in 1966 ed.).

[64] Anon. "De S. Elisabeth, sermo," in *S. R. E. cardinalis Bonaventurae . . opera omnia*, 13:629.

[65] Cenci, "Noterelle su Fr. Giacomo da Tresanti," p. 123.

[66] Arnaud of Serrant, *Chronica XXIV Generalium*, AF 3:222.

[67] Gieben, "I patroni dell'ordine di penitenza," pp. 235-41.

[68] For more on the spiritual-social motivations of the female tertiaries in thirteenth-century Florence, see Carol Lansing, *The Florentine Magnates: Lineage and Faction in a Medieval Comune* (Princeton: Princeton University Press, 1991), pp. 112-24.

[69] T 79r-79v, lines 206-14.

[70] T 80r-80v, lines 249-54.

71 T 88v-90r, lines 617-29.

72 T 82v. The *Dicta* has simply "the ladies of her retinue and members of her household" in the same context; Huyskens, *Quellenstudien*, p. 123.

73 T 81v, lines 298-99.

74 T 81r, lines 287-88.

75 T 92r, lines 743-44.

76 K 126v, lines 865-66.

77 T 86v-87r, lines 523-29.

78 T 82r, lines 320-21; cf. Valenciennes Life, V 67vb, D 12v, lines 160-62.

79 T 90r, K 24ra, lines 672-73; cf. Valenciennes Life, V 70vb, D 15v, lines 294-95.

80 T 86v, lines 511-12.

81 T 86v, lines 522-23.

82 T 87r, lines 545-47.

83 For Conrad's absence on preaching tours, see his letter in Huyskens, *Quellenstudien*, p. 159; testimony in the *Dicta* shows that on another occasion, he was absent in the town of Altenburg; ibid., p. 135.

84 T 86v, lines 516-17.

85 "De B. Margarita," AASS, 9.241, and 7.179; see Coakley, "Gender and the Authority of Friars" for a discussion of this type of spiritual relationship.

86 T 76v, line 85; T 91v, line 737; T 83v, lines 387-88.

87 Huyskens, *Quellenstudien*, p. 147.

88 T 83v, line 382.

[89] K 125va, lines 780-82.

[90] T 92v, K 125r, lines 767-87.

[91] Bynum, *Holy Feast and Holy Fast,* especially pp. 135-36, 193, 203-304, 224.

[92] V 66rb, D 10v, lines 85-86; V 72ra, D, 72r, line 355; T 92r, line 737.

[93] Huyskens, *Quellenstudien,* especially pp. 118-19 and 121-22.

[94] Mooney, "*Imitatio Christi or Imitatio Mariae?*: Clare of Assisi and Her Interpreters," in *Gendered Voices,* pp. 52-77.

[95] For a discussion, see Stark, "Elisabeth von Thüringen," pp. 704-21.

[96] See Anna Benvenuti Papi, "Mendicant Friars and Female Pinzochere in Tuscany," in Bornstein and Rusconi, *Women and Religion in Medieval and Renaissance Italy,* p. 91.

[97] See Lester K. Little, *Religious Poverty and the Profit Economy in Medieval Europe* (London: Paul Elek, 1978).

[98] See Clara Gennaro, "Clare, Agnes and Their Earliest Followers: From the Poor Ladies of San Damiano to the Poor Clares," in Bornstein and Rusconi, *Women and Religion in Medieval and Renaissance Italy,* pp. 39-55.

[99] T 80v, lines 258-60.

[100] T 92r, lines 742-43.

[101] Salimbene, *Cronica,* 1:53 (51 in 1966 ed.).

[102] Cenci, "Noterelle su Fr. Giacomo da Tresanti," p. 123.

[103] T f.79v, lines 224-25.

[104] Bonaventure, *Opera omnia,* 13:629.

[105] Cenci, "Noterelle su Fr. Giacomo da Tresanti," p. 123.

[106] Heidelberg MS, 22v.

[107] Michel Mollat, *The Poor in the Middle Ages: An Essay in Social History* (New Haven, Conn. and London, 1978), pp. 123-35.

Chapter VII

Elizabeth's Influence on The

Women's Franciscan Movement

Introduction

As we have seen, Elizabeth's life and experiences were similar to those of many other women in the thirteenth-century religious movement. This chapter will explore how Elizabeth fits into the context of the Franciscan movement in particular, and how the problems that shaped her life were also faced by other women religious who wanted to follow the Franciscan way of life.

Although the possibilities for women were somewhat more flexible during Elizabeth's lifetime than they were to be later in the century during a period of increasing papal regulation of women's religious lives, she still experienced difficulty reconciling the demands of adherence to Franciscan poverty with those of charitable service. Some of the women who imitated Elizabeth, like Agnes of Bohemia, worked to maintain active lives of charity within the cloister. With the imposition of cloister at the end of the thirteenth century, there were still groups of Franciscan women who undertook to live a non-cloistered life; eventually they were able to gain papal recognition as religious following a rule. Elizabeth's example played an important part in this development, since she seems to have been the first Franciscan woman to live a life of active hospital service.

Because Elizabeth was not the founder of any order, congregation or surviving religious community that can be directly traced back to her, and because her religious life lasted under three years, it might seem difficult to relate it to the lives of other Franciscan women. But because her form of religious life was an inspiration to a number of other medieval women from the thirteenth century on, it is important to examine it. She stands at the fountainhead of a real movement. Elizabeth entered her religious life only three years after the death of St. Francis; this places her very close to the origins of the Franciscan way of life. Also important is the fact that the period the testimonies cover is that of the beginnings of a vocation that was cut short while it was still in development. The testimonies present us with a valuable "snapshot" of the beginning of Elizabeth's religious life. This makes them all the more important, for they are less affected by subsequent biographical tradition that would tend to force Elizabeth's religious experience into the later normative mold. Later biographies of some Franciscan women, for instance, those of St. Clare, which were written after the institutionalization of their religious lives, often present only the later form of life that the women adopted, and give us less about the early days, the experimentation, the uncertainty, and even the compromises they made on their way to achieving it. Because some early documents exist for St. Clare, we can tell something about those days, and with the recovery of early testimonies about Elizabeth, we can do the same for her. These testimonies offer us a clearer picture than do the sources for many other thirteenth-century Franciscan women's lives of the choices that women faced in determining on and launching such daring religious vocations.

I will begin this chapter by examining the relationship between the Franciscan women and the Beguines and other women in the religious movement of the time and the different tendencies in their religious lives. I will then look at how Elizabeth fits into this complex movement. Finally, I will look at a number of groups of women who were influenced by her, or who led similar lives.

The Franciscan Women and the Beguines

The Beguines and the Franciscan and Dominican tertiaries were part of the same women's religious movement. On the outside, the Beguines seemed indistinguishable from the tertiaries; both wore gray habits.1 In other places, too, the Beguines were actually seen as being a part of the Third Order. A document from Toulouse in 1275 refers to the "Order of Beguines of the Third Rule of Blessed Francis."2 As time went on, a number of already-existing groups of Beguines embraced the Franciscan way of life and spirituality as it was offered to non-priests and non-religious. Adopting the way of life of the Beguines was a solution for those who did not want cloistered life, and desired to live a life of active charity. Franciscan women who wanted such a life found the path already traced out for them by the Beguines. But there were both attractions and difficulties in this way of life.

André Vauchez has suggested that there were two basic, though not mutually exclusive, tendencies among those female saints in the Franciscan movement who did not renounce the lay state (by this he means those who did not become cloistered nuns, but who may or may not have lived in non-cloistered, semi-religious communities). The first tendency is "evangelical spirituality, revolving around poverty and love for neighbor manifested by the practice of works of mercy." For him, Elizabeth is the one who best embodies this ideal. The other tendency, which is that of "asceticism, and above all of mystical effusions," led a number of women, like Umiliana dei Cerchi, to gradually abandon practices of charity for the highest contemplation and greater seclusion. This last tendency, he believes, was the one most encouraged by the friars themselves. Vauchez mentions the influence of the friars, but does not consider the institutional factors such as claustration, or societal pressures on women, including those exerted by the male hierarchy,

217

to stay in the private sphere rather than entering the public one.3 Nonetheless, it is true that Elizabeth and a number of female Franciscans did experience a conflict in their souls between the demands of the active life of charity and the desire for contemplation. But charity and poverty were also often at odds.

McKelvie notes that the Poor Clares are often seen as "the most faithful custodians of Francis' legacy of poverty." But, she continues, other women followed Francis faithfully in other ways: "As far as women tertiaries living a common life are concerned –a reality in various places by the mid-thirteenth century – not making a vow of poverty was an integral element in their identity."4 Having resources they could use to benefit the poor and sick was important to them, and required that they have the freedom to use these goods, which they could not if they vowed poverty. Hence there was a tension between the ideal of poverty and that of charity.

We have some very early testimony of a type of life similar to that of the Beguines among Franciscan women. It comes from Bishop Jacques de Vitry, himself a strong supporter of the Beguines, who wrote shortly after his visit to central Italy in 1216:

> I have found one solace in those parts, however; that is many of both sexes who, having left behind all riches and secular things for Christ, have fled the world, and are called the "Lesser Brothers" and "Lesser Sisters." They are held in great reverence by the Lord Pope and the cardinals, but they are not occupied in any way with temporal things; rather with fervent desire and ardent zeal they work every day so that they might withdraw the souls that are perishing from the vanities of the world and lead them with them. And by the grace of God, they have already borne much fruit . . . By day they enter cities and villages, so that they might make their work profitable by their actions; at night they return to the hermitage or a solitary place,

giving themselves to contemplation. The women live together near the cities in various hospices. They accept nothing, but live from the work of their hands (cf. 1 Cor. 4:12); they are very much offended and disturbed, however, because they are honored by the clergy and laity more than they would like.[5]

De Vitry's portrait of the early Franciscan movement is one of great simplicity. He never uses the words "convent" or monastery". Nor is there any word about cloister for the women. The way these women worked with their hands for their livelihood is similar to the life of the Beguines. "Hospice" seems to have been a general term for the dwellings of many of the groups in the women's religious movement of the time, including the Beguines and the Poor Clares.[6] Some of the Beguines were indeed involved in the care of the sick, and perhaps some of the earliest Franciscan women, outside of Clare and her sisters, were as well.

It is possible that de Vitry, as a supporter of the Beguines, was led by his enthusiasm to see the same characteristics as the Beguines in the Franciscan women. There is other evidence, however, of an active life among early Franciscan women during the lifetime of St. Francis. It is found in the *Legend of Perugia*, in a passage describing the conversion of many inhabitants of the Umbrian town of Greccio.

> Through his [Francis'] example and preaching and that of his brothers, by the grace of God, many of them entered the Order. Many women preserved their virginity, remaining in their own homes and adopting a religious habit. And although each one had her own house, each lived the common life virtuously, afflicting her body with fasting and prayer, so that by their way of life it seemed to the people and to the brothers that they were not among lay people and their relatives, but

among holy and religious people who had served
Christ for a long time, although they were young and
very simple. That is why blessed Francis often said
to the brothers in speaking of the men and women of
this town: "There is not one large city were so many
have been converted to penance; and yet Greccio is
only a small town."[7]

As Franciscan scholars Damien Vorreux and Theophile
Desbonnets have noted, these women's way of life had some traits in
common with the Beguines.[8] The fact that they were living in their
own homes and were in the lay state also made them similar in
many ways to the early lay penitential communities in Italy.

According to some scholars, St. Francis was very concerned
about or even hostile towards the continuing inclusion of women in
the order, and failed to support Clare's commitment to complete
poverty.[9] The position of women was clearly a concern in the order.
A passage inserted into the Franciscan Rule in 1221 insisted that
friars not allow women to make vows of obedience to them, though
it was removed in the Rule of 1223.[10] Nevertheless, this account of
the sisters in Greccio seems to be confirmation that Francis desired
to see women as part of the active movement of penitence. Perhaps
he saw the non-cloistered way of life of these early sisters as a
solution to the problem caused by the necessity for the friars to
support cloistered women.

In Germany, there were often ties between the friars and the
Beguines. Later in the thirteenth century, north of the river Main, in
the territory where Elizabeth lived, Franciscan and Dominican friars
ministered to the communities of Beguines, who often lived near
their foundations.[11] Elizabeth's religious community was in some
ways similar to these. We can see a corresponding development in
groups of religious women south of the Main as well. Several
communities in Augsburg, Munich, Nuremberg and other southern
German cities started out as Beguines in the thirteenth century,
gradually accepted the spiritual guidance of the Friars Minor, and

became Tertiaries after the Rule of Nicholas IV was approved in 1289.12

Many women in the Franciscan movement, as well as the Beguines and other religious women, became involved in active works of charity, particularly work with the sick. Their activity could be either formal or informal. This work grew from small beginnings in the thirteenth century. Elizabeth was the earliest woman attached to the Franciscan movement who was known to do hospital work. Others followed her later in the century. Margaret of Cortona (1247-1297), the mistress of a nobleman of Montepulciano, experienced a profound conversion after his death; after joining the Third Order in 1275, she dedicated herself to the service of the sick; in 1278 she founded a hospital in Cortona and a confraternity to serve it. Margaret herself eventually became a recluse.13

Angela of Foligno, a wealthy and worldly woman, experienced a similar conversion. After a mystical experience in Assisi in 1291, and the deaths of her husband and children, Angela joined the Franciscan Third Order under the newly promulgated rule of Nicholas IV. She and her close companion Masazuola served the lepers at the hospital in Foligno.14

Thus there were many similarities between the lives of some non-cloistered Franciscan women and the lives of the Beguines. There were also a number of contacts between the Franciscan friars and Beguine communities. The life Elizabeth lived with the friars in Marburg was quite similar to that of women in German Beguine communities supervised by the friars. In this, Maurer was quite right in saying that Elizabeth lived a Beguine life and spirituality. But this did not prevent her from being a Franciscan as well, and from following Franciscan spirituality, as Clare did even while following the Benedictine rule for a good portion of her religious life. The complete lack of possessions is often thought to be the hallmark of the Franciscan life, and Elizabeth apparently did not vow complete poverty. But she clearly practiced poverty in her everyday life, in the sense of living with the poor, being content with the poorest food and clothing, and accepting want and hardship in order to give to others.

The authors who have written about Elizabeth have put forward different ideas about what makes spirituality Franciscan. Pásztor gives a list of characteristics, such as imitation of Christ, "the poor Christ, the suffering Christ, Christ crucified,"15 while Maurer tends to rely on juridical questions, such as Elizabeth's vow of obedience to Conrad of Marburg, which did not seem to him to fit in with Franciscan tertiary life. The fact that the Anonymous Franciscan was willing to see many similarities between Elizabeth and Clare is a clear indication that it was neither religious practices, such as cloister or fasting, nor the rule that made someone a Franciscan in the eyes of a thirteenth-century friar. A habit and a way of life that were Franciscan in their characteristics were what was important to him. As he quotes the details of Elizabeth's life from the early testimonies, he delights in recounting her Franciscan witness to Christ, while the juridical details seemed somewhat confusing to him. It must have been just as confusing in another way for Elizabeth's contemporaries, who were not looking back in hindsight as he was on institutional developments, and for Elizabeth and her companions themselves, involved in the difficult task of seeking their own vocation and charism within the Franciscan movement.

Elizabeth's Religious Vocation in Light of Her Time

As we have seen, living the life of a wage-earner in service to Christ's poor was the ideal to which Elizabeth dedicated her life, and this led to a conflict with her desire for complete poverty. As Conrad's and Isentrude's testimonies indicate, Elizabeth strongly desired a life of mendicancy. She certainly relied on gifts as well as wages for her support, and this made her in some way like the friars. However, begging from door to door, like Francis and the earliest friars, was forbidden to women. Living as a recluse, enclosed and hidden from view, supported by the alms of others, would have allowed her to pursue perfect poverty. Elizabeth was attracted to both mendicancy and enclosed poverty. The testimony of Brother Gerard indicates that at times Elizabeth's sisters begged for alms from the friars. This may have been a socially acceptable way for the sisters to beg openly, and perhaps also a gesture undertaken to remind them not only of the poverty they should have, but also their fraternal link with St. Francis and his order. Francis himself showed this fraternal link, even to depending on Clare's charity. Once, when he ran out of bread to serve some visiting friars, he sent to St. Clare to ask her for some. The two tiny rolls she sent miraculously multiplied and were enough to feed everyone.[16]

Elizabeth's attachment to manual labor such as spinning was found among the Beguines, but also was an important part of the primitive Franciscan community. Francis stressed it in his Testament, though he must have known the friars were unlikely to follow his wish: "And I worked with my hands, and I wish to work, and I firmly will that my brothers work at some honest occupation."[17]

Apart from her difficult relationship with the very severe Conrad of Marburg, nowhere is there any indication in the sources for Elizabeth's life of a direct conflict between her and the ecclesiastical hierarchy over her way of life. We do not know what Conrad's removal of her closest companions, Guda and Isentrude, who received the gray habit with her, might have meant. We know that he had rejected a wandering life of begging for Elizabeth; perhaps he was unhappy about other aspects of her religious life as well. It may have been that he wanted to break up her sisterhood. Or it may have been that Conrad, chosen by the Pope as her protector, was following the Pope's orders in regard to overseeing Elizabeth's religious life as well as her personal religious needs as a confessor. In this case, restrictions on her unusual life might have represented the Pope's will. We can only speculate, for nothing in the sources really suggests this clearly enough for us to be certain.

Pope Gregory IX, as we have seen, cautioned her not to leave the contemplative life for the active until she was really perfected. Later, by issuing a bull with an indulgence for her hospital in 1229, and by sending relics for it, he clearly showed his approval of the institution and her work there. Yet there is no evidence that he had any intention as yet of imposing a particular rule on Elizabeth as he had for Clare and her sisters and other groups of religious women. In fact, given the Pope's closeness and support, it would have been easy for Elizabeth to have founded a monastery like Clare's. The best explanation is that she was still uncertain about which of the two alternatives she might follow: the life of an enclosed recluse or cloistered sister, or the life of a non-cloistered sister engaged in the active life. Either choice involved a sacrifice of one important aspect of the religious life. This was also an important question for the women who we know for certain directly followed Elizabeth. While all of them cherished Franciscan ideals, some, like Agnes of Bohemia, chose the cloistered life, while others in France, Germany and the Low Countries followed the life of active service. Their stories illustrate the different ways they struggled to combine the various aspects of their Franciscan religious life.

A Cloistered Follower of Elizabeth: Agnes of Bohemia

The first of these alternatives, the cloistered life, was chosen by Elizabeth's first cousin, St. Agnes of Bohemia, another Franciscan woman who has been little known and studied until recently. Born in 1205, thus just two years older than Elizabeth, she was the daughter of King Ottokar I of Bohemia and Constance of Hungary, the sister of Elizabeth's father, Andrew II. Agnes devoted herself to charitable works at an early age, and refused all offers of marriage, including one from the Emperor Frederick II. She first heard about the religious life of the Franciscans when the Friars Minor arrived in Prague in 1225. According to her earliest legend, written by a Franciscan friar,[18] she asked them about the rule and life of Clare and her sisters, and they replied that those who wished to enter this order and live "according to the tenor of the Holy Gospel" should "sell all their property and give it to the poor and serve the poor Christ in poverty and humility." Immediately Agnes said: "This is what I desire, this is what I long for with all my heart."[19] According to Gregory IX's letter to Beatrice of Castile, her vocation was also due to the influence of her cousin Elizabeth. In the letter's long apostrophe to the saint, he said:

> . . .the virgin Agnes, daughter of the King of Bohemia, who you [i. e. Elizabeth] have also inebriated with the draught of this vessel, and in whose so tender age and harsh life we perceive the sign of heavenly preservation, has fled the imperial splendors that were offered to her, as though they were venomous reptiles, and, naked, seizing the triumphant banner of the cross (Mt. 5:21), is already going to meet her Bridegroom with lighted lamps, accompanied by a choir of consecrated virgins.[20]

We do not know what kind of contact there was between Agnes and Elizabeth, although Clare herself counseled Agnes about the religious life and poverty in four surviving letters.[21] It is evident, however, that Agnes was just as strong a personality as Elizabeth and Clare. Unlike Elizabeth, however, she had a definite religious rule and order in mind from the beginning. She sold all of her gold and silver jewels, and distributed the proceeds to the poor. She began founding her convent in 1232, on land donated by her brother, King Wenceslas I; she also built a monastery nearby for the Friars Minor. In 1233, this was followed by the construction of a hospital for the poor, built on land donated by her mother Constance. Agnes then founded the Crosiers of the Red Star, a lay confraternity of men to serve the sick. This group eventually developed into an order which operated more than sixty hospitals in Bohemia, Silesia, Hungary, Poland and Austria. There was also a female branch of this order, dedicated to the care of poor and

abandoned children.[22] The author of Agnes' life says that she did
this in imitation of Elizabeth:

> Finally, in imitation of her cousin, blessed
> Elisabeth, she constructed a religious hospital for the
> sick at the foot of the bridge of the city of Prague in
> honor of the most holy confessor Francis, which she
> enriched with ample income and possessions,
> locating there the Crosiers with a red cross and star,
> so they might direct the care of the above-mentioned
> sick people, and as each one's work might be, they
> might provide what was necessary for all.[23]

Agnes' work was carried out in concert with Pope Gregory
IX. In a letter of April 13, 1234 (*Sincerum animi*), the Pope informed
John, the Minister of Saxony, and Thomas, the *custos* in Bohemia,
that Agnes had decided to join the order of the "poor enclosed
nuns" and ordered them by papal authority to make her the abbess
of the Monastery of St. Francis.[24] He also took her monastery under
the protection of the Holy See. Several Poor Clares from Trent,
already formed in the life of the order, entered the monastery
together with Agnes and her companions, who were all women
from the Bohemian nobility.

In spite of her enclosure, Agnes herself managed to take
some part in the service of the poor at the hospital. Her biographer
gives a graphic picture of this:

> The illustrious virgin. . . also used to send
> special dishes of hers prepared with her most pure
> hands with great devotion to the sick and weak
> brothers, with Martha a solicitous minister of Christ,
> striving to refresh Christ in his poor. . . But also with
> a stupendous excess of humility and forgetting her
> inborn refinement, arranging to have brought to her
> by a pious device the stinking and dirty clothes of
> the sick sisters and the lepers, she washed them with

her tender hands, so that from such frequent rubbing she often had her hands wounded on account of the harshness of the lye and liniments. In addition, she sewed their torn clothing in the silence of the night, not wanting to have any of them as inspector of what she was doing but God, from whom alone she expected the reward for her pious works. . . When this wonderful sanctity reached the ears of the virgin St. Clare, rejoicing at such noble offspring made fruitful by divine grace, she magnified the Most High.[25]

Here there is evidence of Agnes' desire to imitate both Clare and Elizabeth, and Clare's approval of her charitable work. Clare herself was always mindful of her local community in Assisi. We learn from her canonization process that the people of the town would often bring their sick to Clare at San Damiano; she would touch them and make the sign of the cross over them, and they would get well.[26] The author of Agnes' legend says that charity was a lifelong trait of hers: "Both while she lived in the world and while she was in religious life, she turned her compassionate mind toward all the afflicted, and she helped all those who had recourse to her, with pious remedies before God and men."[27]

Thus Agnes was able to preserve both enclosure and poverty, and still engage in some kind of concrete service to the poor in imitation of Elizabeth. This is important, because for the most part Agnes' biographers have concentrated on her battle for poverty, rather than her charitable service. But recently one of her biographers noted, "Already in Elizabeth . . . we find some of those traits of Franciscan spirituality that we also find later in Agnes: the Gospel ideal as a participation in the fate of the disinherited, the care, even material care, of the poor, and mendicancy as a renunciation of security in order to choose a precarious life."[28]

Agnes was preoccupied not only with charity, but with the fight for true Franciscan poverty. The land on which the monastery was built was in the possession of the Holy See. Since the papal decree *Quo elongati* in 1230, and in some cases even before, ownership by the Holy See or some other body or person and *usus* of it by Franciscan religious was the usual solution to the problem of ownership of property. But In 1235, in the letter *Cum relicta saeculi*, Gregory IX, who felt that the sisters must have an income, announced that he was granting them the use of all the income from the hospital, which was to be considered part of the monastery, and offering the nuns even more property if necessary:

> Being inclined to your supplications, we have considered the Hospital of St. Francis, located next to your monastery, which you, daughter, as Abbess, constructed on land of the Roman Church, with all that belongs to it, as perpetually conceded to that same monastery: establishing nonetheless that the same hospital with all that belongs to it may not be separated from the monastery itself in any way or by any device. But an increase of its possessions may be granted for your use and for those who succeed you, safeguarding always the authority of the Apostolic See.[29]

But for Agnes, dedicated to poverty, even this much in the way of possessions was just what she did not want. She must have made her unhappiness with this solution known, for the Pope agreed to the separation in another letter (*Omnipotens Deus*), in which he decreed that the hospital was to be taken under the ownership of the Holy See, and that it was to be separated from the monastery, and that the brothers who took care of the sick there were to be erected into a canonical religious order.[30] On April 15, 1238, the Pope wrote to Agnes again (*Pia credulitate tenentes*):

> . . . since, as it appears from evident signs, you. . . are convinced that it is improper for servants and handmaids to luxuriate in delights when the

only begotten Creator of all things lay in a manger, wrapped in poor swaddling clothes, thus it is that we accept your free renunciation of the Hospital of Saint Francis in the Diocese of Prague together with its rights and pertinences, which was given to you at one time and through you to your monastery. Since you who have held visible things in contempt in order to hasten to the delights of things unseen, are desirous of avoiding that obstacle to seeking unhindered the face of God which is accustomed to arise in the thorns of temporal things. . .we grant to you by the authority of this letter that you cannot be forced against your will to accept any other possessions from this time on.[31]

This was Agnes' "Privilege of Poverty," which had so far been granted only to Clare and her sisters. But Agnes continued to contend with later Popes over her desire to live according to the "form of life" given by Francis to Clare and her sisters. Agnes continued her care for the sick at the hospital until her death in 1282. After popular devotion had considered her "Blessed" for some six centuries, her cult was formally recognized by Pope Pius IX in 1874, and she was canonized by Pope John Paul II in 1989.

The difficulties that Agnes faced in reconciling her life of complete poverty and enclosure with the desire for charity and service were clearly very much like those Elizabeth experienced. Given these difficulties, we can only wonder if Elizabeth might eventually have become cloistered like Agnes – or whether she might have founded an order of active life if she had lived longer. In fact, her influence was very much alive in a number of non-cloistered female communities of active life in the later Middle Ages which were inspired by her example. Let's now turn to them.

Elizabeth's Followers in the Active Life

After Nicholas IV formally promulgated the rule of the Franciscan Third Order by the bull *Supra montem* in 1289, a number of groups of religious women began to follow it, though it was not originally intended for religious but for those in secular fraternities. The religious ran into difficulties because religious community life was seen to be in conflict with the secular nature of the Third Order rule. The papal document *Sancta Roma*, issued in 1317, condemned those "who said they belong to the Third Order of Penance of St. Francis and yet were living in community."[32] This was because living in community was thought to require profession of the three vows of poverty, chastity and obedience–vows which are nowhere mentioned in the Rule of Nicholas IV. Nonetheless, eventually many non-enclosed sisters of the Third Order gained papal permission to follow this rule. Among them were a number who were inspired by Elizabeth's way of life.

Sisters in Service to the Poor

One such early congregation was actually named for her. The Elizabethines were first formed in the thirteenth century among groups of women in Germany, Austria and France devoted to the care of the sick; they were known as Sisters of Mercy or Sisters of St. Elizabeth in France, and the Elizabethines (*Elisabethinen* or *Elisabeterinnin*) in Germany. They began with simple communities of common life which grew up around hospitals, churches and "Houses of Mercy" which served the poor. In time, they slowly transformed themselves into religious, at first with simple vows, and later with solemn vows. They followed the Rule of Nicholas IV, with their own constitutions added. Many of their houses were named for St. Elizabeth. The first congregations began forming at the end of the thirteenth century, through communities of sisters giving birth to daughter houses and the forming of confederations among independent houses. Shortly after the Reformation, there were 3,800 houses in Europe, some of which still survive today.

Other groups gave rise to other institutes which carried on the same work and sometimes had the same name. It is difficult to determine their exact role and influence, however, for they are often confused with the *Soeurs grises* (Gray sisters) or Hospital Sisters discussed below.[33] Raffaele Pazzelli says: "The evolution of the Elizabethan sisters was typical of the transformation of the Third Franciscan Order from secular to regular status."[34]

The *Soeurs grises* and the *Soeurs de la Celle* arose in northern France and Flanders, where groups of women who worked in hospitals began to live a common life.[35] (The "celle" probably refers to a hermitage or small monastery, thus to the smallness of the communities). The first house of the "Soeurs grises" was the Maison de Sainte-Marguerite in Saint-Omer, founded in 1350, where the sisters lived by manual labor and followed the Rule of Nicholas IV; the seven religious of the house pronounced solemn vows on May 1, 1388. The sisters moved into the convent of Sainte-Catherine de Sion in 1433, which was located next to a hospital where they took care of the sick. There were soon a number of other houses. The *Soeurs grises* became a congregation in 1413, when they were approved by John XXIII in the bull *Personas vacantes*. According to the statutes of the sisters, redacted in French and passed at a chapter in 1483 at Wisebecq, their aim was to regulate themselves and "by going out among secular people to practice the works of mercy, to give such a good example that they can give corporal consolation to poor sick people and to edify spiritually all sorts of persons."[36] Great care was taken, however, to have two sisters always go out together, never stay out of each other's sight while talking to seculars, and not to eat or stay the night outside of the convent unless necessary. Much of the rapid growth of the *Soeurs grises* in the fifteenth century is probably due to the aid and protection given to them by Isabel, duchess of Burgundy. Evidence of these sisters' devotion to St. Elizabeth can be found in the names of their convents and hospitals, including the "Maison St. Elisabeth" in Roye, and the "Hôpital Sainte-Elisabeth" in Thuin (Hainaut).

The *Soeurs de la Celle* were sometimes called "Daughters of Bread for God" because they often went begging for bread for the needy; like the *Soeurs grises*, they cared for the sick in their homes. At first, they conformed to the rule of Nicholas IV without pronouncing vows. Then, in 1377, they received permission from a bull of Pope Gregory XI to pronounce vows and to form a community. Around this time they also came to be known as the "Black Sisters" from the color of the mantles they wore over their gray habits. They seem to have begun in Saint-Omer, and spread outwards to found houses in neighboring towns. At the end of the fifteenth century they had convents in the dioceses of Therouanne, Tournai, Cambrai, Arras and Amiens. They also had a number of houses and hospitals dedicated to St. Elizabeth. In 1474, Pope Sixtus IV placed them, at their request, under the obedience of the Friars Minor of the Observance.[37] In 1676, the sisters in Saint-Omer and some other houses were cloistered and were transferred to the Conceptionist Order.[38]

One notable thing about these women was their mobility. They were not bound to their convent. In fact, rather than operate hospitals, they went out into the community to serve the sick, as Elizabeth herself often did. Some houses, such as St. Catherine de Sion in Saint-Omer, did possess and serve at hospitals; the land provided them with some revenues, but also undoubtedly with a great deal of expense, which they may have found it difficult to meet, or which they did not find in agreement with their desire to remain poor. Also, they moved only slowly toward taking solemn religious vows. In fact, it was common among all these groups of Franciscan women for poverty to be the last vow they adopted, because they knew that the care of the sick made the vow of poverty difficult.[39]

The full extent of Elizabeth's influence on other women of her time will probably never be known. We do know that after her death, a number of Beguines who had as their mission the care of the sick began willingly to enter the Franciscan Third Order following her example.[40] Elizabeth herself carried on the tradition of both the Franciscans and the Beguines who came before her in her search for her religious life and vocation.

The Franciscan Beguines

Elizabeth was just one of many women who lived as both Franciscans and Beguines in the thirteenth century. Another example is Douceline of Digne (1214-1274), a Franciscan and Beguine who founded the community called the "Ladies of Roubaud." Although there is no indication that she knew of or consciously imitated Elizabeth, her life is very instructive in regard to some of the questions we have been considering. The life of her written in Provençal around the beginning of the fourteenth century is of special interest because it was apparently written by one of her sisters, most likely Felipa Porcelet (ca. 1250-1316), who succeeded Douceline as head of the little community in 1274.[41] Therefore, it gives a good picture of how the sisters viewed their way of life.

Douceline was the sister of Hugh of Digne, the well-known Franciscan preacher and follower of Joachim of Fiore. Their parents, Berenguier of Digne and Huga of Barjols, were of the merchant class. Douceline's mother died when she was about sixteen, and after she moved from Barjols to Hyères with her father, she devoted most of her time to charity, looking after the poor people her father took into their home. After her father died a few years later, Douceline continued her charitable work at the hospital in Hyères with several other women. She prayed devoutly to God to "let her find an order and a way of living that would please Him more and would put her in the condition that would most please Him." At that time, said her biographer, "there was no religious order of Beguines, nor had they been mentioned in Provence."[42] One day, while she and three of her companions were returning from the hospital, her prayers were answered:

Suddenly two humble ladies, who resembled each other and who were walking very modestly with clear white veils of lace covering their faces, appeared to them on the road. Their clothes were all black. They were leading a little girl who was walking with them. They greeted them very joyously. Stopping in front of [Doucelina], they looked at her. When the holy woman saw them, she was immediately full of marvelous joy. Full of ardor, she asked them who they were and from which order. Then all three together took off the mantels [sic] they wore on their heads saying:"We," they said, "are from that order which pleases God." And showing the veils that they were wearing, they told her: "Take this and follow us." Immediately they disappeared, so that [Doucelina and her companions] never saw where they went . . . But the saint, through the spirit of God, understood immediately how they meant for her to follow them; she proposed firmly in her heart, above all orders, to take this form and this example in its entirety.[43]

Douceline kept this vision in mind, and after she had spent some time with the Poor Clares in Genoa during her brother Hugh's absence, she told him of her vision and her desires; he encouraged her to adopt the habit and way of life she had chosen. She and several companions made their vows of virginity to him around 1240. Douceline also "vowed, in the hands of the holy father, Brother Hugh of Digne, to observe with great ardour the holy poverty of Jesus Christ, just as Saint Francis observed it and gave it, which is to say that she had nothing of her own."[44] Her companions wished to do the same, but Hugh would not permit it. The author of the *Vida* says:

[He preferred] that they should live well and should be able to pay alms, because for women it [poverty] is not a very sure thing and especially for young women. Thus the holy mother, through the counsel of the holy father, wanted them to adopt a moderate poverty so that they could have their need and their necessity, poorly and moderately.[45]

In this way, Douceline and her sisters were able to continue serving the poor in hospitals and in their homes. The community she founded expanded, and soon there was a second one in Marseilles and perhaps others as well.

Douceline, according to the author of the life, always had a strong devotion to St. Francis, and put her sisters under his protection. Indeed, she used to say that "under the wings of St. Francis, all those who persevere and conduct themselves or live under the counsel of the order will be saved; because special grace is given to my lord St. Francis, and special consolation will be done to every person who faithfully followed his counsel and that of his order."[46] In this extravagant claim for the Franciscans, we can see the influence of the Spirituals and of Douceline's brother Hugh and his Joachimite leanings.

While the life clearly describes Douceline and her companions in a number of instances as belonging to a religious order, Salimbene, one of the few other existing contemporary sources for Douceline's life, says that "she never entered any religious order, but lived chastely and religiously in the world. She chose as her spouse the Son of God and as her special object of devotion blessed Francis, whose cord she girded herself with, in sign of his love."[47] Clearly here is another case of confusion about the nature of Beguine /Franciscan life for women – were they actually religious or not?

Perhaps the most remarkable passage in the life of Douceline, however, is one in which the women's various feelings about their devotion to St. Francis, their habit and the criticism of them often expressed by their society are clearly summarized. Some time after Douceline's death, one of the Ladies of Roubaud also died, and another sister had a vision of what happened to her soul when it was met by the saints in the earthly paradise. When the holy ones asked who she was, the sister replied that she was governed under the hand of St. Francis. "Under the hand of Saint Francis you are governed!" they asked suspiciously. "And how do you not wear his habit, nor the habit of Saint Clare, nor of the other orders? Who are you and from what order?" The author continues:

> Then came Jesus Christ, the equitable and compassionate Lord; and he terminated the questions, saying: "What are you asking, you others?" The saints said: "Lord there is a soul whom we don't know, nor do we know from which order she is, nor do we recognize her habit. She said that under the hand of Saint Francis she is governed, but she doesn't wear his habit, nor Saint Clare's, nor that of the other orders; nor is she a nun, nor do we know who she is." The Lord sweetly replied, with a kind face: "I know her. She is," he said, "from an order that I love, which I have in my keeping and which is governed under the hand of Saint Francis. Indeed she says with truth that under his hand it is governed, but she doesn't wear his habit. I know who she is."
>
> So said our Lord, and he saved her and took her aside, just as his Lamb that he had bought dearly. For this reason, it is not important to fear for this holy order, that it might perish under the hand and the administration of Saint Francis, the one which will be continually in the keeping of Our Lord.[48]

Here we find some of the same concerns that we find in Elizabeth's life: these women knew that they were following an unusual way of life and wearing a "different" habit; they were aware that people questioned whether they were part of a religious order or whether they were really attached to the Franciscans, and that some -- perhaps even the saints in paradise -- were suspicious of them. There is a difference, however, perhaps accounted for by the passage of time. Elizabeth's remark about wearing her habit because it was despised, was the statement of a woman at the beginning of her vocation; in the case of Douceline's sisters, who were aware that they were part of a long-standing religious community, concern gives way to an assurance of the special nature of their religious vocation and its protection by God.

Conclusions

Elizabeth's experiences in her active religious life clearly show the fluid, experimental nature of the female Franciscan movement in the early thirteenth century. Elizabeth's life was not limited by an institutional framework, since such a framework did not really exist outside the traditional cloistered life at that time. This gave her some freedom to experiment. Although pressure by the hierarchy toward regularized monastic life and cloister for the new groups of religious women was already underway, there were still a number of possibilities open to non-cloistered women. We can only speculate about what might have happened, but perhaps Elizabeth was simply moving slowly in deciding what form her religious life might take, and it was still only in its preliminary stages at the time of her death.

Nevertheless, she might have found institutional acceptance for her ideas difficult. The pope who guided her first religious steps, Gregory IX, was reluctant to concede that religious women could live a life of complete poverty even when cloistered, as the examples of his interventions with St. Clare and St. Agnes of Bohemia show. He also found it hard to accept the idea of female religious living outside the cloister. Nor would Elizabeth have had an easy time finding any religious rule to follow. Because the Fourth Lateran Council had decreed that all religious must live according to an already-approved rule, the attempts of Clare and Agnes to live according to the "form of life" Francis had given Clare met with opposition from Gregory IX because this form of life had not been approved before the council. No existing rule was sufficiently flexible to meet the needs of those women who, like many of the Beguines and Elizabeth herself, were trying to live lives of service to others amid the social realities of the thirteenth century. The original movement of the Brothers and Sisters of Penance was only conceived for lay people not living in community, and was scarcely beginning to be formed in Elizabeth's lifetime. As yet, it did not have a recognized rule for religious. So it is not surprising that she did not live according to a religious rule. Nor is it surprising that she has often confused modern historians who need to state facts briefly in a structured way, and who find it difficult to determine where she fits into the accepted categories of religious, layperson, penitent or Beguine. In many ways, Elizabeth did not conform completely to any of these states. Wishing to be a Franciscan, but also non-cloistered, she found a partial solution to her difficulties in the way of life of the Beguines. But she is also a sign of, and an inspiration for, changes that were later to take place as new forms of religious life continued to be developed to answer the needs of the time.

It is possible that Elizabeth, understanding the needs of her time as she did, might have actually tried to found a religious congregation devoted to hospital work if she had lived longer. Or perhaps she would have entered a cloister like Agnes of Bohemia or become a recluse like Margaret of Cortona. The possibility of founding a new order, with its almost inevitable conflicts, was left unresolved with her early death. Other women were to carry on her ideals.

In examining the lives of the women who followed her or lived in similar ways, including the cloistered St. Agnes, the Third Order hospital sisters, and Douceline's Franciscan Beguines, all of whom followed the Franciscan ideals, we see the same sort of conflicts that Elizabeth faced. The cloistered Agnes considered it an important part of her vocation to serve the poorest in a personal way, but had some difficulty reconciling the possession of a hospital with poverty. With the later hospital sisters – the Elizabethines, the *Soeurs grises* and *Soeurs de la Celle* – we see the difficulties that professing vows of poverty raised in regard to their active life. While Elizabeth was able to adapt the way of the Beguines to the active life she felt called to, the later hospital sisters happily had the opportunity of adopting the Rule of Nicholas IV and making it work for them. Douceline and her sisters faced possibly being despised by the world because of their religious choice, and they too ran up against the difficulties of vowing poverty and yet being in active service. While their solutions to their problems may have differed from Elizabeth's, these women all shared the same dedication to Franciscan ideals, and the same difficulties in reconciling the need for poverty and service. Elizabeth was one of many women in her century and later feeling their way toward a kind of religious life in which they could serve both God and the poor in the Franciscan way.

Notes

¹ Fiona Bowie, ed., *Beguine Spirituality*, translated by Oliver Davies (New York: Crossroads, 1990), 22; McKelvie, *Retrieving a Living Tradition*, p.58.

² *Prime Manifestazioni*, p. 129.

³ André Vauchez, "L'ideal de sainteté dans le mouvement féminin franciscain," *Movimento religioso femminile e francescanesimo nel secolo xiii* (Assisi: Società Internazionale degli Studi Francescani, 1980), especially pp. 327, 329.

⁴ McKelvie, *Retrieving a Living Tradition*, p. 19.

⁵ R. B. C. Huygens, *Lettres de Jacques de Vitry (1160/1170-1240), Évêque de Saint-Jean d'Acre* (Leiden, 1960), pp. 75-76.

[6] Armstrong, *Clare of Assisi, Early Documents*, p. 314, note b.

[7] *Legend of Perugia*, no. 34. The Latin text is from the critical edition by Rosalind Brooke: *Scripta Leonis, Rufini et Angeli, Sociorum S. Francisci: The Writings of Leo, Rufino and Angelo, Companions of St. Francis* (Oxford, Clarendon Press, 1970 [reprint 1990]), p. 148.

[8] Marion A. Habig., O.F.M., *St. Francis of Assisi: Writings and Early Biographies* (Chicago: Franciscan Herald Press, 1973), p. 1095, note.

[9] McNamara, *Sisters in Arms*, 251-52; Neel, "Origins of the Beguines," pp. 240-41.

[10] First Rule of 1221, ch. XII; in *Die Opuscula des hl. Franziskus von Assisi*, ed. Esser, p. 388.

[11] John B. Freed, "Urban Development and the '*Cura Monialium*' in Thirteenth-Century Germany," *Viator* 3 (1972): 311-327; see also his *The Friars and German Society*, 49-50, and Pazzelli, *The Franciscan Sisters*, pp. 25-26.

[12] Englebert Grau, "Der franziskanische Dritte Ordens in Oberdeutschland im 13. und 14. Jahrhundert," in Mariano D'Alatri, ed., *I frati penitenti de San Francesco nella società del due e trecento* (Rome: Istituto Storico dei Cappuccini, 1977), pp. 125-32.

[13] For Margaret's life and revelations, see her *vita* by her Franciscan confessor Giunta Bevegnati in AASS, Februarii 3:302-363.

[14] Angela of Foligno, *Angela of Foligno: Complete Works*, p. 31.

[15] Pásztor, "Sant'Elisabetta d'Ungheria," p. 93.

[16] This incident was recounted by Bernard of Bessa, St. Bonaventure's secretary in his *De Laudibus* VI, AF 3:673; cited in Vorreux, *Sainte Claire d'Assise: Documents*, pp. 272-73.

[17] Testament, Esser, *Die Opuscula*, p. 440.

[18] This life of Agnes was written about 1328, probably by a Friar Minor of her Monastery of St. Francis in Prague. The Latin text

is in Walter Seton, *Some New Sources For the Life of Blessed Agnes of Bohemia* (Aberdeen: University Press, 1915), with a study of the sources.

[19] Seton, *Some New Sources*, p. 78.

[20] Lemmens, "Zur Biographie," p. 4.

[21] The Latin text of these letters can be found in Walter Seton, "The Letters from Saint Clare to Blessed Agnes of Bohemia," AFH 17 (1924): 509-19. There is an English translation in Armstrong, *Clare of Assisi: Early Documents*, pp. 33-52.

[22] Alfonso Marini, *Agnese di Boemia*, con la collaborazione di Paola Ungarelli (Rome: Istituto Storico dei Cappuccini, 1991), p. 64.

[23] Seton, *Some New Sources*, p. 78.

[24] BF 1:135-36.

[25] Seton, *Some New Sources*, pp. 83-84.

[26] Lazzeri, "Il processo di canonizazione di S. Chiari d'Assisi," p. 473.

[27] Seton, *Some New Sources*, p. 108.

[28] Marini, *Agnes di Boemia*, p. 58.

[29] BF 1:156.

[30] From *Codex diplomaticus et epistolaris regni Bohemiae* III, I, cit., 195-98, no. 160; cited in Marini, *Agnese di Boemia*, pp. 74-75.

[31] BF 1:236-37.

[32] Quoted in McKelvie, *Retrieving a Living Tradition*, pp. 72-73.

[33] Very little has been written about the Elizabethines; even the documents referring to them are scarce. There is some information on them in Pazzelli, *The Franciscan Sisters*, pp. 52-53. See also E. Frascadore, "Elisabettine, Suore," *Dizionario degli Istituti di Perfezione* (Rome: Edizioni Paoline, 1974) 3, col. 1114-15.

³⁴ Pazzelli, *The Franciscan Sisters*, p. 53.

³⁵ Pierre Péano, *Le religiose francescane: Origini, storia e valori constanti* (Rome: Movimento francescani, 1983), 27; quoted in Pazzelli, *Franciscan Sisters*, p. 55.

³⁶ H. Lemaitre, "Statuts des religieuses du Tiers-Ordre Franciscain, dites soeurs grises hospitalières (1483)," AFH 4 (1911): 720.

³⁷ H. Lemaître, "Bulle inédite de Sixte IV (1474) en faveur des soeurs de la Celle," *Revue d'histoire franciscaine* 4 (1927): 361-68.

³⁸ For more on these two groups of sisters, see Jerome Goyens, "Chapitres des soeurs hospitalières en Flandres (1483-1528)," AFH 14 (1921): 199-208, and H. Lemaitre, "Les soins hospitaliers à domicile, données dès le xive siècle par des religieuses franciscaines, les soeurs noires et les soeurs grises: leurs maisons," *Revue d'histoire franciscaine* 1 (1924): 180-208.

³⁹ Pazzelli, *The Franciscan Sisters*, p. 56.

⁴⁰ Ancelet-Hustache, *Gold Tried by Fire,* p. 258.

⁴¹ Joseph Mathias Hyacinthe Albanés, ed., *La vie de sainte Douceline, fondatrice des Beguines de Marseille; composée au xiiie siècle en langue provençale* (Marseille: Étienne Camoin, 1879), pp. xvii-xx.

⁴² From Kathryn Betts Wolfkiel, ed. *"The Life of the Blessed Saint Douceline* (d. 1274): An Edition and Translation with Commentary" (Dissertation, Evanston Illinois, 1993) 2:236.

⁴³ Wolfkiel, *"The Life of the Blessed Saint Douceline,* 2:236-37.

⁴⁴ Wolfkiel, *The Life of Blessed Saint Douceline,* 2:255-56.

⁴⁵ Wolfkiel, *The Life of Blessed Saint Douceline,* 2:259.

⁴⁶ Wolfkiel, *The Life of Blessed Saint Douceline,* 2:332.

⁴⁷ Salimbene, *Cronica,* ed Scalia, 2:833.

⁴⁸ Wolfkiel, *The Life of Blessed Saint Douceline,* 2:377-78.

Chapter VIII

Conclusion

This study has examined the birth, development and nature of the Franciscan vocation of St. Elizabeth of Hungary against the background of the religious movement of the thirteenth century. I have tried to recover her true voice from centuries of traditions that have sometimes been distorted. Even the earliest sources show that there were attempts by contemporaries to control the portrayal of Elizabeth. Conrad of Marburg, her confessor, began trying shortly after her death to fit her into the contemporary mold of a woman saint with an emphasis on her religious life rather than her marriage, while her lady-in-wating Isentrude put forward a more positive view of Elizabeth's marriage. The position of authority of Elizabeth's brothers-in-law, Heinrich Raspe and Conrad, and Conrad's role in overseeing her canonization process may have intimidated the witnesses and kept them from revealing Heinrich's role in her expulsion from her dower castle. The Teutonic Order devoted itself to spreading Elizabeth's cult and writing her biography, perhaps even selecting the testimonies that would be included in the Dicta and omitting others. The Franciscans promulgated their own image of her, though somewhat later than the others.

When facing a complex situation like this, a historian has to deal with some difficult questions: how do we know which witnesses to trust? Can women's lives be recovered when they have been erased from a historiography originating in a patriarchal society? Aren't the lives of saints like Elizabeth a construction based on society's expectations of sanctity rather than historical reality? What about those saints who don't fit the typical pattern?

It is true that most texts are socially constructed in that they reflect something of a society's own views back onto itself. A great deal of what we learn from the documents about Elizabeth does show this construction of various views about her, none of them complete. But a number of aspects of her life find support in a large number of the witnesses, and a partly consistent picture does emerge. In looking for the relationships of saints with individuals and communities, we do find real evidence of personal interactions that are often very enlightening about both individuals and their society. This is what we find in studying Elizabeth's life. The sometimes contradictory views of witnesses about her reflect contradictions and conflicts in her society. The confusion that later writers experience in trying to characterize her life also reflects the often bewildering changes in religious life that were taking place in her time.

Now that we have studied the early testimonies in depth, we find that Elizabeth, like many other women, found a life in poverty and with the poor was an answer to her desire to serve God in the conditions of her time, and an answer to the injustices of her society. She lived her religious life both as a Beguine and a Franciscan though often the sources don't use these specific terms. This was a solution consonant with the needs of the time, and one that was adopted by a number of women, in spite of ecclesiastical pressures toward cloister and the provision of a safe income for women who felt spiritually compelled toward complete poverty. Elizabeth's religious life can be seen as one of real radical poverty both in fact and spirit, even without a vow of poverty, the juridical limitations of which would have prevented her from living an active life of charity for and among the poor. Elizabeth was the first woman religious in the Franciscan tradition to be known for hospital work, and served as an example to other sisters in active life. Elizabeth's struggles and those of the other women opened the way for the active life of women's congregations in the later Middle Ages.

The above summary of the growth and nature of Elizabeth's vocation shows the problems that she and other religious women faced in the context of their times. But not all of the women were alike in their personalities, in the specific problems they faced, in their social backgrounds, or in their conflicts with their families, friends, religious associates and members of the hierarchy. Understanding how individuals differ in response to social conditions shows us something both about those people and their societies. This is true of Elizabeth as well.

One of the questions I encountered in first beginning this study is: was Elizabeth typical or unusual for her time? Comparison of the tradition on Elizabeth with those of other women begins with the nature of the sources that have survived. Many holy women who were Elizabeth's contemporaries are known to us largely through the writings of male clerical biographers. For Marie d'Oignies, we have Jacques de Vitry, for Umiliana dei Cerchi, Vito da Cortona, for Margaret of Cortona, Giunta Bevegnati. For Elizabeth, the major source we possess is her canonization process (one of the relatively few surviving ones from this time). The main testimonies in the traditional version of the Dicta/Libellus are those of the four women who were Elizabeth's closest companions. They open up some unusual perspectives on her life not often found in the writings of male biographers.

Nevertheless, one of the similarities between Elizabeth and other women is that the male view has often prevailed in portrayals of her life. In some of the later lives like that of Caesarius of Heisterbach, Elizabeth's own voice and her own view of her marriage is drowned out by the opinion of her confessor, Conrad of Marburg. The new testimonies from the process included in the Anonymous Franciscan and other stories found in this life add more information about how some of Elizabeth's male contemporaries, the Franciscan friars, saw her. Often the way the friars portrayed their relationship to her was fairly stereotypical and similar to other male portrayals of holy women as being in some ways spiritually superior to the men who directed them. The friars portrayed themselves as relying on Elizabeth for knowledge of their inner lives and her direct contact with God. They felt that her spirituality increased the prestige of the order.

Elizabeth's relationship with the poor was like that of other women in the religious movement in that it was based not only on charity but sharing in the sufferings of the poor. But unlike some other women saints of the period, her social world encompassed both the feudal and the urban worlds and their differing social problems. Elizabeth seems to have gone farther than many in her choice for poverty, particularly in comparison to other women within her royal family. Her niece, Margaret of Hungary, practiced the extremes of being a servant girl within an enclosed Dominican monastery, not in contact with the poor in the streets of the towns. Her aunt St. Hedwig was tied to the older feudal world of a charity that still left a gap between rich and poor.

On the other hand, Elizabeth displayed a number of departures from the pattern expected of a medieval woman saint, a pattern that was marked by aversion to marriage, extreme fasting and other severe ascetic practices, and abundant description of their mystical experiences. Elizabeth is indeed presented as a mystic, but only a part of what we know of her is based on the brief descriptions of her mystical experiences.

Elizabeth was also like other medieval women saints and religious in that her life was one of process and struggle rather than sudden conversion. Most of all, she was fighting against the common difficulties and limitations that all women faced, such as controlling her dower and other property.

Elizabeth's major difference was in being a happily married woman for much of her short life, and a mother as well. This actually presented a major hurdle for her biographers. The

Anonymous Franciscan was uncomfortable about her marriage, addressing Elizabeth: "You always loved virginity, even though you gave birth to children."1 Lay sanctity may have been growing in popularity, but married sanctity caused difficulties for the Church with its exaltation of virginity over married sexuality. Even though she did not have some of the desired attributes, such as an extreme desire for virginity or a practice of marital continence, Elizabeth became a canonized saint perhaps because her prominence and her outstanding example of the virtues of charity and evangelical poverty were exactly the example needed by the Church in her time.

I hope my work will suggest some directions for future studies. The search for historical truth involves the integration of different types of knowledge. Different approaches are also needed for different types of sources, such as the judicial form of testimony in the canonization process on one hand, and literary texts on the other. The way in which the sources appear to portray Elizabeth differently from other women of her time may be due to the lack of certain other sources that might fill in the picture of her. Her own words, if we had them, would certainly add still another way of understanding her.

I believe it is possible to integrate individual in-depth studies like mine on Elizabeth's life with the quantitative surveys or the work done by Bynum, Goodich, and others, which try to find a variety of common characteristics in the lives of many medieval women. Surveys of this type can be valuable, because they show us what the expected characteristics of sanctity were, as they are found in literature and hagiography. But where a variety of sources, including eyewitness testimonies, are available, as in Elizabeth's case, we can form an approach to the saint as an individual. This allows some of the hypotheses about the common social characteristics of medieval women saints to be tested and placed in context.

In Elizabeth's case, an emphasis on the individual helps to balance the large-scale social studies and a concern with individuals. The new methodologies that have been developed for interactive study of different texts have added something to our understanding, as has the study of living saints and their communities. These methods have allowed some pre-conceived notions about saints to be tested. They show that not all writings about saints fit the same stereotypical pattern. Certainly in Elizabeth's case, some of the accepted notions about her marriage or relationship with Conrad of Marburg prove by careful examination of the texts to be more complex than previously imagined. The story of Elizabeth's expulsion after her husband's death, in which the testimonies do not fit preconceived views of a religious conversion, can be easily understood in regard to feudal custom of the time, and can actually reveal much about both a saint like Elizabeth and her society. The future of studies in hagiography and other medieval texts could profitably lie along these lines. This study has revealed, I hope, the possibilities of such work.

Finally, I hope that historians studying the lives of other Franciscan saints and religious will be able to profit by these methods and the insights of modern historians, as I have in studying Elizabeth. Understanding her in the context of her society gives us a clearer picture of her and makes the light of her holiness shine all the more brightly.

Notes

[1] T (90r), K [124ra], lines 673-74.

Afterword

A few medieval works on St. Elizabeth remain in manuscript and have never been examined; others are still unpublished or untranslated. Since this book first appeared, a new edition of the canonization process has been published, including not only Conrad's letter, the *Dicta* and the miracles, but various other pieces as well: Kenneth Baxter Wolf: *The Life and Afterlife of St. Elizabeth of Hungary: Testimony from her Canonization Hearings* (Oxford University Press, 2010). It does not, however, take into consideration the new evidence from the Anonymous Franciscan.

In time I hope to publish the whole of the canonization process, including the portions found in the Anonymous Franciscan. Clearly there is still a great deal to do before all the sources for Elizabeth's life are brought to light and their relationship is clarified. Given her importance and her wide appeal, I believe this will be accomplished before long.

Appendix:

Table of

The Anonymous Franciscan

and His Sources

This table shows the main sources used by the Anonymous Franciscan, as well as the new material he himself added. I am including the Biblioteca Laurenziana life as evidence of a transitional stage between the Valenciennes life and the final version of the Anonymous Franciscan, even though not all the material in it is included in the Anonymous Franciscan. The passages from the sources are arranged chronologically (across) and in the order in which they appear in the Anonymous Franciscan (down), though they are often in a different order in the original sources. I have indicated some of the differences and changes that exist even in similar passages.

Conrad's Letter (1232)	Testimony from Can. Process (1233-35)	Dicta/Libellus (1236-41)	Valenciennes Life (c 1250)	Biblioteca Laurenziana Life (Late 13th century?)	Anonymous Franciscan (1279-1301)
			Therefore Blessed Elizabeth, the daughter of the king of the Hungarians, nobly brought up in a palace and in purple, imbued with the Catholic faith…	Therefore Blessed Elizabeth, the daughter of the king of the Hungarians, nobly brought up in purple and refinements, imbued with the Catholic faith…	Therefore Blessed Elizabeth, the daughter of the king of the Hungarians, brought up in a palace and in noble purple, imbued with the Catholic faith…
	Her youthful games and virtues	Her youthful games and virtues	Youthful games and virtues		Her youthful games and virtues
	Her love for John the Baptist	Her love for John the Baptist			Her love for John the Baptist

Conrad's Letter (1232)	Testimony from Can. Process (1233-35)	Dicta/Libellus (1236-41)	Valenciennes Life (c 1250)	Biblioteca Laurenziana Life (Late 13th century?)	Anonymous Franciscan (1279-1301)
			She often gives charity to the poor in front of the king's palace.	As a small child she gave to the poor.	She used to visit kitchens at the king's palace, to get bread which she would give to the poor.
				Bread for the poor is miraculously changed into flowers in Elizabeth's apron	Bread for the poor is miraculously changed into roses in her apron
		Libellus: a number of people at court oppose her marriage; her betrothed consoles her; no reluctance to marry.	On reaching marriageable age, she is married to the "duke of the Thuringians". (Nothing about reluctance to marry). She obeyed him as Sarah did Abraham.	On reaching marriageable age, she is given to the "duke of the Thuringians" as his wife. (Nothing about reluctance to marry).	"Deceived by enticements of parents" she reluctantly agrees to be betrothed to "the Landgraf, the duke of the Thuringians." Later tearfully regretted it, obeyed him as Sarah did Abraham, etc.

Conrad's Letter (1232)	Testimony from Can. Process (1233-35)	Dicta/Libellus (1236-41)	Valenciennes Life (c 1250)	Biblioteca Laurenziana Life (Late 13th century?)	Anonymous Franciscan (1279-1301)
			She is a kind mother to the poor	She is a kind mother to the poor	She conforms herself to the miseries of poor like a mother
	She takes her children to church for purification.	She takes her children to church for purification.	Births of Elizabeth's children (number and sex); she takes them to church for purification.		Births of her children (number and sex); she takes them to church for their purification
	On rogation days, she follows the procession of the cross barefoot.	On rogation days, she follows the procession of the cross barefoot.	On rogation days, she follows the procession of the cross barefoot.		On rogation days, she follows the procession of the cross barefoot.
			She is the mother of the Friars Minor	She loves the Friars Minor as the true poor of Christ	She is a special mother to the Friars Minor in Eisenach and provides for their needs.

Conrad's Letter (1232)	Testimony from Can. Process (1233-35)	Dicta/Libellus (1236-41)	Valenciennes Life (c 1250)	Biblioteca Laurenziana Life (Late 13th century?)	Anonymous Franciscan (1279-1301)
		Buries the poor like Tobias (intro to *Libellus*)	Buries the poor like Tobias		Buries the poor like Tobias
	Becomes godmother to poor.	Becomes godmother to poor.	Becomes godmother to poor - passage from Galatians		Became godmother to poor - passage from Galatians
	Builds a hospital at Wartburg	Builds a hospital at Wartburg	She establishes a hospital		Builds a hospital and visits the poor
	In her husband's absence, spends time in vigils, discipline and prayers	In her husband's absence, spends time in vigils, discipline and prayers			In her husband's absence, spends time in vigils, discipline and prayers
	Refuses to eat food from profit of officials.	Refuses to eat food from profit of officials.		Refuses to eat food gathered by officials.	She refuses to eat food plundered by officials

Conrad's Letter (1232)	Testimony from Can. Process (1233-35)	Dicta/Libellus (1236-41)	Valenciennes Life (c 1250)	Biblioteca Laurenziana Life (Late 13th century?)	Anonymous Franciscan (1279-1301)
				She gives eyes to boy blind from birth.	Cures a small boy blind from birth who had no eye sockets
				Her mother appears to her, and is freed from purgatory by her prayers.	Her mother appears to her and is freed from purgatory by her prayers; she confesses to a Franciscan, and asks for a penance for oversleeping
		Ms. of *Libellus* in Brussels has story of crown and angel		She receives a robe and crown from an angel; hearing of it, her husband decides to serve God.	Arrival of nobleman; miracle of angel bringing robe and crown
			The Landgraf dies overseas	Elizabeth's husband dies overseas.	Her husband, moved by miracle, goes overseas and dies in the service of the cross.

Conrad's Letter (1232)	Testimony from Can. Process (1233-35)	Dicta/Libellus (1236-41)	Valenciennes Life (c 1250)	Biblioteca Laurenziana Life (Late 13th century?)	Anonymous Franciscan (1279-1301)
	Her husband's bones are brought back and buried, her prayer beside his bones.	Her husband's bones are brought back and buried, her prayer beside his bones.	Her husband's bones are brought back and buried (no prayer)		Her prayer on meeting her husband's bones
	After his burial, everyone in Thuringia ignores her interests.	After his burial, everyone in Thuringia ignores her interests.			Persecution in Thuringia –
	Tells maidservant she is rejoicing because husband's soul freed from Purgatory				Tells maidservant she is rejoicing because husband's soul freed from Purgatory
	To Irmingard, about the life of the "sisters in the world": "If there were a more despised life, I would have chosen it." Description of habit by Brother Gherard	To Irmingard, about the life of the "sisters in the world": "If there were a more despised life, I would have chosen it."			With her handmaids she puts on religious habit. Description of her patched habit by Brother Gherard; if she had found a poorer one, she would have worn it, etc.

Conrad's Letter (1232)	Testimony from Can. Process (1233-35)	Dicta/Libellus (1236-41)	Valenciennes Life (c 1250)	Biblioteca Laurenziana Life (Late 13th century?)	Anonymous Franciscan (1279-1301)
					Her seal had an image of Friars Minor.
	Names of other friars who testified about her habit				Names of other friars who testified about her habit
					King Stephen of Hungary visits Esztergom, and has Elizabeth's portrait repainted barefoot and with cord.
	She is professed and puts on gray habit in Marburg, clothed by Brother Burchard(?)	She is professed and puts on gray habit in Marburg (Isentrude)			How she had herself tonsured in the House of the Friars Minor, Master Conrad celebrating Mass, and builds her house next to their church.

Conrad's Letter (1232)	Testimony from Can. Process (1233-35)	Dicta/Libellus (1236–41)	Valenciennes Life (c 1250)	Biblioteca Laurenziana Life (Late 13th century?)	Anonymous Franciscan (1279-1301)
Her religious vocation and renunciation of the world in Church of the Friars Minor					Quotation from Conrad's letter to Pope about her religious vocation and renunciation of the world.
	She washes the feet of the lepers and spoke kindly to them.	She washes the feet of the lepers and spoke kindly to them.	Like another Mary Magdalen, she washes the feet of the poor and kisses feet of lepers	Like another Mary Magdalen, she washes the feet of the lepers	Like another Mary Magdalen, she washes the feet of the poor and kisses feet of lepers
	Washes dishes, etc.	Washes dishes, etc.			Washes dishes, etc.

Conrad's Letter (1232)	Testimony from Can. Process (1233-35)	Dicta/Libellus (1236-41)	Valenciennes Life (c 1250)	Biblioteca Laurenziana Life (Late 13th century?)	Anonymous Franciscan (1279-1301)
	Elizabeth, her handmaids and children are ejected from the castle by some of her husband's vassals; she goes to the Church of the Friars Minor and asks them to sing the "Te Deum"	Elizabeth, her handmaids and children are ejected from the castle by some of her husband's vassals; she goes to the Church of the Friars Minor and asks them to sing the "Te Deum"	Elizabeth, her maidservants and children are ejected from the castle by some of her husband's vassals		Elizabeth, her handmaids and children are ejected from the castle by some of her husband's vassals; she goes to the church of the Friars Minor to ask them to sing the Te Deum
	Old woman pushes her in mud	Old woman pushes her in mud	Old woman pushes "our pearl" in mud.	Old woman pushes her in the mud.	Old woman pushes "our pearl" in the mud.
	She sends her children to different places to be brought up	She sends her children to different places to be brought up	She sends her children to different places to be brought up		She sends her children away
	Vision in church; vision of Christ: "If you want to be with me," etc.	Vision in church; vision of Christ: "If you want to be with me," etc.	Vision in church; vision of Christ: "If you want to be with me," etc.	Vision of Christ, "If you want to be with me," etc.	Vision of Christ: "If you want to be with me," etc.

Conrad's Letter (1232)	Testimony from Can. Process (1233-35)	Dicta/Libellus (1236-41)	Valenciennes Life (c 1250)	Biblioteca Laurenziana Life (Late 13th century?)	Anonymous Franciscan (1279-1301)
	She challenges a young man who is dressed in a secular way; when she prays for him, he grows hot at her prayer; he joins the Friars Minor	She challenges a young man who is dressed in a secular way; when she prays for him, he grows hot at her prayer; he joins the Friars Minor	She challenges a young man who is dressed in a secular way; when she prays for him, he grows hot at her prayer; he joins the Friars Minor	Young man grows hot at her prayer; becomes a Friar Minor.	Visited by Gertrude and Berthold, who is dressed in a secular way; when she prays for him, he grows hot at her prayer; he joins the Friars Minor
	Her uncle, bishop of Erfurt, wants her to marry again, says she will cut off nose.	Her uncle, bishop of Erfurt, wants her to marry again, says she will cut off nose.	She providentially escapes her relatives' urging to marry again		Her uncle, bishop of Erfurt, wants her to marry again, says she will cut off nose.
	She moves to Marburg at Master Conrad's request	She moves to Marburg at Master Conrad's request	She moves to Marburg and builds hospital for the poor there.	She builds hospital.	Follows Master Conrad to Marburg, and builds hospital, named after St. Francis by order of Pope Gregory IX.

Conrad's Letter (1232)	Testimony from Can. Process (1233-35)	Dicta/Libellus (1236-41)	Valenciennes Life (c 1250)	Biblioteca Laurenziana Life (Late 13th century?)	Anonymous Franciscan (1279-1301)
					Gregory wishing to encourage her spiritual friendship for Francis, sends her a relic of his blood.
	She cares for poor in hospital, carrying them, etc.	She cares for poor in hospital, carrying them, etc.			How she cared for poor in hospital, carrying them, and burying the dead, etc.
	She milks a cow for a sick man.	She milks a cow for sick man.			She milks a cow for sick man.
	On Holy Thursday, gathers lepers together and washes their feet.	On Holy Thursday, gathers lepers together and washes their feet.			On Holy Thursday, gathers lepers together and washes their feet.

Conrad's Letter (1232)	Testimony from Can. Process (1233-35)	Dicta/Libellus (1236-41)	Valenciennes Life (c 1250)	Biblioteca Laurenziana Life (Late 13th century?)	Anonymous Franciscan (1279-1301)
Conrad speaks of a leper girl whom he "threw out."					Excerpt from Conrad's letter, about leper girl, who he "firmly orders be separated from her."
Conrad speaks of Elizabeth's contemplation.					Excerpt from Conrad's letter, about her contemplation.
	Her father, hearing of her misery, sent count Paviam as an emissary. He sees her spinning with her maids (Perhaps more than one testimony)	Her father, hearing of her misery, sent count Paviam as an emissary. He sees her spinning with her maids (Testimony of Irmingard)	Her father, hearing of her misery, sent count Paviam as an emissary. He sees her spinning with her maids		Her father sends a count to bring her home; he finds her spinning wool for clothes of Friars Minor, based on testimony of Guda and "Ysenguldis"
She gives her husband's grain away at time of famine.	While the Landgraf was still living, she gave his grain to the poor at time of famine.	While the Landgraf was still living, she gave his grain to the poor at time of famine.	While the Landgraf was still living, she gave his grain to the poor at time of famine.		While her husband was living, she gave out grain from his at time of famine.

	Conrad's Letter (1232)	Testimony from Can. Process (1233-35)	Dicta/Libellus (1236-41)	Valenciennes Life (c 1250)	Biblioteca Laurenziana Life (Late 13th century?)	Anonymous Franciscan (1279-1301)
Elizabeth's acts of charity		And the remainder of what she brought from her father in Hungary she sold, and gave to the poor.	And the remainder of what she brought from her father in Hungary she sold, and gave to the poor. Introduction to the *Libellus* – gives not half, like Zaccheus, but all like Lawrence.	She gives away two thousand five hundred marks she had received for her dower. And the remainder of what she brought from her father in Hungary she sold, and gave to the poor; not half, like Zaccheus, but all like Lawrence.		She gives away five hundred marks and more from her dowry; she gave not half, like Zaccheus, but all like Lawrence.
						Quotation from Conrad about her acts of charity
					She miraculously supplies fresh fish for a sick man.	Miraculously procures fish for a poor man during Lent.
					She heals a mute and paralyzed (boy or man?)	Gives speech and movement to a mute paralyzed boy.

Conrad's Letter (1232)	Testimony from Can. Process (1233-35)	Dicta/Libellus (1236-41)	Valenciennes Life (c 1250)	Biblioteca Laurenziana Life (Late 13th century?)	Anonymous Franciscan (1279-1301)
					She wishes her son were a Friar Minor
					She says that if God had made her a man, she would be a friar
	Woman and her husband who abandoned child	Woman and her husband who abandoned child	Woman and her husband who abandoned child		Man and wife who leave child behind.
	Brother Gerard of Guerles, her confessor, testifies about her spirit of poverty and desire to be a recluse.				Brother Gerard of Guerles, her confessor, testifies about her spirit of poverty and desire to be a recluse.
	She asked brother Henry to sell a fish for her.	She asked brother Henry to sell a fish for her.			Her poverty was often such that she did not have necessities. Asked brother Henry to sell a fish for her.

Conrad's Letter (1232)	Testimony from Can. Process (1233-35)	Dicta/Libellus (1236-41)	Valenciennes Life (c 1250)	Biblioteca Laurenziana Life (Late 13th century?)	Anonymous Franciscan (1279-1301)
					The brothers take counsel and advise Elizabeth to entrust herself to Master Conrad. A brother (Henry, Andrew?) goes to Rome for her. He obtains Apostolic letters and secures return of her dowry.
					Her mantle, a gift from St. Francis through Gregory IX. Brothers of the Teutonic Order saw it, and famous preacher Brother Berthold saw and touched it in Weissenberg; gave it to a female companion as she was dying

Conrad's Letter (1232)	Testimony from Can. Process (1233-35)	Dicta/Libellus (1236-41)	Valenciennes Life (c 1250)	Biblioteca Laurenziana Life (Late 13th century?)	Anonymous Franciscan (1279-1301)
				She heals Master Conrad's brother's lethal wound.	She heals Master Conrad's brother's lethal wound.
					She grants the knight who saw her hair shirt a request, later after her death, she frees him from prison
	As she was about to die, she heard a bird singing and singing is heard in her throat.	As she was about to die, she heard a bird singing and singing is heard in her throat.			As she was about to die, she heard a bird singing and singing is heard in her throat.
	Tells the devil to flee.	Tells the devil to flee.			Tells the devil to flee.

Conrad's Letter (1232)	Testimony from Can. Process (1233-35)	Dicta/Libellus (1236-41)	Valenciennes Life (c 1250)	Biblioteca Laurenziana Life (Late 13th century?)	Anonymous Franciscan (1279-1301)
	"Now the hour is approaching when the Virgin gave birth." She is weak but doesn't feel any sickness. Her handmaids' words.	"Now the hour is approaching when the Virgin gave birth." She is weak but doesn't feel any sickness. Her handmaids' words.	In her final illness, she tells the devil to flee. "Now the hour is approaching when the Virgin gave birth…"		"Now the hour is approaching when the Virgin gave birth." She is weak but doesn't feel any sickness.
					How Henry, who went to Rome for her, obtained her recommendation to join the Friars Minor
			Christ says to her, "Come my love, my perfect one, my dove".	Christ appears to her, and says, "Come my chosen one and enter the eternal tabernacle, my beloved bride."	Christ tells her, "Come by beloved, my perfect one…"

Conrad's Letter (1232)	Testimony from Can. Process (1233-35)	Dicta/Libellus (1236-41)	Valenciennes Life (c 1250)	Biblioteca Laurenziana Life (Late 13th century?)	Anonymous Franciscan (1279-1301)
Death of Elizabeth	Death of Elizabeth	Death of Elizabeth	Death of Elizabeth	Death of Elizabeth	Death of Elizabeth
	She remains unburied for four days; a sweet odor comes from her body; people come and cut off parts of her body for relics.	She remains unburied for four days; a sweet odor comes from her body; people come and cut off parts of her body for relics.	She remains unburied for four days; a sweet odor comes from her body; people come and cut off parts of her body for relics.	A fragrant odor comes from her body.	She remains unburied for four days; a sweet odor comes from her body; people come and cut off parts of her body for relics.
	Abbess of Wetter hears the birds singing at her funeral.	Abbess of Wetter hears the birds singing at her funeral.	Abbess of Wetter hears the birds singing at her funeral ; comparison to Blessed Francis who preached to the birds; invitation to friars to mourn her.		Abbess of Wetter hears the birds singing at her funeral ; comparison to Blessed Francis who preached to the birds; invitation to the friars to mourn her.

Conrad's Letter (1232)	Testimony from Can. Process (1233–35)	Dicta/Libellus (1236–41)	Valenciennes Life (c 1250)	Biblioteca Laurenziana Life (Late 13th century?)	Anonymous Franciscan (1279–1301)
					As an example of her love for the Franciscans, tells how Elizabeth served the visiting friars and asked to wash their feet.
			Her most holy body is buried in chapel of the hospital of St. Francis; miracle of the oil.		Her most holy body is buried in the chapel of the hospital of St. Francis; miracle of the oil
			Miracles described. Sixteen dead people raised to life	Series of posthumous miracles from the canonization process	Miracles described. Sixteen dead people raised to life
				Her canonization	Her canonization

Conrad's Letter (1232)	Testimony from Can. Process (1233-35)	Dicta/Libellus (1236-41)	Valenciennes Life (c 1250).	Biblioteca Laurenziana Life (Late 13th century?)	Anonymous Franciscan (1279-1301)
					Her brother Bela's devotion to her and to the Franciscans
					About Cunegunde, Iolenta and Salomeya, and other women following Elizabeth
			Doxology		Doxology

Bibliography

Primary Sources

Manuscripts

Valenciennes Life

Manuscript

Valenciennes. Bibliothèque Municipale, Ms. 508 (467 -- T. 4. 25). Parchment. 13th century, fol. 64r-74r.

Description:

Molinier, A. "Manuscrits de la Bibliothèque de Valenciennes." *Catalogue general des manuscrits des bibliothèques publiques de France. Departments* 25 (1894), p. 407.

Partial edition:

Király, Ilona. "Egy XIII századi szent Erzsébet-legenda." *Egyetemes Philologiai Közlöny (Archivum Philologicum)* 59 (1935): 64-72.

Manuscript:

Douai. Bibliothèque Municipale, Cod. 864. Parchment, 13th century, fol. 209-17.

Description:

"Catalogus codicum hagiographicorum latinorum bibliothecae publicae duacensis." AB 20 (1901): 415-16.

Manuscript:

Cambrai. Mediathèque Municiaple, ms. 34-35. 13th century. (2 vols. of a breviary belonging to the cathedral in Cambrai).

Cambrai. Mediathèque Municipale, MS. 91. 14th century. (Summer breviary).

Description:

Institut de Recherche et d'histoire des textes. *Manuscrits datés des bibliothèques de France. 1: Cambrai,* par Denis Muzerelle, et al. Paris: CNRS Editions, 2000, 6-7, 17.

The Anonymous Franciscan

Manuscript:

Koblenz. Landeshauptsarchiv. Abt. 701. No. 122. 15th century, ff. 123r-126v.

Description:

Archiv der Gesellschaft für altere deutsche Geschichtskunde, 11:741.

Manuscript:

Trier. Stadtbibliothek. Cod. 1173/475 8. 15th century, fol. 74v-92v.

Description:

"Catalogus codd. Hagiogr. Latinorum Bibliothecae Civitatis Treverensis." *Analecta Bollandiana* 52 (1934): 234-35.

Keuffer, Max, ed. *Handschriften der Stadtbibliotehk zu Trier. Vol. 8: Verzeichnis der Handschriften des historischen Archivs.* Trier: Kommisionsverlag der Fr. Lintzschen Buchhandlung Friedr Val. Lintz, 1914. (Reprint Wiesbaden: Otto Harrassowitz, 1973).

Edition:

Pieper, Lori, SFO. "A New Life of St. Elizabeth of Hungary: The Anonymous Franciscan." *Archivum Franciscanum Histori-*

cum 93 (2000): 29-78; also published in idem, "Elizabeth of Hungary and the Franciscan Tradition," Dissertation. New York: Fordham University, 2002.

Heidelberg Life

Manuscript

Heidelberg. Universitätsbibliothek. Cod. Pal. Germ. 105. 15th cent., fol. 1r-36r.

Description:

Bartsch, Karl. *Katalog der Handschriften der Universitätsbibliothek in Heidelberg* 1 (1887): *Die altdeutschen Handschriften.* Heidelberg: Verlag von Gustav Koester, 1887.

Published Sources

Acta Sanctorum. Paris: Apud Victorem Palme, 1863- .

Angela of Foligno. *Angela of Foligno, Complete Works.* Translated, with an Introduction by Paul Lachance, O.F.M., Preface by Romana Guarnieri. New York/Mahwah, N. J.: Paulist Press, 1993.

Anglade, P. Maria Paschalis, O.F.M. "Descriptio novi codici dicta iv ancillarum s. Elisabeth exhibentis." *Archivum Franciscanum Historicum* 6 (1913): 61-75.

Anonymous. [*Cronica Anonyma*]. *Analecta Franciscana* 1 (1885): 279-300.

Anonymous. "De S. Elisabeth, sermo." In *S. R. E. cardinalis S. Bonaventurae . . . Opera omnia.* Paris: L. Vivès, 1868, 13:628-30.

Anonymous. [Zwettl Life]. "Vita sanctae Elisabeth, landgraviae Thuringiae, auctore anonymo, nunc primum in lucem edita." ed. Diodorus Henniges, OFM. In *Archivum Franciscanum Historicum* 2 (1909): 240-68.

-----. Boccali, Giovanni, OFM. "Codice francescano nel monastero delle Clarisse di Bressanone." *Archivum Franciscanum Historicum* 84, n. 3-4 (1991): 491-98.

Armstrong, Regis, OFM Cap, ed. *Clare of Assisi: Early Documents.* St. Bonaventure, NY: Franciscan Institute, 1993.

-----, J. A. Wayne Hellmann, O.F.M. Conv., William J. Short, O.F.M., *Francis of Assisi: Early Documents.* New York: New City Press, 199- .

Arnaud de Serrant. *Chronica XXIV Generalium Ordinis Minorum (1209-1374),* in *Analecta Franciscana* 2 (1897): 221-23.

Berthold von Regensburg. *Berthold von Regensburg. Vollständige Ausgabe seiner Predigten,* mit Einleitungen und Anmerkungen von Franz Pfeiffer und Joseph Strobl. Berlin: Walter de Gruyter, 1965.

Biblioteca Hagiographica Latina medii aevi. Bruxelles, 1898-1901. Supplements 1911, 1986.

Bihl, Michael. "Descriptio novi codicis Dicta iv ancillarum S. Elisabeth Thuringiae et Legendam S. Clarae auctore Fr. Thomas de Celano continentis." *Archivum Franciscanum Historicum* 6 (1913): 522-27.

Bozon, Nicole. [Life of St. Elizabeth]. Klenke, Sr. M. Amelia, ed. *Seven More Poems by Nicholas Bozon.* St. Bonaventure NY: Franciscan Institute, 1951.

-----. Karl, Louis. "La vie de Ste. Elisabeth par Nicole Bozon." *Zeitschrift fur Romanische Philologie* 34 (1910): 294-314.

Caesarius of Heisterbach. "Die Schriften des Caesarius von Heisterbach über die heilige Elisabeth von Thüringen." Ed. A. Huyskens, in A. Hilka ed., *Die Wundergeschichten des Caesarius von Heisterbach* (Bonn, 1937), 3:331-390.

Catalogus Codicum Hagiographicorum antiquorium Saeculo XVI qui asservantur in Bibliothecae Nationali Parisiensis. Ed. hagiographi Bollandiani. Brussels: apud editores, 1889.

Catalogus codicum Hagiographicorum Bibliothecae Regiae Bruxellensis. Ed. Hagiographi Bollandiani. Bruxelles, 1886.

Cazelles, Brigitte. *The Lady as Saint: A Collection of French Hagiographic Romances of the Thirteenth Century.* Philadelphia: University of Pennsylvania Press, 1992.

"Cronica Reinhardsbrunnensis." ed. O. Holder-Egger, *Monumenta Germaniae Historica. Scriptores,* 30: 490-658.

Dietrich of Apolda. *Die Vita der heiligen Elisabeth des Dietrich von Apolda.* Ed. Monika Rener. Marburg: N. G. Elwert, 1993. (Veroffentlichen der Historischen Kommission für Hessen, 53).

Elemosina, Fra. *Cronica.* Excerpt in Gieben, Servus (von St. Anthonis). "Bruder Elemosinas Doppelbericht zum Leben der hl. Elisabeth von Thüringen." *Collectanea Franciscana* 35 (1965): 166-76.

Francis of Assisi, Saint. *Die Opuscula des hl. Franziskus von Assisi: neue textkritische Edition.* Ed. Cajetan Esser, O.F.M. Grottaferrata: Editions Collegii S. Bonaventurae, 1976.

Giacomo da Tresanti. [3 sermons on St. Elizabeth]. Cenci, Cesare, OFM. "Noterelle su Fr. Giacomo da Tresanti, lettore predicatore." *Archivum Franciscanum Historicum* 86 (1993): 119-128.

Giordano of Giano. *Chronica Fratris Iordani.* In *Analecta Franciscana* 1 (1885): 1-19.

-----. Translated in Hermann, Placid., ed. *Thirteenth Century Chronicles.* Chicago: Franciscan Herald Press, 1961.

Glassberger, Nicholas. [*Cronica*]. *Analecta Franciscana* 2 (1887).

Gregory IX, Pope. [Letter to Elizabeth]. Heinisch, Klaus J. "Ein Brief Gregors IX an die hl. Elisabeth." *Franziskanische Studien* 25 (1938): 379-82.

-----. In Wenck, Karl. "Die heilige Elisabeth und Papst Gregor IX." *Hochland* 5 (1907-1908): 129-47.

Habig, Marion A., O.F.M. *St. Francis of Assisi: Writings and Early Biographies*. Chicago: Franciscan Herald Press, 1973.

Haggh, Barbara. *Two Offices for St. Elizabeth of Hungary: Gaudeat Hungaria and Letare Germania*. Ottowa: Institute of Medieval Music, 1995.

Henniges, Diodorus. "Prologus et epilogus in dicta IV ancillarum S. E. Thuringiae lantgraviae." *Archivum Franciscanum Historicum* 3 (1910): 463-490.

Huyskens, Albert. *Quellenstudien zur Geschichte der hl. Elisabeth, Landgrafin von Thüringen*. Marburg: N. G. Elwert, 1908.

-----. *Der sogennant Libellus de dictis quattuor ancillarum s. Elisabeth confectus*. Kempten und Munchen: Verlag der Jos. Kösel'schen Buchhandlung, 1911.

Jacobus de Voragine, O. P. *Legenda aurea: edizione critica a cura di Giovanni Paolo Maggioni*. Tavarnuzze: SISMEL: Edizioni del Galluzzo, 1998. 2 v.

Jacques de Vitry. *Lettres de Jacques de Vitry (1160/1170-1240), Évêque de Saint-Jean d'Acre*. Edition crit. by R. B. C. Huygens. Leiden, 1960.

Lazzeri, Zefferino, ed. "Il processo di canonizzatione di S. Chiara di Assisi." *Archivum Franciscanum Historicum* 13 (1920): 403-507.

Lemaitre, H. "Statuts des religieuses du Tiers-Ordre Franciscain, dites soeurs grises hospitalières (1483)." *Archivum Franciscanum Historicum* 4 (1911): 713-31.

-----. "Bulle inédite de Sixte IV (1474) en faveur des soeurs de la Celle." *Revue d'histoire franciscaine* 4 (1927): 361-68.

Lemmens, L. "Zur Biographie der heiligen Elisabeth, Landgrafin von Thuringen." *Mitteilungen des historischen Vereins des Diözeses Fulda*, 4 (1901): 15-19.

-----. "Zum Rosenwunder der hl. Elisabeth von Thüringen," *Der Katholik* 82 (1902): 381-84.

Mechtild of Magdeburg. *The Flowing Light of the Godhead.* Translated and introduced by Frank Tobin, preface by Margot Schmidt. New York/Mahwah, N. J.: Paulist Press, 1998.

Meersseman, G. G. "Le deposizioni delle compagne di S. Elisabetta di Turingia in un frammento conservato nell'Archivio di Stato a Friburgo." In *Palaeographica, diplomatica et archivistica: Miscellanea in onore di G. Battelli*, vol. I, Rome, 1979, pp. 367-80.

Porcellet, Felipa de. *La vie de sainte Douceline, fondatrice des beguines de Marseille; composée au xiiie siècle en langue provençale.* Ed. by Joseph Mathias Hyacinthe Albanés. Marseille: Étienne Camoin, 1879.

-----. "*The Life of the Blessed Saint Douceline* (d. 1274): An Edition and Translation with Commentary." Ed. Kathryn Betts Wolfkiel. Ph.D. Dissertation. Evanston Illinois: Northwestern University, 1993.

Robeck, Nesta De. *Saint Elizabeth of Hungary: A Story of Twenty-Four Years.* Milwaukee, Wisc.: Bruce Publishing Co., 1954.

Robert of Cambliegneul. *Chi commenche de Sainte Yzabiel.* Edited as a supplement in Jubinal, Achille, *Oeuvres complètes de Rutebeuf.* Paris: Pannier, 1839. 2:360-412.

-----. In Karl, Louis, ed. "Vie de Sainte Elisabeth de Hongrie." *Zeitschrift für Romanische Philologie* 34 (1910): 708-733.

Rutebeuf. *La vie sainte Elysabel.* In Edmond Faral and Julia Bastin, *Oeuvres complètes de Rutebeuf.* Paris: Editions A. and J. Picard, 1960. 2:60-123.

Salimbene d'Adam. *Cronica.* Edidit Giuseppe Scalia. Turnhout: Brepolis, 1998-99.

-----. *The Chronicle of Salimbene de Adam.* Ed. by Joseph Baird, Giuseppe Baglivi and John Robert Kane. Binghampton, New York: Medieval and Renaissance Texts and Studies, 1986.

Sedulius, Henricus (Vroom) OFM, 1547-1621. *Historia Seraphica vitae B. P. Francisci Assisiatis illustriumque virorum et feminarum qui ex tribus eius ordinis relati sunt inter sanctos.* Antwerp, 1613.

Seton, Walter. *Some New Sources for the Life of Blessed Agnes of Bohemia, Including a Fourteenth-Century Latin Version (Bamberg, Misc. Hist. 146, E. VII, 19) and a Fifteenth-Century German version (Berlin, Germ. Oct. 484).* Thesis aproved for the degree of doctor of literature in the University of London. Aberdeen: University Press, 1915.

-----. "The Letters from Saint Clare to Blessed Agnes of Bohemia." *Archivum Franciscanum Historicum* 17 (1924): 509-19.

Siegfrid of Balnhusin. *Historia universalis et compendium Historiarum.* ed. O. Hoder-Egger. *Monumenta Germaniae Historica. Scriptores,* 25: 700-702.

Temperini, Lino. *Santa Elisabetta d'Ungheria secondo le fonti storiche.* Rome: Editrice Franciscanum, 2006.

-----. *Santa Elisabetta d'Ungheria (1207-1231) gloria dei penitenti francescani.* Rome: Editrice Franciscanum, 2002.

Two Lives of Marie D'Oignies: The Life by Jacques de Vitry, Translated by Margot H. King; Notes by Margot H. King and Miriam

Marolais; *Supplement to the Life by Thomas of Cantimpré,* Translated, with Notes, by Hugh Feiss, OSB. Fourth edition: Toronto, Ontario: Peregrina Publishing Co., 1998.

Wadding, Luke. *Annales Minorum.* Quaracchi: Collegio San Bonaventura, 1931-.

Winter, Ursula. "Ein neues Fragment der *Dicta Quattuor Ancillarum S. Elisabeth.*" *Philologus: Zeitschrift für klassische Philologie* 115, 1-4 (1971): 328-33.

Secondary Works

Abate, Giuseppe. *S. Rosa da Viterbo, terziaria francescana (1233-1251): Fonti storiche della vita e loro revisione critica.* Rome: Editrice Miscellanea Francescana, 1952.

Ancelet-Hustache, Jeanne. *St. Elisabeth de Hongrie.* Paris: Editions Franciscaines, 1947. English translation: *Gold Tried by Fire: St. Elzabeth of Hungary.* Chicago: Franciscan Herald Press, 1963.

Atkinson, Clarissa. *The Oldest Vocation: Christian Motherhood in the Middle Ages.* Ithaca and London: Cornell University Press, 1991.

Barratt, Alexandra. "The Revelations of St. Elizabeth of Hungary: Problems of Attribution." *The Library* (Series 6) 14, no. 1(1992): 1-11.

Battes, Julius. "Das Vordringen der Franziskaner in Hessen und die Entwicklung der einzelnen Konvente bis zur Reformation." *Franziskanische Studien* 18 (1931): 309-350.

Bauer, Hermann. *St. Elisabeth und die Elisabethkirche zu Marburg.* Marburg: Hitzeroth, c1990.

Bell, Rudolph. *Holy Anorexia.* Chicago: University of Chicago Press, 1985.

Benvenuti Papi, Anna. "La Serva-Patrona," in her *In castro poenitentiale:" santità e società femminile nell'Italia medioevale.* Rome: Herder Editrice e Libreria, 1990, 264-303.

Beutin, Heidi. "'Soror in saeculo.' Elisabeth von Thuringen: Landgrafin, Visionarin, Heilige." in *Europäische Mystik vom Hochmitelalter zum Barock.* Ed. Wolfgang Beutin - Thomas Bütow. Frankfurt am Main-Berlin-Bern-New York-Paris-Wien: Lang, 1998, 97-118.

Beyreuther, Gerald. "Elisabeth Thüringische Landgräfin und heilige." *Fürstinnen und Stadterinnen: Frauen im Mittelalter.* Heraus. von Gerald. Beyreuther, Barbara Patzold, Erik Vitz, (Frauenforum Herder). Freiburg: Herder, 1993, pp. 15-39.

Bihl, Michael. "Die heilige Elisabeth von Thüringen als Terziarin." *Franziskanische Studien* 18 (1931): 259-93.

-----. "De tertio ordine S. Francisci in Provincia Germaniae Superioris sive Argentinensis." *Analecta Franciscana* 14 (1921): 138-98, 442-60; 15 (1922): 349-81; 17 (1924): 237-65; 18 (1925): 63-89.

Blumenfeld-Kosinski, Renate and Timea Szell, eds. *Images of Sainthood in Medieval Europe.* Ithaca, N.Y.: Cornell University Press, 1991.

Bolton, Brenda. "Daughters of Rome: All One in Christ Jesus." *In Women in the Church,* ed. W. J. Sheils and Diana Wood. Cambridge, MA: Blackwell, 1990, pp. 101-16.

-----. "*Mulieres sanctae.*" *Studies in Church History* 10 (1973): 77-95.

Börner, G. "Zur Kritik des Quellen für die Geschichte der heiligen Elisabeth, Landgrafin von Thüringen." *Neues Archiv der Gesellschaft für altere deutsche Geschichtskunde* 13 (1888): 431-515.

Bornstein, Daniel, and Roberto Rusconi. *Women and Religion in Medieval and Renaissance Italy.* Trans. by Margery J. Schneider. Chicago and London: Univerity of Chicago Press, 1996.

Boros, Fortunatos, O.F.M. "Die hl. Elisabeth in der ungarischen Geschichte." *Franziskanische Studien* 18 (1931): 233-41.

Bowie, Fiona, ed. *Beguine Spirituality.* Translated by Oliver Davies (New York: Crossroads, 1990).

Busse-Wilson, Elisabeth. *Das Leben der Heiligen Elisabeth von Thüringen: Das Abbild einer mittelalterlichen Seele.* Munich: C. H. Beck'sche Verlagsbuchhandlung, 1931.

Bynum, Caroline Walker. "Fast, Feast and Flesh: The Religious Significance of Food to Medieval Women." *Representations* 11 (1985): 1-16.

-----. *Fragmentation and Redemption: Essays on Gender and the Human Body in Medieval Religion.* New York: Zone Books, 1992.

-----. *Holy Feast, Holy Fast. The Religious Significance of Food to Medieval Women.* Berkely: University of California Press, 1987.

-----. "Women Mystics in the 13th Century: The Case of the Nuns of Helfta." In her *Jesus as Mother: Studies in the Spirituality of the High Middle Ages.* Berkely: University of California Press, 1982, pp. 170-247.

Carney, Margaret. *The First Franciscan Woman: Clare of Assisi and Her Form of Life.* Quincy: Franciscan Press, 1993.

"Cat. cod. Lat. Bibl. Neap." *Analecta Bollandiana* 30 (1911):179-80.

Cenci, Cesare. "De constitutionibus Praenarbonensibus." *Archivum Franciscanum Historicum* 83 (1990): 90-91.

Coakley, John. "Gender and the Authority of the Friars: The Significance of Holy Women for Thirteenth-Century

Franciscans and Dominicans." *Church History* 60 (1991): 445-60.

Congar, M. J., O.P. "Sainte Elisabeth: La charité de la Croix." *Vie Spirituelle* 30 (1932): 51-73.

Convegno di Studi Francescani (3rd: 1979, Padua, Italy). *Il movimento francescano della penitenza nella società medievale: atti del 3. Convegno di studi francescani*. Roma: Istituto storico dei Cappuccini, 1980.

D'Alatri, Mariano. *Aetas poenitentialis: l'antico Ordine francescano della penitenza*. Rome: Istituto Storico dei Cappuccini, 1993.

D'Avray, David. "Marriage Sermons in 'ad status' Collections of the Central Middle Ages." *Archives d'histoire doctrinale et littéraire du moyen âge* 47 (1980): 71-119.

Delehaye, Hippolyte. *The Legends of the Saints: An Introduction to Hagiography*. London: Longmans, Green, 1907.

Delooz, Pierre. "Towards a Sociological Study of Canonized Sainthood in the Catholic Church." *Saints and Their Cults: Studies in Religious Sociology, Folklore and History*, ed. Stephen Wilson. Cambridge/New York: Cambridge University Press, 1983, pp. 189-216.

Elisabeth, der Deutschen Orden und ihre Kirche: Festschrift zur 700jahrigen Wiederkehr der Weihe der Elisabethkirche Marburg 1983; herausgegeben im Auftrag der Philipps- Universität Marburg von Udo Arnold und Heinz Liebing. Marburg: N. G. Elwert Verlag, 1983.

Elliot, Dyan. *Spiritual Marriage: Sexual Abstinence in Medieval Wedlock*. Princeton: Princeton University Press, 1993.

Folz, Robert. *Les saintes reines du moyen âge en occident (vie-xiiie siecles*. Bruxelles: Societé des Bollandistes, 1992.

Frascadore, E. "Elisabettine, Suore." In *Dizionario degli Istituti di Perfezione*, (Rome: Edizioni Paoline, 1974), 3, col. 1114.

Freed, John B. *The Friars and German Society in the Thirteenth Century*. Cambridge: Mediaeval Academy of America, 1977.

-----. "Urban Development and the *Cura Monialium* in Thirteenth-Century Germany." *Viator* 3 (1972): 311-27.

Geary, Patrick. "Saints, Scholars and Society: The Elusive Goal." In his *Living with the Dead in the Middle Ages*. Ithaca: Cornell University Press, 1994, pp. 9-29.

Gieben, Servus. "I patroni dell'ordine della penitenza." *Collectanea Franciscana* 43 (1973): 229-45.

Goodich., Michael. "Ancilla Dei: The Servant as Saint in the Late Middle Ages," in Suzanne Wemple and Julius Kirschner, *Women of the Medieval World: Studies in Honor of John H. Mundy* (Oxford: Basil Blackwell, 1985), pp. 119-78.

-----. "The Countours of Female Piety in Later Medieval Hagiography." *Church History* 50 (1981): 20-32.

-----. "The Politics of Canonization in the Thirteenth Century: Lay and Mendicant Saints." *Saints and Their Cults: Studies in Religious Sociology, Folklore and History*, ed. by Stephen Wilson. Cambridge/New York: Cambridge University Press, pp. 169-187.

-----. *Vita Perfecta. The Ideal of Sainthood in the Thirteenth Century*. Stuttgart: Anton Hiersemann, 1982.

Goyens, Jerome. "Chapitres des soeurs hospitalières en Flandres (1483-1528)." Archivum Franciscanum Historicum 14 (1921): 199-208.

Grundmann, Herbert. *Religious Movements in the Middle Ages*. Notre Dame/London: University of Notre Dame Press, 1995.

Haselbeck, Gallus. "Die hl. Elisabeth und ihre Beichvater Br. Rodeger und Konrad von Marburg. Ein Kritik der Hypothesis Wencks." *Franziskanische Studien* 18 (1931): 294-308.

Hay, Denys. *The Church in Italy in the Fifteenth Century.* Cambridge, England: Cambridge University Press, 1977.

Herlihy, David. "Women in Medieval Society." In his *The Social History of Italy and Western Europe, 700-1500.* London: Variorium Reprints, 1978, pp. ix, 3-17.

Helyot, Pierre. *Histoire des ordres monastiques.* Paris, 1721.

Heymann, E. "Zum Ehegüterrecht der hl. Elisabeth." *Zeitschrift des Vereins für thuringische Geschichte* N. F. 19 (1909): 1-22.

Jurgensmeier, F., ed. *So also, Herr. . .Elisabeth von Thüringen (1207-1231).* Frankfurt am Main: Verlag J. Knecht, 1982.

Kaiser, Denise Adele. "Sin and the Vices in the *Sermones de dominici* by Berthold of Regensburg." Columbia University Dissertation, 1983.

Klaniczay, Gábor. *Holy Rulers and Blessed Princesses: Dynastic Cults in Medieval Central Europe.* Translated by Éva Pálmai. New York: Cambridge University Press, 2002.

Kleinberg. Aviad. *Prophets in Their Own Country: Living Saints and the Making of Sainthood in the Late Middle Ages.* Chicago: University of Chicago Press, 1992.

Lansing, Carol. *The Florentine Magnates: Lineage and Faction in a Medieval Comune.* Princeton: Princeton University Press, 1991.

Le Goff, Jacques. "Apostolat mendiant et fait urbain dans la France medievale: l'implantation des ordres mendiants." *Annales: Economies, sociétés, civilisations* 23 (1968): 335-52.

Lemaitre, H.. "Les soins hospitaliers à domicile, données dès le xive siècle par des religieuses franciscaines, les soeurs noires et les soeurs grises: leurs maisons." *Revue d'histoire franciscaine* 1 (1924): 180-208.

Levardy, F. "Il Leggendario ungherese degli Angiò conservato nella Biblioteca Vaticana, nel Morgan Library e nel'Emitage." *Acta Historiae Artium Academiae Scientarum Hungariae* 9 (1963): 75-108.

Little, Lester K. *Religious Poverty and the Profit Economy in Medieval Europe.* London: Paul Elek, 1978.

McKelvie, Roberta A, O.S.F. *Retrieving a Living Tradition: Angelina of Montegiove: Franciscan, Tertiary, Beguine.* St. Bonaventure, NY: Franciscan Institute, 1997. (Franciscan Institute Publications).

McNamara, Jo Ann. *Sisters in Arms: Catholic Nuns Through Two Millennia.* Cambridge, MA./ London: Harvard University Press, 1996.

Makowski, Elizabeth. *Canon Law and Cloistered Women: Periculoso and Its Commentators, 1298-1545.* Washington, D. C.: The Catholic University of America Press, 1997.

Manselli, Raoul. "La chiesa e il francescanesimo femminile." *Movimento religioso femminile e francescanesimo nel secolo xiii.* Assisi: Società internazionale degli studi francescani, 1980, pp. 241-61.

-----. "Royal Holiness in the Daily Life of Elizabeth of Hungary: The Testimony of Her Servants." *Greyfriars Review* 11 (1997): 1-20.

Maresch, Maria. *Elisabeth von Thüringen.* Bonn: Verlag des Buchgemeind, 1931.

Marini, Alfonso. *Agnese di Boemia*. Con la collaborazione di Paola Ungarelli. Roma: Istituto storico dei cappuccini, 1991.

Martel, Gerard de, ed. "Trois sermons inédits du xiiie siècle sur Ruth 3, 11." *Archivum Franciscanum Historicum* 89 (1996): 379-424.

Matter, E. Ann, and John Coakley, eds. *Creative Women in Medieval and Early Modern Italy: A Religious and Artistic Renaissance*. Philadelphia: University of Pennsylvania Press, 1994.

Maurer, Wilhelm. "Zum Verstandnis der hl. Elisabeth von Thuringen." *Zeitschrift für Kirchengeschichte* 65 (1953-54): 16-64.

Meersseman, G. G. *Dossier de l'ordre de la pénitence au xiiie siècle*, 2nd edition. Fribourg: Éditions Universitaires Fribourg Suisse, 1982.

Menestó, Enrico. "The Apostolic Canonization Proceedings of Clare of Montefalco, 1318-1319." Daniel Bornstein and Roberto Rusconi, eds., *Women and Religion in Medieval and Renaissance Italy*. Chicago and London: University of Chicago Press, 1996, pp. 108-110.

Menge, Gisbert. "Zur Elisabethforschung." *Franziskanische Studien* 19 (1932): 292-314.

Michael, Emil. S. J. "Ist die heilige Elisabeth von der Marburg vertrieben werden?" *Zeitschrift für katholische Theologie* 33 (1909): 41-49.

Mollat, Michel. *The Poor in the Middle Ages: An Essay in Social History*. Trans. by Arthur Goldhammer. New Haven: Yale University Press,1978.

Montalembert, Charles, comte de. *Histoire de Sainte Elisabeth de Hongrie, Duchesse de Thuringe (1207-1231)*. Paris: Lecoffre, 1861. Most recent edition: *La vie de saint Elisabeth de Hongrie*.

Pref de Guy Bedouelle, OP. Paris: Cerf, 2005. (Collection sagesses chretiennes).

Mooney, Catherine M., ed., *Gendered Voices: Medieval Saints and their Interpreters.* Philadelphia: University of Pennsylvania Press, 1999.

Neel, Carol. "The Origins of the Beguines," in *Sisters and Workers in the Middle Ages,* ed. Judith M. Bennett, Elizabeth A. Clark, Jean F. O'Barr, et al. Chicago and London: University of Chicago Press, 1979, pp. 240-260.

Newman, Barbara. *From Virile Woman to Woman-Christ: Studies in Medieval Religion and Literature.* Philadelphia: University of Pennsylvania Press, 1995.

Nicholson, Barbara. *Templars, Hospitallers and Teutonic Knights: Images of the Military Orders, 1128-1291.* Leicester/ New York: Leicester University Press, 1993.

Oliger, L. "Servasanto da Faenza, O.F.M. e il suo '*Liber de virtubus et vitiis.*'" *Miscellanea Francesco Ehrle* I, (Studi e Testi 37), Rome, 1924, pp. 166-170.

Pásztor, Edith. "Sant'Elisabetta d'Ungheria nella religiosità femminile del secolo XIII." *Annali della Facoltá di lettere e filosofia dell'Universitá di Siena* 5 (1984): 83-99.

Paul, Jacques. "Témoignage historique et hagiographique dans le procès de canonisation de Louis d'Anjou." *Provence historique* 23 (1973): 305-317.

Pazzelli, Raffaele. *The Franciscan Sisters: Outlines of History and Spirituality.* Steubenville, Ohio: Franciscan University, 1989.

----- and L. Temperini. *Prime manifestazioni di vita communitarie maschile e femminile nel movimento francescano della Pentitenza (1215-1447).* Atti del Convegno di Studi Francescani, Assisi, 30 giugno-3 luglio, 1981. Rome: Analeta TOR, 1982.

Petrakopoulos, Anja. "Sanctity and Motherhood: St. Elizabeth of Thuringia." *Sanctity and Motherhood: Essays on Holy Mothers in the Middle Ages*. Ed. by Anneke B. Mulder-Bakker. New York/London, 1995, pp. 259-96.

Petroff, Elizabeth A. *The Consolation of the Blessed*. New York: Alta Gaia Society, 1979.

Pieper, Lori, SFO. "In Search of Sanctity: St. Elizabeth of Hungary," unpublished paper, Fordham University, 1996.

Préfontaine, Vinot. "Le couvent des soeurs grises de Beauvais." *Revue d'histoire franciscaine* 5 (1928): 288-326; 6 (1929): 129-72.

Roisin, Simone. "L'efflorescence cistercienne et le courant feminin de pieté au xiiime siecle." *Revue d'histoire ecclesiastique* 39 (1943): 342-78.

Ruether, Rosemary R. *Sexism and God-Talk: Toward a Feminist Theology*. With a new Introduction. Boston: Beacon Press, 1993 (originally published 1983).

Rusconi Roberto. "L'espansione del francescanesimo femminile nel secolo xiii." *Movimento religioso femminile e fracescanesimo nel secolo xiii*. Assisi: Società Internazionale degli Studi Francescani, 1980, pp. 265-313.

Salvà, B., T.O.R. "Exordia Tertii Ordinis Regularis. Documenta et adnotationes." *Analecta T.O.R.* 1 (1933-1936): 154-64.

Sankt Elisabeth: Fürstin, Dienerin, Heilige. Aufsatze, Dokumentation, Katalog. Sigmaringen: Jan Thorbecke Verlag, 1981.

Schuchman, Anne M. "Literary Collaboration in the *Life* of Umiliana dei Cerchi." *Magistra: A Journal of Women's Spirituality in History* 7, 2 (Winter 2001): 5-22.

Schulenburg, Jane Tibbetts. "The Heroics of Virginity: Brides of Christ and Sacrificial Mutilation," in Mary Beth Rose, ed.,

Women in the Middle Ages and the Renaissance: Literary and Historical Perspectives. Syracuse, NY: Syracuse University Press, 1986, pp. 29-72.

Schüssler-Fiorenza, Elisabeth. *In Memory of Her: A Feminist Theology of Deconstruction of Christian Origins.* New York: Crossroads, 1983.

Stark, Brigitte. "Elisabeth von Thüringen. Die Entdeckung individueller Züge in der Biographie einer Heiligen," in *Individuum und Individualität im Mittelalter.* Berlin/New York: W. de Gruyter, 1996, pp. 704-21.

Stoeckli, Alban (ab Hermetschwil), OFM Cap. "S. Elisabeth Hungariae, sodalis Tertii Ordinis et Ordinis 'sororum Paenitentium.'" *Tertius Ordo* 23 (1962): 29-35.

Stuard, Susan Mosher. "Ancillary Evidence for the Decline of Medieval Slavery." *Past and Present* no. 149 (1995): 3-28,

Takács, Innocenz. "Die Verehung der hl. Elisabeth in Ungarn." *Franziskanische Studien* 18 (1931): 242-58.

Third Order Regular of St. Francis, Minister General. "We Have Come to Believe in Love: Letter for the Eighth Centenary of the Birth of St. Elizabeth, Princess of Hungary and Franciscan Penitent." Rome: Basilica of Sts. Cosmas and Damian, 2006.

Tobin, Frank. *Mechtild von Magdeburg: A Medieval Mystic in Modern Eyes.* Columbia, SC: Camden House 1995.

Toews, John E. "Intellectual History After the 'Linguistic Turn': The Autonomy of Meaning and the Irreducibility of Experience." *American Histoircal Review* 92 (1987): 879-907.

Vauchez, André. "Charité et pauvreté chez Sainte Elisabeth de Thuringe, d'après les actes du procès de canonisation." In

Mollat, Michael, ed. *Études sur l'histoire de la pauvreté.* Paris: Publications de la Sorbonne, 1974, 1:163-73.

-----. "L'ideal de sainteté dans le mouvement féminin franciscain." *Movimento religioso femminile e francescanesimo nel secolo xiii.* Assisi: Società Internazionale degli Studi Francescani, 1980, pp. 317-37.

-----. "Jacques de Voragine et les saints du xiiie siècle dans la *Légende Dorée*," in *Legenda aurea: Sept Siècles de diffusion.* Actes du colloque international, l'Université du Québec à Montreal, 11-12 mai 1983. Montreal: Editions Bellarmin/Paris: Librairie J. Vrin, 1986, pp. 27-56.

-----. *La sainteté en occident aux derniers siècles du moyen age, d'apres les proces de canonisation et les documents hagiographiques.* Rome, 1981. (Bibliothèque des Etudies Francaises det Athenes et de Rome, 241).

Weinstein, Donald and Rudolph M. Bell. *Saints and Society: The Two Worlds of Western Christendom, 1000-1700.* Chicago: University of Chicago Press, 1982.

Wenck, Karl. *Die heilige Elisabeth.* Tübingen: J.C.B. Mohr/Paul Siebeck, 1908.

-----. "Quellenuntersuchungen und Text zur Geschichte der hl. Elisabeth. I. Ueber die *Dicta quattuor ancillarum sanctae Elisabeth.*" *Neues Archiv der Gesellschaft für alter deutsche Geschichtskunde* 34 (1908): 427-502.

Werner, Matthias. "Die Elisabeth-Vita des Dietrich von Apolda als Beispiel spätmittelalterlicher Hagiographie." *Geschictsschreibung und Geschichtsbewusstsein im späten Mittelalter* (Vorträge und Forschungen 31), herausgegeben von. H. Patze. Sigmaringen: Jan Thorbecke Verlag, 1987, pp. 523-541.

Wies, Ernst W. (Ernst Wilhelm). *Elisabeth von Thuringen: die Provokation der Heiligkeit*. Esslingen: Bechtle, c1993.

Wiethaus, Ulrike. "Feminist Historiography as Pornography: St. Elisabeth of Thuringia in Nazi Germany." *Medieval Feminist Newsletter*, no. 24 (Fall 1997): 46-54.

-----. "Naming and un-naming violence against women: German historiography and the cult of St. Elisabeth of Thuringia," *Medievalism and the Academy*, ed. Leslie J. Workman, Kathleen Verduin and David D. Metzger (Cambridge: D.S. Brewer, 1999), 1:187-208.

-----. "Sexuality, Gender and the Body in Late Medieval Spirituality: Cases from Germany and the Netherlands." *Journal of Feminist Studies in Religion* 7 (1991): 35-52.

Wieser, Klemens, ed. *Acht Jahrhunderte Deutscher Orden in Einzeldarstellungen*. Bad Godesburg: Verlag Wissenschaftliches Archiv, 1967.

www.ingramcontent.com/pod-product-compliance
Lightning Source LLC
LaVergne TN
LVHW051253080426
835509LV00020B/2950

Readers' experiences with the *Book of Days*...

This volume makes the first even more profound, showing just how much our relationship with the Divine affects how we relate with ourselves and everyone and everything in life. Having planted the seeds in the Spring with volume 1, the metaphor flows beautifully into the blossoming of Summer, and the self.

— **Jodi Lynn**, Actor (New York, NY)

I connected with this material especially when I saw that one of my own birth angels, dealing with my life purpose, coincided with an issue I've been dealing with my whole life. By the time I got through the first 41 days of angel wisdoms in this volume, I had been brought gently to my own Incarnation Angel in a way that allowed me to finally approach my issues with authority. I realized that my discomfort with outer authority was calling me to claim my own clearer voice of self-sovereignty and a willingness to take responsibility for my actions and reactions, without being too persuaded or misused by the "authorities" of the outer world. Working with the daily wisdoms EVERY DAY has also made me realize that spiritual work cannot be an occasional or one day a week thing. This daily work of spiritual awareness has enabled me to experience the sacred potential in everything that happens and with everyone who crosses my path. It's like the sacred is hiding in plain sight all around us.

— **Stacie Florer**, jewelry artist, Human Design Guide (Roanoke, VA)

Thank you for this beautiful and resonant Angel series...The daily wisdoms e-mails are also wonderful to spark heart connection and fuel inspiration each day - lovely when traveling and also during times when picking up a book, especially early in the day, is not likely.... Each message has a very special way of touching me in the just-exactly-what-is-needed way.

— **Sarah Gallant**, Visioning with Heart Facilitator and Guidess (Cincinnati, Ohio)

The daily wisdoms offer reminders, sign posts, guidance for my daily living and interactions with my world. They really do help me to be more mindful of how I'm living on all levels – to thine own self be true in all ways..do unto others as I would have them do unto me...don't sweat the small stuff...remember how very much I am loved and that my life matters.

— **Aletheia Mystea**, psychotherapist & founder of Green Theology Ministries: Earth Rites, Animal Rites, Human Rites (Fort Collins CO)

The messages in this volume are conveyed in such a positive and loving way that helped me to begin each day as though wrapped in a blanket of gentle optimism. The daily wisdom fully prepares me to deal with whatever presents itself with calmness and a feeling of acceptance and encouragement. I'm very grateful for the benefits I receive from this material.

— **Paula Mooney**, nurse, gardener & herbalist (Bigelow, AR)